IMPRESSIONS

AND OPINIONS

IMPRESSIONS
AND OPINIONS

BY

GEORGE MOORE

NEW YORK
BRENTANO'S

PR 5042
M 82 i

PREFACE

I

A PUBLISHER will not bring out a new edition without a preface, and we find prefaces difficult to write. Three weeks were spent on the preface to *Spring Days*, for a long screed had been contemplated containing many new and ingenious theories of literature ; but as these did not seem to prepare the reader's mind for the book he was going to read, an anecdote was substituted, and a hundred newspapers related that the author had bought up and pilfered as many copies of the original edition as he could, and had thrown them into the Thames. We have nothing so picturesque to tell in the present preface, but merely that the author was sinking in a flood of public disfavour caused by *Spring Days*, and the book that followed *Spring Days* (its name we fear to pronounce), when *Impressions and Opinions*, like a big Newfoundland dog, dived after him and brought him to shore. And all that we have to tell of the further career of this book is that it seems to have retained the admiration it first inspired, and to have made some friends in the last twenty years. Those who read us and do not possess this book seem anxious to possess it, and those who do possess the book will not part with it except at extravagant prices. We have heard of three pounds ten shillings being asked for a copy, and when it became necessary to procure one for the preparation of this edition, we were asked fifty shillings. It would have been distasteful to us to spend so much money on our own writings. The story got about, and the book was brought to us one morning in a basket. Our butcher's son had been collecting our writings for some years, and had slipped it in with the beef; and looking at the copy which had come to us in so unexpected a way, we see that we may attribute to David Nutt the great store set upon the first edition of *Impressions and Opinions*. A book's first life, it is true, depends upon its contents, but two or three years after publication the pagination, the print, the paper, the cover, and the shape of the book begin to attract, and year by year they attract more and more until the book attains the glory of a Chinese vase in which there is nothing but a little dust.

We should have liked to reproduce the original edition of *Impressions and Opinions*, but the time comes when an author begins to look round the corner after a uniform edition of his works. The form in which *Spring Days* was published was chosen with that intention, and it was therefore an obligation that *Impressions and Opinions* should be uniform with *Spring Days*. A slight mistake was made in the pagination of *Spring Days*, but that will be rectified when the book is printed again, and as soon as that is done the two books will not too painfully disfigure the shelves of an old mahogany bookcase. In their new form they may be laid upon a satinwood table,

while the reader dozes or lies back to consider whether
he prefers our earlier to our later style; both books
are strictly in our first manner, and the reader will
not be deceived by the fact that a short article on
Zola has been replaced by a longer article; we have
dared this alteration because the longer article seemed
to us a more energetic affirmation of our early style
than the rejected article. It was written while *Impressions and Opinions* was being written, and may
be taken as an example of a style which many critics
prefer to our later and more polished style. Among
these critics is Mr T. D. O'Bolger of Pennsylvania
University who, while in England, did us the great
compliment of enquiring out a copy of *Impressions and
Opinions*, and when he had obtained one, of writing
to us his appreciations, remarking that *Impressions
and Opinions* was a much better book than *Memoirs
of my Dead Life*. There was no page in this latter
book, he said, that could compare with any page of
Impressions and Opinions unless, perhaps, the opening
pages of *Ninon's Table D'hôte*. Mr O'Bolger's literary
perceptions are remarkable, for the opening pages of
Ninon's Table D'hôte were printed *verbatim* from an
earlier version of the story. But Mr O'Bolger's preference for the early manner is not so individual. It
seems to us to be part of the literary humour of the
present time, which is always to sneer at artistic
accomplishment, and to praise the rude and rough
manifestations of untutored genius. In the taste of
the present day Assyrian sculpture is better than
Egyptian, and Phidias is looked upon as being no
better than Turgueneff. Balzac has had his day

of favour, but is giving way to the more unculti-
vated imaginations of Dostoevsky. Even grammar
is out of fashion; peasant speech yields a richer
flavour; and as we would win by hook or by crook
some of the popularity of our great contemporaries,
we have not corrected any mistakes, but tried to
see them as beauty spots.

II

Three weeks ago it had seemed to us that all the
beauty spots might be accepted without demur, but
on looking into the book again the article entitled
"Art for the Villa," seemed to us such a ravelled
skein that we could not do else than strive to knit it
together; and as this proved to be a task beyond our
skill a new article has been substituted entitled, "Une
Rencontre au Salon," written, we admit it, in our later
style. We might have parodied ourselves, put on paint,
and powder, and patches; but Mr O'Bolger would be
the first to detect such artifices, and we should have
found ourselves for ever out of his favour.

G. M.

CONTENTS

IMPRESSIONS AND OPINIONS

BALZAC

AS a traveller in the unknown East, standing on the last ridge of the last hill, sees a city, and in awe contemplates the walls fabulous with terraces and gates, the domes and the towers clothed in all the light of the heavens, so does the imaginative reader view the vast sections into which the Human Comedy is so eloquently divided—scenes from private life, scenes from provincial life, scenes from Parisian life, scenes from political life, scenes from military life, scenes from country life, philosophical studies, analytical studies. These are the streets and thoroughfares which intersect and divide this great city of thought; in each division the titles of the volumes rise like spires and pinnacles, and unconsciously the reader passes from story to story like a sightseer through palaces and gardens inexhaustible.

Jonah marched three days into Nineveh before he began to preach : Nineveh was small compared with the Human Comedy. I have walked many years in its streets and mused many years on its terraces, but so abundant is that city of thought with all beauty of imaginative design, so resplendent with all jewels of wit, so full of the many enchantments of various love, so terrible with all accents of pain, grief, sorrow, and pathetic melancholy, that the mind may retain only a portion of the wonders there displayed. With Balzac it is as with a great city, neither can be learnt completely; at each fresh acquirement the mind loses something hitherto its own. And, when we close the fiftieth volume and take up the first, which we read ten, maybe twenty, years before, what we have not forgotten we read with new lights, for the light of middle age is different from that of youth.

Impossible it is then to write an article on Balzac as it is to write one on life itself, and the guide that comes forth from the city to meet the stranger will do well to limit the range of the first excursion. If he is a wise guide he will say, " Let us not attempt too much this first day, let us pass it in some quiet suburb rather than in the torrid magnificences of the town ; come with me and we will examine at leisure some quaint interesting places where the characteristics and the genius of the city may be studied." And even so would I address the reader wholly unacquainted with the Human Comedy.

Just as a guide meeting a traveller climbing the last ridge of the last hill would I address the reader : " Come with me," I say, "we will spend the day in a suburb where you will learn much, but the city you must explore yourself, for all who have attempted to explain its beauties have failed. There was Sainte-Beuve, there was Janin ; both fell into memorable disaster ; and the first discredited the critical labour of his life by failing to understand the great genius of his age."

The lot of critics is to be remembered by what they failed to understand. That Sainte-Beuve understood Hugo, who cares? but his failure to understand Balzac will assure him of the sneers of many a generation. The same with Ruskin ; who cares that he understood Turner? We know that he did not understand Whistler, and the "pot of paint flung in the face of the public" will survive his finest prose passage. And the unfortunate Janin, writing of *Les Illusions Perdues*, one of Balzac's very greatest works, depreciates, indeed he even tries to turn into ridicule, Balzac's constant reference to the exact sums of money that Lucien spent daily in the restaurant. These pecuniary details appeared to Janin to indicate a low and sordid mind. Janin failed to understand how by thus apportioning out the daily expenditure of Lucien, showing how the young poet might live on his little fortune while educating himself, Balzac was introducing a new element into fiction—the value of money. Balzac was the first to perceive "that money was as necessary to a young man in the nineteenth century as a coat of mail was in the fifteenth."

Zola himself was not successful in his study of Balzac. He told me that of all his critical studies his Essay on Balzac was the one he was least satisfied with. And he is right; his Essay on Balzac does not compare, for instance, with his Essay on Flaubert. So, having regard for the celebrated failures that have preceded this attempt, it occurred to me that possibly the only way to a suggestion of the vastness of Balzac lay through the minor pieces. However this may be, and before we start on our adventure, let us for a moment view the city from this last ridge, whence we can see it spreading over the plain, beautiful in its magnitude—famous public ways and squares clearly defined; and far away, under the horizon, vapoury indications of rampart and outlying fort.

The works of no other writer offer so complete a representation of the spectacle of civilised life as the Human Comedy. That sensation of endless extent and ceaseless agitation, which is life, the Human Comedy produces exactly. If we think of its fifty volumes, we are impressed with the same perplexed sense of turmoil and variety as when we climb out of the slum of personal interests and desires, and from a height of the imagination look down upon life, seeing image succeeding image and yet things remaining the same, seeing things tumbling forward, hastening always, passing away, and leaving no trace. The Human Comedy justifies its name; it is the only literature that reproduces the endless agitation and panoramic movement of civilised life. To do this may not be the final achievement, the highest artistic aim: I contest not the point, I state a fact: alone among writers Balzac has succeeded in doing this.

For in the fifty volumes you find all that represents civilisation. Civilisation in the nineteenth century is money, and Balzac, with his unerring wisdom which saw into the heart of things, knew, or rather felt, that money would be the stake for which Christianity would fight its last great battle. Therefore the grim faces of misers meet you at every turning. All varieties of misers are to be found in the Human Comedy: the sordid wine-making peasant counting the sugar in the bowl, starving his wife; the hideous country miser and usurer, holding the entire village in his grip, receiving the first fruits of farmyard and garden; the terrible and cynical miser, conscious that he is the type and epitome of the evil of the city —terrible indeed is the Père Gobseck, and terrible is the signature that precedes and announces him. There are others, and around misers and usurers and money-makers hundreds of human souls float round and round as in a vortex; the usurer everywhere, each governing his own section as he governs it in life. We find all classes of society represented in the Human Comedy, and all types of men. There are peasants working in fields and drinking in *cabarets*, there are courtesans in the streets and in palaces, there are old men being preyed upon by unscrupulous women, who in turn

are the victims of unscrupulous young men. There are
men who sacrifice their lives to art, and others who
sacrifice their lives to pleasure, there are poets who
waste their talents in love-dreams, there are poets who
waste their talents in *bon-mots*. There are full-length
portraits, half-length, heads and silhouettes. The
characters pass and repass, and as in life you stumble
unexpectedly upon acquaintances.

This innumerable and unceasing eruption of souls
is accompanied with a poignant and searching criticism
of life. Sometimes the criticism is direct and personal,
more often it proceeds experimentally by comparison
with the immediate past; we find allusions full of
anticipatory insight into those problems of clairvoyance
and hypnotism and auto-suggestion, which modern
science is rescuing from the pollution of supernatural
belief, and classifying within the natural.

Balzac's intuitive knowledge of the latent forces in
things, which circumstances might at any moment
develop into active forces, led him to see that if peasants
combined the laws would prove powerless to tear from
them either the rent or the land, and that by passive
resistance and secret murder the landlords could be
forced to sell their properties to the peasants at nominal
prices. No Irish agitator could draw up a plan of cam-
paign more effectually than Balzac did in *Les Paysans*,
written fifty years ago. In this book will be found
every incident of the land war in Ireland ; indeed, the
murder of the bailiff differs not at all from the many
such murders we have read of in Ireland in these last
ten years, and the boycotting of the general might
be included with very little alteration in Captain
Boycott's memoirs ; and the schemes for land reform
propounded in that wonderful chapter, *En quoi le
cabaret est le parlement du peuple*, wonderful from the

title to the closing word, might pass without exciting suspicion for extracts from one of Michael Davitt's speeches. To have looked so far into the future, and with such precision and graphic detail, constructing a world to come from a single fact, as Cuvier constructed a past animal from a single bone, must strike even the casual reader as a most extraordinary intellectual feat, and quite beyond the reach of any other novelist.

It will be asked how Balzac could have written so much and yet found time to experience the life he was describing.

The vulgar do not know that the artist makes but little use of his empirical knowledge of life, and that he relies almost entirely upon his inner consciousness of the truth. In Balzac perception of the truth extended over an inconceivably wide area ; the perception was not so pure as in Shakespeare, but it was wider. Living as Balzac did in the giddiness and exaltation of an unceasing creation, I can imagine him lifting his face from the paper like one still under the influence of the dream, unable for the moment to bear with the intensity of the enchantment. In the somnambulism of his genius he lived peopling a perfectly imagined world with souls as troubled with passions and all the racking inquietude of existence as those who wander in that moment which we are pleased to call real life. Of his own soul and his own troubles he must have lived nearly unconscious, hardly aware of their existence. He often mentions in his letters that he has been working eighteen hours, and it is not infrequent to find him saying that he rose at two in the morning; he would then continue his cerebral debauch till noon. And the story of the improvisation of the *Cousine Bette* in six weeks is one of the wonders of literary history. Think of the book! To have woven such a fabric, to have created so many souls, and to have lived through it all in six weeks! . . . Surely no one who reads these lines need wonder why my illustrious predecessors failed to write any adequate essay on Balzac; and surely all, even should they find no further wisdom in this essay, will admit that it was fortunate in conception, and that probably the only way to convey a suggestion of the genius of the great novelist lies through the minor pieces.

I will begin with *Les Secrets de la Princesse de Cadignan.*

" The revolution of July destroyed many aristocratic " fortunes upheld by the Court, and Madame la Princesse " de Cadignan had the cleverness to lay at the door of " these political crises her ruin, which was really due to " her prodigalities. The Princess heretofore so celebrated " —queen of all queens of fashion under her first name " La Duchesse de la Maufrigneuse, retired from the world " to a small *appartement*, consisting of no more than five " rooms, where she devoted herself to her son's education." The Princess was married when she was sixteen to her mother's lover, the Duke de Maufrigneuse, and when the Princess tells the story of her life to D'Arthez, the great writer whom Balzac probably meant for himself, she speaks thus of the Duchesse d'Uxelles.

" Well, I never was angry with the Duchesse for " having loved Monsieur de Maufrigneuse better than " poor Diana, and this is why. My mother knew very " little of me ; she had forgotten me ; but she conducted " herself towards me in a way which is wicked between " women and horrible between mother and daughter. " I knew nothing ; I was incapable of guessing the secret " of this alliance. I had a handsome fortune. Monsieur " de Maufrigneuse was overwhelmed with debt. If " I learnt later what it was to have debts I was at the " time too ignorant of life to suspect it. The economies

"the Duke was enabled to make by the help of my
"fortune sufficed to appease his creditors. He was thirty-
"eight when I married him, but those years were like
"those of the campaigns of military men, and should
"count double. Ah! he was in truth more than seventy-
"six. At forty my mother still had pretensions to good
"looks, and I found myself between two jealousies.
"What an existence was mine for ten years! Ah! if it
"were known what this poor, little, suspected woman has
"suffered, watched by a mother jealous of her daughter!
"Good heavens, you who write dramas will never invent
"anything so black, so cruel, as that! Oh, my friend,
"you men cannot guess what life is with an old man
"*à bonnes fortunes*, a man accustomed to the adoration
"of women of the world, and who finds neither incense
"nor censor at home, dead to everything and jealous
"for that very reason. I desired when the Duke de
"Maufrigneuse was wholly mine to be a good woman;
"but I came in rough contact with all the asperities
"of a chagrined mind, with all the caprices of power-
"lessness, with all the puerilities of folly, with all the
"vanities of self-sufficiency, with a man who was in fine
"the most tiresome elegy in the world, who treated me
"like a child, and amused himself by humiliating my
"self-esteem at every turn, overwhelming me with his
"experience, and proving me ignorant in all things."

So did the Princess coo in the ears of the great man
who sat at her feet listening to her "as a neophyte
in one of the first days of the Christian faith might have
listened to the epistle of an apostle."

Understand that the actors in this scene from Parisian
life are a princess who has dissipated many fortunes, her
own and those of her lovers, who knows all sensations
except love, whose drawing-room is her temple, and
whose ritual is love confidences; the other is a man
of genius, who knows the world theoretically, as Balzac

knew it, and who in practice was as child-like as Balzac himself. Arthez was chosen for that very reason, for as the Marquise d'Espard said to the Princess when the two friends sat together regretting they had never loved any one of their many lovers : " Fools love well some-"times," said the Marquise. " But," replied the Princess, "for this " (that is to say, to believe in the speakers) "even fools would not be sufficiently credulous." " You "are right," said the Marquise, laughing. " But it is "neither a fool nor yet a man of talent that we should "seek. To solve such a problem a man of genius is "necessary. Genius alone has child-like faith, the "religion of love, and willingly allows his eyes to be "banded. Look at Canalis and the Duchesse de "Chaulieu. If you and I have met geniuses, they were "perhaps too far from us, and we were too occupied, "too frivolous, too carried away, too taken up with "other things." " Ah! I would not leave the world "without knowing the delights of true love," cried the Princess. " It is nothing to inspire it," said Madame d'Espard, " the difficulty is to feel it. I see many "women who are only pretexts of a passion instead of "being at once the cause and the effect."

It is out of conversation, a few sentences, one of which I have translated, between the Princess and Madame d'Espard that the action of the story springs. *Qui a bu, boira*, the Princess grown tired of solitude and motherly duties, yearns for a new emotion, and Daniel d'Arthez is sought, Rastignac and de Trailles are commissioned to draw him from his studies. Infinite genius meets infinite worldly sagacity, and with what art is the web spun, and with what art is the accomplished charmer shown waiting, her lovely head leaned upon her long white fingers in the lamplight, an exquisite expression of tender melancholy. She is determined that this is to be no passing caprice, if she gives herself again it will be to a lover who believes her innocent, pure, incapable of untruth. The poor man of genius, sceptical, when sitting at his writing table, as Mephistopheles, is candid as a little child, sitting at the feet of the Princess. How true this is! The philosopher is as a child when he strives to put his knowledge into practice, the man of the world is a child when he strives to put his knowledge into words.

Les Secrets de la Princesse de Cadignan might be entitled the seduction of genius by experience. It is animated by a sublime comprehension of the fascinating perversities of cerebral passion, and the confiding simplicities of a great man who, wearied, like Faust, with learning, desires the repose and consolation of love. *Les Secrets de la Princesse de Cadignan* might also be entitled the philosophy of the drawing-room. It is the drawing-room in essence. The Princess is a being born of the drawing-room; she has been formed and coloured by the drawing-room as an insect by the chemical qualities and the colour of the plant upon which it lives. Her ideas of love, literature, art, and science are drawing-room ideas of love, literature, art, and science. The intonations of her voice, and every inflection of accent, have been produced by the drawing-room. Her weariness of life is drawing-room weariness of life. She is a creature of the drawing-room as the horse is a creature of the stable, as the eagle is a creature of the cliff. Balzac saw that the drawing-room was the great feature of civilisation.

Since Dickens, no one in England has had sufficient strength of imagination to get outside of his habit and seek the pathetic and the picturesque where Morris wall - papers and Liberty silk are unknown; and although an immense amount of wholly unnecessary scribbling is done concerning drawing - rooms, their decoration and flirtations, none has attempted to understand and to raise the drawing-room out of a dreary fictional *lieu commun*. To say that Lady So-and-so's drawing-room is furnished in pink is sufficient for the English writer. But Balzac went deeper; he saw that the drawing-room is perhaps the last expression of an exhausted civilisation, and he expressed the drawing-room in the *Princesse de Cadignan*.

I have said elsewhere than in this article that a book of maxims surpassing those of La Rochefoucauld might be garnered in Balzac's novels. Here are a few taken from this little story which does not consist of more than forty pages. "Yes, when we are young we are full of fatuous stupidities; we resemble those poor young men who play with a tooth-pick to make believe that they have dined well." "What is to be gained by leaving your husband? In a woman it is an admission of feebleness." "One of the glories of society is to have created woman where Nature made a female, to have created a continuity of desire where Nature only thought of perpetuating the species; in fine, to have invented love."

Adieu is an example of Balzac's romantic manner, and we shall see the enchantment he weaves about the beautiful word. Two sportsmen, tired after a hard day, wander out of the sun's way into the cool of a large wood, seeking a house or habitation of some kind. Presently they come upon open spaces, at the end of which is an Abbey partly in ruins. "What disorder," cried Monsieur d'Albon, after taking pleasure for a "moment in the sombre impression that the ruins gave "to the landscape, which appeared to have been struck "as if by a malediction." Then, after a detailed description of the place, we catch a glimpse of a woman passing lightly as the shadow of a cloud from beneath the walnut-trees growing by the iron gate. The men

find their way to the ruined Abbey, which they discover
to be still used as a habitation. The strange woman
again appears, and this is how she is described :—

" The two men were astonished to see her jump on
" the bough of an apple-tree and swing there with the
" lightness of a bird. She seized the fruit, ate, and then
" let the apples fall with that gracious softness which we
" admire in squirrels. Her limbs possessed an elasticity
" which relieved every slightest movement from appear-
" ance of effort or difficulty. She played upon the
" ground, rolled there as might a child ; then suddenly
" throwing her feet and hands forward remained stretched
" on the grass with the abandonment, the grace, and the
" naturalness of a young cat asleep in the sun.

" ' Adieu !' she cried, and her voice was soft and
" harmonious, but it lacked that accent of human feel-
" ing which the men waited for impatiently."

But one of the men recognises the woman ; he cries
her name, and his emotion on seeing her is so great
that he faints, and is taken home by his friend, who
returns on horseback at his earnest request to make
enquiries as to the identity of the mysterious woman.
He learns her story from her uncle, who lives in the
ruined Abbey.

The scene is on the banks of the Beresina ; and
Maréchal Victor had left there a thousand men in guard
of the bridges, which they were charged to destroy
when the Russians appeared. But instead of crossing
the river the remnant of Napoleon's army encamped in
the snow, feeding on horse-flesh, cooked before fires
made of broken carts and wagons.

" The apathy of these poor soldiers cannot be under-
" stood except by those who have traversed those vast
" deserts of snow, without other perspective except a
" horizon of snow, without other drink than snow, without
" other bed than snow, without other nourishment than

"a frozen beet-root, a handful of meal, or a piece of
"horse-flesh. . . . Although the artillery of the left wing
"of the Russian army fired without ceasing on this mass,
"sometimes seen as a great black stain, sometimes as a
"great blaze in the middle of the snow, the indefatigable
"bullets seemed no more to the torpid crowd than one
"more discomfort."

I would I had space to give some of the extraordinary
details by which Balzac evokes the very motion, colour,
smell, and sound of awful war. Among these war-
stricken fugitives there is a general and his wife, and
Philip de Susy is striving to save their lives, striving to
get them to the bridge before it is destroyed by the
troops on the other side. But his last horse has been
seized and eaten. He steals, however, horses from
the Russian sentries which are tied to the carriages,
and they drive over the bodies of sleeping soldiers.
"'You can't make an omelette without breaking the
eggs,' cries the grenadier, pricking the horses with his
sword-point." But the bridge is burnt before they can
reach it; a raft is constructed, place is made for the
woman, and she cries "Adieu" to Philip. But the
husband was thrown from the raft and killed among
the ice, and, without a protector, lost in the disaster of
the retreat, she followed the track of the army for two
years, the plaything of every ruffian. In a word, she
knew all the misfortunes of war, hunger, thirst, cold, and
cruelty, until she was at last rescued from a madhouse
in Germany and brought back to France. No words
except Balzac's can tell how her lover in the woods
about the lonely ruined abbey strives to win her back
to reason. . . . Ah! the infinite pity of his efforts to
coax her, as he might a wayward animal, with lump-
sugar, and all his various hopes and disappointments,
until the old uncle finds him one day loading his pistols
to shoot her.

"'Poor little one,' cried her uncle, pressing the poor
"crazy thing to his breast, 'he would have killed you,
"egoist that he is ; he would kill you because he suffers.
"He knows not how to love you for yourself, my child
"We will forgive him, shall we not? He is insane, and
"you are only crazed. Go! God alone should call you
"to Himself. We think you are unhappy because you
"can participate no longer in our miseries—fools that we
"are! But,' said he, placing her on his knees, 'you are
"happy, nothing annoys you ; you live like the bird, like
"the hind.'"

"She rushed and caught a young blackbird, crushed
"it, looked at it, and left it at the foot of a tree without
"thinking anything more about it.

"'Come,' cried Philip, taking her in his arms, 'do you
"not feel my heart beating? I love you always. Philip
"is not dead. He is here, you lean upon him. You are
"my Stephanie, and I am your Philip.'

"'Adieu,' cried she, 'adieu!'"

Balzac carries the story further, but for our purpose
it is not necessary to follow it to its exquisite conclusion.
The magic must have been already perceived by the
reader. The imagination is exquisite, and its pathetic
simplicity might have been equalled by Shakespeare
if he had written prose fiction ; he might have given an
equally pure picture of the return of the human, through
suffering, to the pure animal—that gracious wiping out,
by benevolent nature, of thought when the burden
became too great to bear.

There is in Ophelia much tender appreciation of the
little breadth that divides the sane from the insane and
the immensity of the responsibility which the transition,
slight in itself, involves ; but is the very haunting
question, if we have gained in happiness since we have
acquired the power of looking before and after, so
tenderly-insinuated?

In these days, when the domestication of literature is proceeding apace, and our standard of literary ability seems a negative one, namely, to write nothing that young ladies may not openly discuss in their drawing-rooms, the marvellous story of *Sarrasine* will find little favour; not because it is immoral, but because it is unconcerned with the accepted ideals of the nineteenth century, the tea-table, the curate, the young lady who wants to be married, etc. To the nineteenth century, the abnormal is intolerable, even frank sensuality receives a better welcome. And as education proceeds, natural taste, that is to say, individual taste, withers, and man becomes blinder every day to the charms of the bizarre, and more intolerant to the exotic. But the abnormal is found in all great writers, and though not their flesh, it is their heart. The abnormal must always be felt, although it may rarely form the subject of picture or poem. To make the abnormal ever visible and obstrusively present is to violate the harmony of Nature; to avoid the abnormal is to introduce a fatal accent of insincerity. But Balzac's mind being irreproachably pure, and his genius wholly valid, he was led to give the abnormal exactly the same prominence in the Human Comedy as it has in Nature; and his treatment and comprehension of it was nowise inferior to his treatment and comprehension of the great and primal emotions. Balzac has called genius a terrible malady: he was qualified to define it. But there is a marked element of health in all great work. Shakespeare's genius was unquestionably healthier than that of any of his contemporaries, yet he wrote the Sonnets; Balzac's genius was unquestionably saner than any of his contemporaries, if we except Hugo's, and yet Balzac wrote *La Fille aux Yeux d'Or*, *La dernière Incarnation de Vautrin*, *Une Passion dans le Désert*, *Séraphita*, and *Sarrasine*. Therefore it may be said

that the final achievement of genius is the introduction
and artistic use of the abnormal.

And this for a reason which will not be suspected by
the casual student of fiction, and which when first stated
will seem like paradox. But it surely is true, except
for those who stand high among the highest, that the
choice of any but the most ordinary theme will lead
into commonplace. Even in the hands of a man of
talent the abnormal slips into sterile eccentricity, which
is the dreariest form of commonplace; but let the man
of talent choose an ordinary every-day story, and in
developing it any originality of mind and vision he may
possess will appear to its very best advantage. Genius
can, we know, do all things — it can even make the
abnormal interesting: but even genius does not find
in the abnormal the sublime moments of the soul that
it finds in the normal, and truly it cannot be said that
La Fille aux Yeux d'Or is worth *Le Curé de Tours*, or
that any one would hesitate if choice were given him
between *Sarrasine* or *Une Vieille Fille*.

Although somewhat lost amid numberless *chefs-
d'œuvre*, although rarely cited as a striking example of
Balzac's genius, *Une Vieille Fille* is one of the first
among the minor pieces. *Une Vieille Fille* seems to
me to epitomise the most completely and the most
perfectly the resources of a mind at once so profound,
and, at least in the conception of subject, so unfailingly
artistic. I say so because I find in *Une Vieille Fille*
that philosophic criticism of his own time, that power
of contrasting and opposing it with its immediate past,
so peculiar to Balzac, which no other writer of fiction
has possessed before or since. I find also in this story
three characters conceived with rare philosophic and
imaginative incisiveness, and executed with an elaborate-
ness and alertness of thought only to be found in his

very best work; and I find, although these qualities
predominate almost to excess in the one hundred and
sixty-five pages which form the story, some two or
three rare and exquisite dramatic moments. Nothing
more exquisite, according to me, than the scene where
the fair laundress slips into the chevalier's room and
confesses her trouble to him. He is far too cunning to
show that he disbelieves her story. With phrases, in
delicious harmony with the traces of prosperous days
that linger about the room — traces of the eighteenth
century — he sends her away to lay the charge of
seduction at the door of his rival Du Bousquier. The
scene with Du Bousquier is equally good, for in it
Balzac achieves his intention, which was to portray,
and, in portraying, to show how these two old bachelors,
who are both intriguing one against the other for the
hand and fortune of Mlle. Cormon, represent the
ideas and outward appearance of two distinct epochs—
the Chevalier de Valois, the aristocracy and elegance of
the eighteenth century, Du Bousquier, the vulgarity and
commercialism of the nineteenth. Another exquisite
moment is when Mlle. Cormon hears that the Vicomte
de Troisville is a married man, and yet another when
the Chevalier comes to ask the hand of Mlle. Cormon.
"But this fine gentleman could only be killed in one
"way: he had lived by the Graces, and it was right that
"he should die by their hand. While the Chevalier
"had been putting the finishing hand to his toilette Du
"Bousquier entered the drawing-room of the disconso-
"late maid."

The soul of the story is the desire of Mlle. Cormon
to be married, and the difficulties which beset her
project. Through this simple subject Balzac passes
as with a lantern in his hand, showing us how the
conscription had affected the marriage market and how
the republican spirit persisted, and, notwithstanding the

restoration, was beginning to make itself felt in the social life of the remote provinces ; we are made to feel too that the monarchy is ephemeral and that republicanism is the abiding force, that its eclipse is more apparent than real.

Yet the machinery of this story, in which so many grave subjects enter, is the very simplest, and it is put in motion by one of Madame Lardot's laundresses, who, as we have seen, thought first of laying a charge of seduction against the elegant Chevalier, but who was easily persuaded that it would be to her far greater advantage to lay the charge against his rival Du Bousquier. Here are a few extracts from Balzac's description of the elegant Chevalier which seem to me to display higher power of mind than any that Fielding, Dickens, Thackeray, and George Eliot would have revealed had they been called upon to describe an elderly gentleman, long, dry, and penniless, the greater part of whose youth had been passed in Paris, where, when he was about thirty, the revolution had surprised him in the midst of his conquests, but who now lived "en Province" in two rooms above Madame Lardot's laundry, in the midst of grisettes, whom he looks kindly upon, making them presents of bits of ribbon and slight packets of chocolate creams.

" He dined out every day and he played cards every " evening. He passed for being a witty man, thanks to " a defect which consisted in telling numberless anecdotes " concerning the reign of Louis XV. and the beginning of " the revolution. When these stories were heard for the " first time they were considered to be well told. Though " the Chevalier de Valois never ascribed his witticisms to " himself, nor spoke of his love affairs, his graces and his " smiles were deliciously indiscreet. This good gentleman " availed himself of the privilege of an old Voltairean " noble not to attend mass, but his irreligion was looked

"upon indulgently on account of his devotion to the
"Royal cause. One of his graces, and the most remarked,
"was his manner, doubtless imitated from De Molé, of
"taking snuff from an old gold box ornamented with the
"portrait of the Princess Goritza, a charming Hungarian,
"celebrated for her beauty in the reign of Louis XV.
"Attached in his youth to this illustrious stranger, he
"never spoke of her without emotion; and it was on her
"account that he had fought with Monsieur de Lauzun.

"The Chevalier was now fifty-eight, he admitted to
"fifty; but he could permit himself this harmless decep-
"tion, for amid the many advantages of those who are
"thin and blonde he preserved that juvenility of figure,
"which saves men no less than women from the appear-
"ance of age. Learn that all life, or all elegance which
"is the expression of life, exists in the waist. Among
"the Chevalier's belongings must be numbered the nose
"which nature had presented him with. This nose
"vigorously divided his pale face into two sections that
"did not match, for one reddened during the labour of
"digestion. This fact is worthy of remark in a time
"when physiology occupied so much attention. The
"incandescence was on the left side.

"Although the long, slim legs, the lank body and
"the pallid complexion of Monsieur de Valois did not
"proclaim a healthy constitution, he ate like an ogre,
"and sought to excuse his excessive appetite by pretend-
"ing to be afflicted with a malady known 'en Province'
"as a hot liver. The flushing of his face gave a certain
"credence to this story. But in a country where meals
"lengthen into thirty or forty dishes and last for four
"hours, the stomach of the Chevalier must have seemed
"a gift from Providence to the town. According to
"certain doctors the flushing of the left side of the
"face denotes a prodigal heart. The fast life of the
"Chevalier confirmed these assertions, happily relieving

"the historian from all responsibility.   Notwithstanding
"these symptoms Valois had a nervous constitution, con-
"sequently vivacious.   If his liver burnt (*ardait*), to use
"an old expression, his heart did not burn less.   If his
"face was lined, if his hair was silvered, a trained observer
"would have detected there the stigmas of passion and the
"furrows of pleasure.[1]   'En la *patte d'oie* caractéristique
"et les *marches du palais* se montraient ces élegantes
"rides si prisées à la cour de Cythère.'   In this spruce
"Chevalier everything pointed to 'un homme à femmes'
"(*ladies' man*).   He was so minute in his ablutions that
"his cheeks were a pleasure to look upon ; they seemed
"to have been washed in some miraculous water.   That
"part of the skull which the hair refused to cover shone
"like ivory.   Constant combing gave a false appearance
"of youth to his hair and eyebrows.   Without using
"perfume the Chevalier exhaled a perfume of youth that
"'rafraichissait son air.'   His gentlemanly hands, cared
"for like those of a 'petite maîtresse,' attracted the eye
"by their rose-coloured nails carefully trimmed.   If it
"were not for his majestic and superlative nose he would
"have been 'poupin.'   We must, however, spoil this
"portrait by an admission of a weakness.   The Chevalier
"put cotton in his ears, and still continued to wear in
"them two little negroes' heads in diamonds, admirably
"fashioned it is true ; and he strove to justify these
"singular appendages by saying that since he had
"had his ears pierced he no longer suffered from
"neuralgia.   We do not offer the Chevalier as an
"accomplished man, but should we not forgive old
"bachelors whose hearts send so much blood to their
"faces ? and their adorable absurdities, are they not
"founded, perhaps, upon sublime secrets?   Besides,
"the Chevalier made up for the negroes' heads by so

[1] A mixture of *patois* and bad grammar renders any but a conjectural
translation an impossibility.

"many other graces that society considered itself
"sufficiently indemnified."

This long quotation seems to me to justify itself. For
pure power of mind, combined with astonishing alertness of mind, I think it is unmatchable. It would be
easy to set examples that surpass it in all qualities,
except an excessive alertness to seize every aspect of the
subject, and a power to see deep down into it, noting at
once the hidden reason for every peculiarity of structure.
It reminds me of a fine Holbein; it is as incisive as
Holbein, but it has a dash that recalls the manner of
Hogarth.

I pass over the interview between the enterprising
laundress and Du Bousquier, from whom she extorted
six hundred francs, going immediately afterwards to
lay her distressful case before Madame Granson, the
treasurer of La Société Maternelle. It was necessary
that Madame Granson should have a son who likewise
aspired to the hand of Mlle. Cormon; but I confess that
I fail to see why Balzac thought fit to hamper the action
of his story, hitherto so simple and direct, by making
Suzanne in love with the melancholy young poet.
Indeed the error is more grave than would appear at
first sight. For the suggestion that Suzanne is in love
with Athanase turns what would have been a perfect
short story into a novel which has accidentally been cut
down to the limits of a short story. And if a critic
were to urge this reason for assigning a higher place to
the *Curé de Tours* than to *Une Vieille Fille,* I confess
that I should find myself unable to advance any valid
argument against his plea.

Balzac then paints the portrait of Mlle. Cormon's
country, her house and her history. We see the *salon*
lighted up and the guests arriving on the famous
Thursday evenings—the elegant Chevalier producing his
box, gazing for a moment on the features of the Princess

Goritza, and then taking snuff. We see the brutal and arrogant Du Bousquier, and the pale and melancholy poet who loves Mlle. Cormon sincerely; we hear the shrewd poverty-stricken mother Madame Granson whispering to him, " Look at the Chevalier : study him, " imitate his manners, see with what ease he presents " himself; his air does not seem borrowed like yours. " For goodness sake speak : one would think you knew " nothing, you, who know Hebrew by heart." There is the Abbé de Sponde, Mlle. Cormon's uncle. All these people assemble in the great square reception room, with four doors and four windows, and modestly wainscoted with grey painted wood. One oblong mirror above the chimney-piece, and the windows are draped with heavy green curtains. Everything breathes the old and unalterable *province*. Having painted with rare insight her house and her surroundings, Balzac sets to work to paint the portrait of *la vieille fille* Mlle. Cormon.

" . . . One gave one reason, another gave another, " but the poor girl was as pure as an angel, healthy as " a child, and full of goodness, for nature had intended " her to receive all the pleasures, all the happiness, and " all the labours of maternity.

" Nevertheless Mlle. Cormon did not find in her " appearance any aids to her desire. She had no other " beauty but that which is improperly called *la beauté* " *du diable*, and which consists in the coarse freshness " of youth, which, theologically speaking, the devil could " not have unless we may justify the expression by the " constant desire to cool himself. The heiress's feet were " large and flat ; her leg, which she often showed, but " quite unintentionally, when she lifted her dress after " rain, and when she stepped out of St Leonard, could " not be taken for the leg of a woman ; it was a sinewy " leg with a small calf, hard and pronounced like a sailor's. " A thick healthy waist, a bosom like a nurse's, strong and

"dimpling arms, red hands. Everything about her
" harmonised with the rounded form and the fat white
" beauty of Normandy. Prominent eyes of an undecided
" colour gave to the face, whose outlines were without
" nobility, an air of astonishment, of sheep-like simplicity,
" not unsuitable to an old maid; if Rose had not been
" innocent she would have looked as though she were.
" Her aquiline nose contrasted with the smallness of
" her forehead, for it is seldom that a nose of this shape
" does not of necessity imply a fine brow—notwithstand-
" ing the thick red lips, indicative of a great goodness,
" the forehead announced too few ideas for it to be
" possible that the heart was directed by the intelligence :
" she was probably good without being gracious. There-
" fore virtue is often reproached for her faults whilst one
" is full of indulgence for those of vice. Her light brown
" hair so strangely long lent to her face that beauty
" which comes of force and of abundance, the two principal
" characteristics of Rose Cormon. In her best days Rose
" affected a three-quarter view of her face, so that a very
" pretty ear might be seen showing between the azured
" whiteness of her neck and her temples, and the ear was
" brought into still further evidence by the enormous
" head-dress. Seen in this way in a ball-dress she might
" appear to be good-looking. Her protuberant form, her
" waist, her vigorous health, drew from the officers of the
" Empire this exclamation : 'What a fine slip of a girl ! '
" But with years the plumpness, increased by a life of
" virtue and tranquillity, had become insensibly so badly
" distributed over the body that it had destroyed its
" primitive proportions, and now no pair of stays could
" find her waist or her hips, and she appeared to be made
" in one straight block. . . . "

Skipping some few lines of too minute physiological
examination we come upon this passage :—

" But the poor girl was already over forty ! At this

"moment, after having fought so long to acquire those
"interests which make a woman's life, but nevertheless
"being forced to remain a maid, she fortified her virtue
"by the most severe religious practices. She had had
"recourse to religion, that great consolation of carefully
"guarded virginities. Her confessor for the last three
"years had foolishly advised Mlle. Cormon in the theory
"of mortification, and had counselled the use of the
"scourge. These absurd practices had begun to spread
"a monastic tint over the face of Rose Cormon, and
"seeing her white skin taking those yellow tones which
"announce maturity she despaired. The light down
"which adorned the corners of her upper lip threatened
"to increase and spread like a whiff of smoke. The
"temples had begun to look glassy. In fine, decadence
"had commenced. It was known in Alençon that she
"suffered from heating of the blood ; she took the
"Chevalier into her confidence, enumerating the number
"of foot-baths, and consulting him concerning cooling
"medicines. The sly dog drew forth his snuff-box, and
"for form of conclusion contemplated the Princess
"Goritza."

I do not think it too much to say that this passage is
the origin of the intention of all that has been done
since in fiction, and indeed of a great deal of writing
outside of fiction. I will try and justify this assertion.

It will not be denied that what differentiates the
literature of the nineteenth century from that of all
preceding centuries is the attempt on the part of the
pen to compete with the brush. Until the end of the
eighteenth century literature and painting were separable
arts: literature being occupied exclusively with thoughts,
and not concerned with the folds of the dress, their
shape, and the tones they took in the shadow, and
again the tones they took when the lady bade her

lover good-bye, passing as she said the words into the light of the lamp which stood on a small table, and whose pink shade was clearly defined on the rich purple of the window curtains. It was not until the middle of the eighteenth century that women began to shriek and sob amid the blue cushions of the sofa, and it was in 1880 that Angelica stood in her ecstasy looking through the whiteness of the room. No fact is more indisputable than that the appearance of the purely pictorial in literature dates from the beginning of this century, and since the death of Balzac the discovery has been pursued with unabated vigour in almost every European language. In France and England hardly a great writer has refrained from the new method of expression. It would be curious to note the many talents the new art has called into existence, and how in turn it has been developed and burlesqued; but here I am only interested to state that the finest piece of pictorial writing was achieved by Balzac, the inventor of the method. He employed the method unconsciously, whereas, in Gautier and in Zola, the knowledge of the means they were employing introduced an element of exaggeration which is not atoned for even by the many great qualities which enabled them to use the new method in a more striking manner than its inventor could.

But besides the merit of unconsciousness—that first form of sincerity—Balzac's description of Mlle. Cormon is something more than mere picturesque description; it is something more than Zola's phrase "in ecstasy Angelica looked through the whiteness of the room." For by being quite sincere, that is to say unconscious that he was laying the foundation of a new art, Balzac did not forget the intention of the old art, which was to lay bare the soul, and in writing the passage under consideration his intention was merely to give you Rose Cormon's soul, his genius leading him to do so by a road which had not been traversed before. For every physiological detail is a surprising revelation of the soul within, whereas Gautier's or Zola's description of surfaces reveal the soul rather less than did the brushes of the Dutch painters. And yet, notwithstanding his psychological intentions, Balzac's description of Rose Cormon is the most successful piece of pictorial description in existence. Is there another writer from whose work ten painters would be more likely to produce ten pictures that would not widely differ one from the other? The soul of Becky Sharp is certainly distinct enough, but of her physical appearance we can form hardly an idea; we may imagine her soul in a hundred fleshly forms, but Rose Cormon's soul we can imagine only in the form that Balzac placed it in. When I came upon the description of her leg, the book dropped from my hand in admiration of the master's genius. The whole of Rose Cormon is in that wonderful leg. But the leg that would have meant so much to another was but an accent in Balzac's picture; he was sure of being able to give a culminating touch when he wished, no matter what had gone before, and with physiological detail he created the soul of Rose Cormon, endowing it with a life intense as any in fiction. She stands outside of the little drama in which Balzac saw her involved, and may be imagined in different dramas; we can see her outside of all story, as some one we have known intimately in real life. Greater praise I cannot give. For to create soul is to accomplish the work of God.

The story, too, is full of the most charming details, for Balzac possessed as strong a hold over dialogue as he did over description, and he rarely failed to supply his characters with the right words. For

instance, how admirably suited to the occasion this
is :—

"Mademoiselle," said he, in great haste, "your uncle
"has sent you an express messenger : the son of Mother
"Grosmort has arrived with a letter. The fellow started
"from Alençon before daylight, and he has arrived all the
"same. He ran like Penelope (Penelope is Mlle. Cormon's
"bay mare). Shouldn't he have a glass of wine?"

"What can have happened, Josette? My uncle, could
"he——"

"He would not have written," said the lady's-maid,
who had guessed her mistress's fears.

"Quick! quick!" cried Mlle. Cormon after having
read the first lines. "Let Jacquelin harness Penelope
"at once. And do you, my good girl, see that everything
"is packed in half an hour. We return to town at once."

"Jacquelin!" cried Josette, stimulated by the sentiment which Mlle. Cormon's face expressed ; and instructed by Josette, Jacquelin came forward, saying :—

"But Penelope is eating her hay!"

"What does that matter ; I want to start at once."

"But Mlle., it is going to rain."

"Well, then, we shall get wet."

"The house is on fire," said Josette, a little piqued by
her mistress's silence, for after reading her letter she
re-read it again and again.

"Finish your coffee at least ; do not upset yourself ;
"see how red you are."

"I am red, Josette," said she, going to a glass whence
the quicksilver was peeling, and therefore gave back a
distorted reflection of her face. "My goodness," thought
Mlle. Cormon, "if I should look ugly."

Her worthy uncle had written to his niece that
Monsieur de Troisville, a military officer who had seen
service in Russia, the grandson of one of his firmest
friends, intended to come and live at Alençon, and had

asked for hospitality, whilst reminding him of the friendship which the Abbé had borne for his grandfather the
Vicomte de Troisville, *chef d'escadron* under Louis XIV.
The importance of this visit in the life of Mlle. Cormon
was like that of Waterloo in the life of Napoleon. Of the
household arrangement I will only tell that Mlle. Cormon
turned her boudoir into a bedroom, and a new bed was
bought to suit the room, and she faints in full view of all
her guests on hearing the Vicomte reply to a question
put to him by the Chevalier, that he has been married
for the last fifteen years, and has four children.

Rose's disappointments in her marriage, her desire of
children, the entire philosophy of the married life of an
old maid who has married an old man, is given with
an insight and a power of wide comprehension of life
and things that Balzac has never surpassed, because the
last pages of *Une Vieille Fille* are unsurpassable.

One excellent reason for believing that the genius of
Balzac can be approached through the minor pieces
is the existence of the *Curé de Tours*. In this short
story, which hardly reaches to a hundred pages, his
genius attains its highest, purest, and completest form.
The *Curé de Tours* is the genius of Balzac in epitome;
and a reader of first-rate intelligence, reading it for the
first time, knowing nothing of the author, would say "this
man is great among the great ones of the world, the
brains herein are inferior to none."

It is the finest short story ever written. Look at it
from every side and you will find no fault. Unlike many
of Balzac's short stories it is not a novel reduced to the
limits of a short story—a bundle of events excellently
well imagined, but hastily arranged, and showing bad
cutting and awkwardly sewed seams on every side.
The *Curé de Tours* is perfectly proportioned: it begins
at exactly the right point; the development proceeds

without long waits; nowhere is there an unnecessary
line; and it ends in sequences rhythmical and as final
as those which unite the parts of Beethoven's finest
symphony. It would be vain to look anywhere for fault
or flaw. The art displayed in the composition is equal
even to that which seemed to be always at the command
of Turgueneff—the art is as fine, as delicate, and as
decisive as the Russian's ; I will not compare it with
that implacable directness which in Maupassant has
captivated the minds of the unwary and the superficial.
Not Turgueneff nor Maupassant nor Bret Harte has
exceeded the mastery of handling manifested in this
story.   True that Turgueneff, Maupassant and Bret
Harte in their best short stories are far too consummate
artists to leave fag-ends unclipped or litter lying about.
True that they do exactly what they want to do. The
difference between their work and this story is that
Balzac was more ambitious than they, and gained his
greater ends as easily as they did their lesser.

Rhapsodies have been written about the simplicity of
Shakespeare's means in *Othello*, the mere dropping of a
handkerchief.   In the *Curé de Tours* the means are
even slighter.   True that neither murder nor suicide
results, and some will call it a storm in a teapot ; but
storms that threaten to overwhelm the lives and the
happiness of human beings, are equal ; whether a
man is killed by a meteor from the skies, or a tile
from the roof, his death is equally impressive, and
Balzac composed the *Curé de Tours*, with the intention of exhibiting this truth, too often disregarded or
not understood. This is obvious almost in the first
lines, when he shows us the Abbé Birotteau going
home, happy at heart, for he has spent a delightful
evening at Madame de Listonière's. His prospects
of being made a canon have been discussed, and all
there agreed that he would be appointed. There

are other reasons for his feeling singularly content with himself and the world. It is not very long since the Abbé Chapelaud left him by will the books and the furniture which the poor Abbé had not coveted, but which had been his *hoc erat in votis* for the last dozen years.

The hope of a lifetime, realised only a year ago, and the memory still an active principle in him, and the pleasure of assurance that still further fortune awaited him, combined to render him almost indifferent to the danger of the shower in which he had been caught, and the possible touch of gout it might result in. It seemed to him strange, however, that Marianne should keep him waiting some minutes before opening the door; and when Marianne, to excuse herself, said that she had only obeyed orders received from Mademoiselle, the Abbé received a shock, the more violent because it fell in the midst of his happiness. But when he found that his candlestick had been left outside his door instead of in the kitchen, according to custom, he entered his apartments in mute amazement. There another surprise awaited him—there was no fire; and the time that Marianne took to light one!

The Abbé lay in the handsome bed which he had inherited from the Abbé Chapelaud, unable to sleep, overcome and terrified by the presentiment of immeasurable misfortune. For he could not banish from his mind the thought that the delay in opening the door, the removal of the candlestick, and the absence of the fire in his bedroom could hardly be attributed to accident. And the poor Abbé fell asleep, hoping that the morning would enlighten him concerning the motives of Mlle. Gamard's displeasure.

But the secret motives of Mlle. Gamard's displeasure were destined to remain for ever unknown to him. Mlle. Gamard was an elderly maiden lady who always had priests as boarders. The Abbé Chapelaud had lived with her in the most perfect comfort for over a dozen years—nowhere a grain of dust, beautifully washed linen surplices, and albs smelling of iris, etc. On the ground floor the tall, angular, yellow-tinted Abbé Troubert, liked by nobody and not received by Madame Listonière, lived in a damp, bare apartment. He, too, had his eye on the wide, airy apartment on the first floor, filled with the beautiful furniture that the Abbé Chapelaud had left to the Abbé Birotteau, and he says when the Abbé Birotteau is away spending the evening at Madame de Listonière's: "The Abbé Birotteau does not find us amusing. He is a wit—a *gourmet!* He likes fashionable society, brilliant conversation, and the gossip of the town." It is thus that we hear for the first time of the terrible Abbé Troubert, who afterwards becomes so powerful: "his hands in Paris and his elbows on his table in Tours." But a word of explanation is necessary to make clear the terrible significance of the Abbé Troubert's words. It had long been Mlle. Gamard's ambition to have an "at home," and when the Abbé Birotteau came to occupy the apartment of the Abbé Chapelaud, he lingered after dinner in Mlle. Gamard's drawing-room, played *Boston* with her, and helped her and himself to pass an agreeable evening. The Abbé Birotteau, although quite witless, was good, kind, and amiable, and his presence in Mlle. Gamard's drawing-room attracted several other friends, and for a moment it seemed as if Mlle. Gamard was about to realise the ambition of her life. But the Abbé, although himself a fool, like many another fool, could not bear the conversation of fools, and when he took to passing his evenings at Madame Listonière's, he brought away with him many other guests, and Mlle. Gamard was obliged to give up her *soirées.*

It is easy to imagine how this cruel thwarting of her

social ambitions engendered in the heart of this old maid a ferocious hatred of the Abbé; it is easy, I say, to imagine this hatred; yes, it is easy to do so as we imagine things; but Balzac's imagining is quite different from ours; and using this simple theme as a loom he weaves a world of human passion, folly, goodness, and fashionable selfishness. The short story is a foretaste of the Human Comedy. For no writer of the first magnitude ever epitomised thus concisely all the great qualities of which his genius was composed. In *La Vieille Fille* we have the great thinker and the great social critic, but we have not the great artist; in the *Curé de Tours* we have the thinker, the critic, and the artist, and, as it should be, each enforces the other.

The story is one of pure observation—a great mind directed on what is commonly termed the minutiæ of life. But are not things only great and small in proportion as we think of them? The world is but man's thought, and in the envelope of Balzac's mind the little folk in the city of Tours rise up at once as large, as mean, and as pathetic as life itself—the little folk who are determined for a moment to defend the dear Abbé in the persecution that is being directed against him, but who, a moment after, are forced to abandon him to protect their own interests, which are being menaced by the terrible Abbé Troubert.

The story is fortunate in every way. Besides the even more than usually brilliant envelope of thought, in which Balzac never failed to enfold all he wrote, the *Curé de Tours* is extremely well written. The composition is balanced within and without, and so evenly, that no one of the epigrams that light up the pages starts out of its setting or frets, or, for one moment, fatigues the eye. Here are a few:—

"Every fresh choice implies disdain for the object that has been refused."

"If great things are simple to understand and easy to explain, little things demand an elaboration of detail."

"Morality and political economy are opposed to the individual who consumes without producing, who holds a place without distributing good or evil; for evil is but good, the results of which are not at once visible."

"Nevertheless these trifles made up the sum of his entire life; his dear life full of occupations in emptiness, full of emptiness in occupations; a life colourless and grey, and where deep sentiments were pain, and the absence of emotion felicity."

"Jealousy in Touraine, as is usually the case in provincial life, formed the substance of the language."

"Celibates replace sentiments by habits."

"If we do not always know where we are going we always know the fatigues of the journey."

Out of this handful of maxims there are at least four that would hold their own against the best that could be found in La Rochefoucauld, and they were gathered almost at haphazard from a short story written in the space of a couple of nights, printed with others in one of the fifty volumes which form the Human Comedy!

We have seen therefore that among the minor pieces the *Curé de Tours* is the finest example of Balzac's realistic method; in *Adieu* he touches high-water mark in his romantic manner. Among his studies of the abnormal *Une Passion dans le Désert* and *Sarrasine* are the best. The former is founded on a story, told to him by a showman, of a pantheress, that met a soldier starving in the desert, and taken with a sudden fancy galloped off and brought him back the hind quarter of an antelope, and in such wise continued to feed the soldier for many months. A cat when it likes you will bring in a rat and lay it at your feet; and Balzac tells the story of this strange caprice with rare intensity, and a subtle comprehension of the affections of the feline. *Sarrasine* is a rare and wonderful piece of work, but the conventionalities of this century prevent me from speaking of it.

After the *Curé de Tours* perhaps the most celebrated among the minor pieces is *Massimilla Doni*. I am aware of the great admiration in which students of Balzac hold it; but I confess that I do not share this admiration. There are some exquisite passages in this story, but it is disjointed and ill-proportioned. This is my opinion, but I am bound to say that Balzac himself held this story in the very highest esteem. Therefore it is incumbent upon me to attempt to justify my disparagement.

In the first place, the musical criticism seems to me to be a grievous disfigurement. On the subject of digression we should be indulgent, if the digression is interesting or valuable. But the eulogy of the *Moses in Egypt* shows no critical discernment, nor does it reveal any natural love of music. A naïve notation of his own impressions would have been more interesting, but crude technical praise of a work which has not stood the test of time is never very interesting, however eminent the critic.

It has been said that Balzac had not time to live; it might be added that he had not time to think. Thoughts came to him intuitively, as notes come to a bird. He had never time to hear, he had never time to think about music. But one of the vulgarly seductive phrases of the *Moses* haunted in his ear, and before it had departed some plausible criticism must have met his eye and generated in his mind a scheme for a musical novel — the Israelites languishing in Egyptian captivity. . . . The modern equivalent ?—

the Venetians under Austrian rule. That is the genesis of Massimilla Doni.

Emilio is a young Venetian whose whole fortune does not consist of more than sixty or seventy pounds a year; he lives in the palace of his ancestors amid precious marbles and works of the highest art, no portion of which he may sell. He is in love with Massimilla Doni as Dante was in love with Beatrice, and one night, after an ecstatic evening, as he returns home in his gondola, he sees his palace decorated and lighted as if for festival. Thinking that it is some surprise that Massimilla Doni is preparing for him, he asks no questions, but seats himself at the supper table, which he finds spread with rare comestibles and wines. He eats and drinks so heartily that he immediately afterwards yields to an overpowering somnolence. Soon after a woman enters, a woman that "reminded one of a fantastic English engraving invented for a forget-me-not, *une belle assemblée*, or a Book of Beauty." The Prince trembles with pleasure. "His soul, his heart, his reason turned from the thought "of any infidelity; but the brutal and capricious infidelity "dominated his soul." But the woman is not alone; she is followed by a monster—a fearful duke, who is of course Massimilla Doni's husband. The duke is a melomaniac, and the last pleasure left to him is music. The lady with him is a great singer, upon whom he expends fortunes so that he may accompany her voice on the violin, for certain harmonies convulse him with delight. But it would be profitless to follow the story into its many circumlocutions, and tell how the great singer is persuaded to yield the young man to Massimilla Doni, and how Massimilla Doni is induced to descend from the palace of reserve and purity. The intrigue surely savours of comic opera. So beautiful a theme— a young man hesitating between the real and the ideal

—should have been worked out on the simplest and most natural lines. That the beauty of the theme survives the vulgarity of the treatment is the highest tribute I can here pay to Balzac. *C'est du mauvais romantisme* . . . that is the true criticism of this story. And the second-rate romanticism of the composition penetrates and permeates the execution. An extract will explain my meaning. This is how Balzac describes the monster, the melomaniac who accompanies the woman :—

"Like that of Neapolitans the costume of the "unknown consisted of five colours, if the black of the "hat be admissible as a colour; the trousers were olive, "the red waistcoat glittered with gilded buttons, the "coat verged upon green, and the linen inclined to "yellow. This man seemed to have accepted the task "of justifying the truth of the Neapolitan that Gerolamo "always introduces into his theatre of marionettes. The "eyes seemed to be of glass. The nose shaped like an "ace of clubs was odiously prominent; and it kindly "covered a hole which would be a libel upon man to "call a mouth, and where showed three or four white "tusks loose in their sockets, lapping one over the "other. The ears drooped by their own weight, giving "to this man an odd resemblance to a dog. The com-"plexion, apparently containing several metals infused "into the blood according to the prescription of some "Hippocrates, verged upon black. The pointed fore-"head, badly hidden by flat sparse hairs which fell like "filaments of spun glass, crowned with red lumps a "grotesquely comic face. Lastly, although thin and of "ordinary height, this gentleman had long arms and "broad shoulders; but notwithstanding these deformities, "and although you would have said he was seventy, he "was not without a certain cyclopean majesty; his "manners were aristocratic, and he had that air of

"security which belongs to the rich. For those whose
"stomachs were sufficiently strong to observe him his
"story was written by passions upon a noble clay that
"had turned to mud. You would have divined the great
"lord, who, rich in his youth, had sold his body to
"Debauch at the price of excessive pleasures. Debauch
"had destroyed a human creature and made another to
"its purpose; thousands of bottles had passed beneath
"the purple arches of that grotesque nose, leaving their
"lees upon the lips. Long and wasting indigestions had
"carried away the teeth. The eyes had faded in the
"light of gaming-tables. The blood was charged with
"impure principles which had exhausted the nervous
"system. The play of the digestive forces had absorbed
"intelligence. Love had scattered the brilliant tresses
"of the young man. Like a greedy inheritor, every
"vice had left its mark upon a still living corpse.
"When we observe Nature, we discover in her jests
"a very superior irony; Nature has placed toads next
"to flowers, and in such wise was this duke near to
"this rose of love."

"Le style c'est l'homme" is an old saw, and one that
has been repeated in and out of season; my excuse
for citing it is that perhaps no better exemplification
of it could be found were all literature ransacked for
vindication of its truth. How easily we see the intellectual giant in this description, pushing forward in
mad haste, crazed with ideas, impetuously fumbling
for the right words, and finding expression at last.
To show Balzac as he is, I have translated word for
word, preserving, as well as I knew how, every ungainly
edge. Sometimes, it is true, I have not understood,
and I admit my entire inability to understand, and,
therefore to translate adequately, the following phrase
descriptive of the Duke's mouth: "Et où se montraient
trois ou quatres défences blanches douées de mouvement

qui se plaçaient d'elles-même les unes entre les autres." The looseness of the original French is, of course, magnified in the translation, for in the original an association of ideas unites, or rather blends, the words, as an effect of light blends the different parts of a landscape; this enveloping film is, of course, removed in translation, and I have preferred to leave the body naked rather than to weave for it a veil upon my own loom.

. . . But no, this is but subterfuge; far better tell the truth about Balzac's style. It has been said that Balzac had not time to live, it might be added that he had not time to *write*. He lived in ideas: ideas were always about him — ideas on all subjects; and writing was merely the operation of noting them down. In Balzac there is neither question of bad style nor of good style; he simply did not *write*; he noted down his ideas, and his ideas are always so interesting that you read without noticing the impossibilities of verbal expression he constantly slips into. It is not until you translate Balzac that you fully realise his deficiencies. For instance, the phrase I left untranslated in the description of the Chevalier de Valois, *En la patte d'oie caractéristique et les marches du palais se montraient ces rides élégantes, si prisées à la cour de Cythère. Patte d'oie* I always understood to be the French equivalent for crowsfeet; it is impossible even to conjecture what he means by *les marches du palais*, but letting that pass, I find myself quite unable to explain the grammatical construction of *se montraient* in the sentence. We find another equally bad on the same page: *Ses sourcils comme ses cheveux jouaient la jeunesse par la régularité que leur imprimait le peigne.* And what I can explain still less than the meaning of his ungrammatical sentences is the fact that until you come to translate or to read very, *very* attentively, the page appears to you to be not only well but magnificently well written. The constant supply of ideas, I suppose, is the explanation of so astonishing a deception. . . . But I see no sufficient reason to pursue the subject further. When it has been said that Balzac did not *write*, but that he found an idea for every sentence, all has been said that is worth saying.

Balzac lived in the midst of the romantic movement, and had his genius not been infinitely high and durable it would have succumbed and been lost in that great current which bore away all but himself. But the realistic and critical method, of which he was inventor and creator, lived too strongly in him, and the romance that swept about him only tended to purify and ventilate the abundance of his genius : it was the romantic movement that saved him from drifting among the mudbanks and shallow shores of Naturalism. Rembrandt, a romanticist at heart, lived in an age of plain realism, and for many a year he strove to reconcile the principle which he individually represented with the spirit of the time he lived in. I think he failed to do this in *Ronde de Nuit*, and I think he succeeded in that incomparable picture, the Good Samaritan in the Louvre ; and in just the same way I think Balzac succeeded in reconciling two discordant principles in *Adieu*, *Seraphita*, *La Peau de Chagrin*, *Sarrasine*, and failed to do so in *Massimilla Doni* and *Une ténébreuse Affaire*.

It would be foolish to argue that *Vanity Fair* is superior to the *Père Goriot*, that the *Mill on the Floss* is more beautiful than *Eugénie Grandet*, that *David Copperfield* is preferable to *La Cousine Bette*, or that *Tom Jones* is worth *Les Illusions Perdues*, but any one or all of these propositions would be more tenable than, for instance, that Thackeray or George Eliot or Dickens came, in their shorter works, within range of such marvels as *Le Curé de Tours*, *Jésus-Christ en Flandre*, *Une Vieille Fille*, *La Maison Nucingen*, or any other handful of stories that may be gathered on the endless shore of the Human Comedy. The Human Comedy is littered with stories, and each is a supreme invention, and each reveals absolute power to attain the end desired. To write a novel without a love-interest is a feat that only the very strongest may attempt, and this feat Balzac accomplishes whenever he chooses, as a matter of course. In *La Maison Nucingen* he sets himself a still more difficult task. As a party of friends are finishing dinner in a private room in a fashionable restaurant, another party sits down to dinner in the room on the other side. The walls are thin, and what they say is overheard. This dinner party consists, as Balzac puts it, of the four most celebrated vultures of Parisian society. Their conversation fills sixty - eight closely printed pages ; and they tear Paris, plunging their beaks into the very entrails, dragging them forth. After sixty-eight pages of the most astonishing conversation, one of the party says, " There is some one next door." Bricou answers significantly, " There is always some one next door."

The volume which contains *Les Secrets de la Princesse de Cadignan* commences with *La Maison Nucingen*, and closes with a short tale, some half a dozen pages, called *Facino Cane*. Facino Cane, a Venetian nobleman, is, when the story opens, a poor blind musician who plays the flageolet at servants' weddings. But he was in his youth the hero of many an adventure. He was imprisoned in a Venice dungeon, whence by the aid of a broken dagger he dug his way through the wall, and all the while he is digging he sees the darkness full of gold and diamonds, for he is, according to his account, gifted by Nature with the faculty of seeing gold. He stops, he says now, before the jewellers' shops, and the yellow of the dear metal flows through the empty orbs to his brain. After many months' toil he reached the vaults in which the treasures of the Doges were concealed. Then he entered into a conspiracy with his gaolers, and escaped by the sea, carrying a great part of the treasure with him. Being a writer of fiction myself I am not deceived by those superficial likenesses which are gathered by shallow critics and flung in the face of contemporary writers. Most foolish charges of plagiarism were urged against Mr Rider Haggard on the publication of *She;* he was even severely criticised for introducing verses not written by himself into one of his books. While the controversy was raging, I remember wondering why the erudite Mr Lang did not defend his friend by citing Balzac's conduct in precisely similar circumstances. The sonnets and verses that Lucien is supposed to have written are not by Balzac. The names of the authors are, I believe, known; but be sure every student of French verse can read the name of its author in the last lines of that exquisite sonnet "La Tulipe":—

"Mais la nature, hélas! n'a pas versé d'odeur
Dans son calice fait comme un vase de Chine."

As plainly as the author of *Les Emaux et Camées* is recognisable in that last verse, that thief Dumas is seen stealing *Monte Cristo* from *Facino Cane.* I have no faintest notion as to the date of the first publication of *Monte Cristo*, but were I possessed of all the riches of the Doges, I would stake all, yea, and my life to boot, that *Monte Cristo* was published after 1836. That is the date of *Facino Cane.*

To secure great work two things, as Mr Matthew Arnold said, are necessary—the man and the moment; in other words, a man is great when all men are great.

And Balzac lived when a concurrence of natural causes
had combined to render France especially sensible to
the reception of ideas. The revolution had loosened
the founts of human thought; Napoleon had passed
like a wild dream through Europe, the fields of conventionality were laid waste, religious, political, and
literary, rendering the French mind once more, as it
were, virgin soil, ready and in season to receive the
seed. In our own great literary epoch was it not even
so? Was it not the Reformation and the discovery of
America which resulted first in Marlowe and then in
Shakespeare? And as Shakespeare seems to have
expressed all the ideas that poetry may sing, so does
Balzac seem to have expressed all the ideas that
prose may speak. The rivalry between these two great
men seems to be between verse and prose, rather than
between French and English genius. Is it better to
reign despotically over a single country or to stretch
your power vaguely over an entire continent? Balzac's
empire is wider than Shakespeare's; his subjects are
more numerous, and his sovereignty not quite so secure.
But between him and any other writer working in
prose fiction there is little comparison. He peopled
his vast empire with surely a greater number of souls
and ideas than did Dickens or Thackeray, or Fielding,
or George Eliot, or Turgueneff, or Tolstoï. On this
point there can be no difference of opinion; and he
spoke truly when he said, "The world belongs to me
because I understand it." To me there is more wisdom
and more divine imagination in Balzac than in any
other writer; he looked further into the future than
human eyes could see; and that I am finishing these
pages with tears in my eyes, that I have written so
many upon five or six short stories, and could have
written as many more, so rich in thought is his very
slightest page, is a tribute to his genius, if such a

rushlight as myself may pay tribute to such a miracle of glory as he. Some will deem this hysterical and exaggerated praise, but only those who do not know the master, or those who think they know him because they have read the *Père Goriot*. To arrive even at a fragmentary and superficial knowledge you must read at least thirty of the fifty volumes which go to make up that city of thought so well named "The Human Comedy." As God is said to have created Adam from a handful of clay, so did Balzac create the French novel. Flaubert, Zola, Daudet, Goncourt, Bourget, and Maupassant have only taken and developed that part of Balzac which individually they superficially represent. In conclusion, I will say that as I understand criticism more as the story of the critic's soul than as an exact science, I confess that I would willingly give up *Hamlet*, *Macbeth*, *Romeo and Juliet*, etc., for the yellow books.

TURGUENEFF

THE first and last time I saw Turgueneff was at the Elysée Montmartre. It had just come on to rain, and everybody had fled from the gardens into the ball-room ; the band was clanging, the crowd was forming into quadrilles. Some one said to me, "That is Turgueneff, the great Russian novelist." I turned, and saw one immense man walking as if through a crowd of pigmies. A great, grey face, sad and weary alike of the world's folly and wisdom ; a man about sixty ; a man in whose face you read Russian in the first glance ; *enfin, l'homme de ses œuvres*. All this is as clear and certain in my mind as if it were a memory of yesterday—why, I cannot say, for at the time I do not think I was much impressed. We sat down at one of the beer-tables. Knowing I was English, and as I had been introduced as a poet — a much-abused word in the *quartier*— Turgueneff spoke of Rossetti and Swinburne. He spoke of the former as a *décadent*, and he deprecated that labouring after old forms of speech, that harkening after old ideals of beauty : "In Rossetti I note the first signs of decadence in the English tongue. Swinburne, notwithstanding some imitation of Victor Hugo, is a genius ; he is——" What further criticism would have been pronounced on Mr Swinburne must remain un-recorded, for at that moment I caught sight of the girl to whom I was engaged for the dance, and, regardless of the dignity of the person I was sitting with, I said,

"Vous m'excuserez, je suis engagé pour cette danse."
Turgueneff smiled, bowed; he was evidently a little
amused, but the author of *Torrents of Spring* was not
a man to be angry because a very young man preferred
dancing a quadrille to discussing English poetry at the
Elysée Montmartre. When I returned, he said, as he
may be easily imagined saying, "Eh bien, vous vous
êtes bien amusé?" "Very much indeed," I replied.
"You were speaking of Swinburne——" But the conversation was now firmly fixed in French fiction
and the naturalistic method—*l'Assommoir* was then
appearing in *La République des Lettres.* "For the first
time Zola has created a human being; Gervaise is a
a woman: I feel her; I know her; she is true. . . .
Still the same vicious method pervades the book—the
desire to tell us what she felt rather than what she
thought. *Je me demande qu'est-ce que cela peut me
faire si elle sue au milieu du dos ou sous les bras?*" It
is difficult to conceive the vexed and difficult question
of how far a writer should proceed in physical description better put than Turgueneff put it in this pithy
sentence: What does it matter? The most specious
sophistry would fail to convince the veriest dullard
that it mattered much; and any one gifted with a ray of
artistic understanding will see that as everything cannot
be related, if for no other reason, for want of space,
a selection is inevitable. Shall we tell how people
perspire or how people think? It will not do to
venture out on the treacherous ice of theory and
attempt definitions of what is worthiest of selection;
far better say let perspiration be admitted into the
domain of art, but let perspiration take the place in
art that it does in Nature. So think the physiological
school, but the school of adventure is of a different
opinion: never mind how she thinks; give us the spot
of perspiration; tell us how So-and-so killed the negro

As there is no difference (thought being abstracted) between a spot of perspiration and the killing of a negro, it will be seen that Mr Rider Haggard is a disciple of M. Zola, both being recorders of mere facts. For it is thought, and thought only, that divides right from wrong; it is thought, and thought only, that elevates or degrades human deeds and desires; therefore turgid accounts of massacred negroes, and turgid accounts of fornicating peasants, are in like measure distasteful to the true artist. Whether the writer should intrude his idea on the reader, or leave it latent in the work, is a question of method; and all methods are good. What I wish to establish here is that the narration of any fact is useless unless it has been tempered and purified in thought and stamped by thought with a specific value. This seems to me a suggestive comment on Turgueneff's happy remark, and hereby we arrive at a more comprehensible classification of novelists than has hitherto been attempted— the thought school, and the fact school; the identification is surely less liable to misinterpretation than the Romantic and the Naturalistic, the Realistic and the Idealistic.

To the thought school Turgueneff belonged from the first, and he was true to it just as much when he sought after a plain and passionless narration of physical phenomena, for example in the volume entitled *Strange Tales*, as when he stepped to the edge of the gulf of didacticism in "Virgin Soil." His desire was always to give utterance to a thought, to awake consciousness of that thought in the reader. His idea of things, not the things themselves, was what he longed and laboured to express; and this love of the idea was so constitutional and so inveterate in him that, had he not been the marvellous artist he was, his pursuit of his idea would have lured him into disaster, and he would have been overwhelmed and lost in the shoaling waters and quicksands of instruction and purpose. But although he steered his bark perilously near those dangerous shores he always was able to put the helm up in time and get off into the deep water of human emotion without a started plank or loss of a single spar. The most skilful yachtsman that ever lived was not more completely master of his craft than he of his art. His artistry is unfailing ; it is invincible ; and so delicate and subtle was his power over his material that he leads the reader at will ; the reader follows helplessly ; go he must, although he may feel certain that the path leads nowhere, that there is no fruit nor even haws to gather. But there is always a suggestion in the end which is equivalent to fruit. In *A Sportsman's Sketches* the slightest events are fashioned into marvellous stories. The wheel of a carriage becomes loose, the sportsman has to spend a night at an inn ; there he meets—no, not a young girl, but a dwarf, who is supposed to be an adept in *sortilège*. The dwarf begs to be allowed to accompany the sportsman out shooting ; they find no birds, and, lying on the grass, the sportsman questions the dwarf on his mode of life. A long dialogue ensues : a little girl appears ; she is strangely like the dwarf. That is all ; but that told by Turgueneff is a *chef d'œuvre*, and is as superior to our ordinary magazine short stories as a ballad by Villon is to a ballad by me. This excessive delicacy and certainty of touch has caused some eminent writers to speak of him as *une plante un peu grêle*. This is not surprising ; it is certain that these qualities forbid him the fire and explosion of Balzac, and in reading him we are conscious of a thinness, of an irritating reserve. He has often seemed to us to have left much unsaid, to have, as it were, only drawn the skin from his subject. Magnificently well is the task performed; but we should like to have seen the carcass disembowelled and hung up. Balzac would have done this no doubt; but we do not propose to compare one with the other. Balzac was greater than Hugo, and equal to Shakespeare; he was lyrical, analytical, and metaphysical at will, and he blended and made all three styles his own, and carried you away in the tempest of his genius. Turgueneff wisely refrained from attempting to measure his strength with Balzac; he loved his country; he felt her to the ends of his finger-tips; he watched her face from near and from afar; he strove to reproduce each line and lineament; Russian thought was in his brain, and you find it in his pages unadulterated.

An idea has been improvised from a knowledge of his long residence in France that he is more western in form than his illustrious compeers Tolstoy and Dostöevsky; but it would be hard to point to a trace of this denaturalisation in his works. Tolstoy I have not read, but Dostöevsky I know to be little more than Gaboriau with psychological sauce, and that of an inferior kind. For the origin of Turgueneff's literary finish we must look further back than his residence in France. His taste for scholarship was pronounced from the first, and in this natural taste and the opportunities fortune gave him for developing it, we find the seeds of the qualities which enabled him to pioneer Tolstoy and Dostöevsky, and prepare the western mind for the immense bumpers or vats of admittedly *real* Russian home-brew which are being now consumed in every civilised country. I once heard Henry James say, speaking of a well-known novelist, "He gives me the idea of a man who had never spoken to a lady in his life." I cannot say that the reverse of this is true of Turgueneff; that would mean that he only cared for those who are in society. Turgueneff knew the serf as the gentleman knows the serf; he knew the gentleman as the gentleman knows the gentleman; and he looked on and judged both as a scholar and a philosopher, without small-beer cynicism or that air of which Thackeray could never divest himself, of having been in society after the success of one of his books. While reading him we are always conscious of being in the company of a gentleman and a scholar—a scholar who has chosen to work in the novel, and who is putting into it the highest and best thought. We also know, and very well too, that we are with one who has suffered, who is sad at heart, a pessimist who believes little in regeneration, who is convinced that we turn and turn in a circle, uttering little cries until overtaken by the great oblivion. But he is not the ferocious cynic who, having drunk and found gall, would spit gall into every cup within reach; he is a man who, having learned the lesson thoroughly well, knowing that we must live, since Nature has so willed it, is inclined towards kindness and pity; who would say, "Obey Nature's laws, be simple and obey; it is the best that you can do." In various forms this philosophy finds expression in his books. His advice to young people is always to marry; only in the calm and naturalness of home is happiness found. For an exemplification of this theme let us look into the charming novel, *Smoke*.

Smoke begins amid the babel of the Baden of old days. Idleness and sunlight, bands in the open spaces, chairs under the trees, the odour of restaurants, the glitter of gold, a town of generals from all countries, of strange costumes, of ephemeral passions, above all, a town of Russians—Russians talking of the future of Russia, of *l'œuvre nationale et spontanée*, Russians declaring that Russia had invented nothing, that her most important productions, the samovar, bark shoes, and the knout were not even invented by her. There we find Litvinof, a young man of eight-and-twenty, waiting for his *fiancée*. One day, on entering his hotel, he found a letter on the table. "It is from Tanea!" he cried. But as he was about to break the seal his attention was stayed by a penetrating and agreeable odour not altogether unknown to him. He looked up and saw a bunch of heliotrope in a glass. It reminded him of something far away, of something he had almost forgotten, and could not quite recall to mind. He rang the bell, and asked the servant if he knew who had brought the flowers. The servant said a lady had brought them. The lady refused to give her name; but he thought she must be a Russian countess. "Why do you think she is a Russian countess?" "Because she gave me two florins." Litvinof then read his letter; it was not from his *fiancée*, but from her father; it came from the steppes, and it reminded him of the hard, rude life there, and it seemed to him especially opportune to read this letter at Baden. He went to bed, but he could not sleep; the odour of the heliotrope pursued him. Remembering that the odour of flowers is unhealthy in a room at night, he placed the bouquet in an adjoining room; but still the fatiguing and enervating perfume followed him; it swept over his pillow, it slipped under the sheets. Then came thin and shallow sleep, and suddenly starting up he exclaimed, "Is it she? It is not possible!" For, some years ago, Litvinof was engaged to be married to a beautiful girl; she jilted him. Irene is now the wife of a general officer; she is now in Baden, and she seeks out her former lover. She cannot deceive a second time, and, full of remorse, fear, and anguish, he is drawn into the temptation and overpowered by it. One day Irene comes and throws herself into his arms.

Then he exists but for her; he writes a cruel letter to his *fiancée*, breaking off his engagement; he tells Irene that they must go to the ends of the earth and live for one another; he has sacrificed all for her. She consents; but when the time comes to go she writes to say she cannot. "I cannot; I am yours for ever; "but to fly with you, to leave everything. . . . No, no, "no! . . . Ah, how delicious it would be! but how "impossible! Oh, my friend, treat me as a feeble, "worthless woman, but do not abandon me. . . . We are "returning at once to St Petersburg; come there; *nous* "*t'y trouverons de l'occupation. 'Nous t'y trouverons de* "*l'occupation!'* cries Litvinof. *'Voudrait-on faire de moi* "*un gentilhomme de la chambre, par hasard? Qu'est-ce* "*nous?'"* It would be difficult to praise too highly, and it would be impossible to give sufficient idea of the intense charm of the scenes in which the young man is led, as if by a silken thread, into destruction—scenes for the most part in dialogue, where no one phrase is remarkable or striking when read separately, but when taken with the context continues the picture—a picture tense with emotion, a well-nigh fabulous photograph of the mind.

Painters speak of indications; some are peculiarly happy in indications, and an object skilfully indicated has a charm that the complete painting cannot have. Turgueneff was peculiarly skilful in his indications. He had, when he showed us Irene in girlhood, to indicate the writer of the letter that was latent in the girl. This is how he does it : "Once he ran from the "university to see her in a worn and seedy frock-coat, "his hands covered with ink. She came towards him "with her usual impulsiveness. Suddenly she stopped. "'You have no gloves,' she said, insisting on each word "and then she added, 'Fie, you are only a—student. "'You are too impressionable,' replied Litvinof. 'Oh, "you are only a student, *vous n'êtes pas distingué,*' and "turning her back upon him she left the room. It is "true that an hour after she begged of him to forgive "her." Turgueneff is full of these subtle and soul-revealing touches.

Torrents of Spring treats of the same subject: the theme is the same, the variation consists in working it out through simple and honest middle-classes instead of the effete, elegant and corrupt society of Baden, in choosing the spring-time rather than the summer of life. As the title indicates, everything is fresh, innocent, and impulsive in *Torrents of Spring*. In 1840 Sasine, a young Parisian, was walking through the street of Frankfort on his way home after a pleasant and instructive journey in Italy. Suddenly he was surprised to see a young girl of the most astonishing beauty rush out of a confectioner's shop, her shoulders and arms bare, her hair undone. She seized him, he being the nearest person to her, and begged of him to succour her brother who was dying. He was dragged through the shop, and in a back room he found a boy about fourteen in an apoplectic fit; he loosed his collar, sprinkled his face with water, and the boy was restored to consciousness. One word followed another: the people in whose house he was were half Italians; he spoke of Italy; they asked him to call on the following day. Then he was introduced to the young girl's *fiancé*. She was called Gemma, and her *fiancé* was a young shopman of elegant appearance. He professed himself very grateful for the assistance Sasine had so kindly lent in a moment of extreme difficulty, and he invited him to lunch in the country on the following Sunday. A glance from Gemma made him accept the invitation. But at the restaurant a most unfortunate incident occurred. There were some officers lunching at an adjoining table, and one who had lunched a little

too well came to their table, drank Gemma's health
insolently, and took away a rose she had laid on the
table. The *fiancé* contented himself with abusing the
military, and refusing to tip the waiter, but Sasine, who
had already fallen in love with Gemma, went over to
where the officers were sitting, and in very plain
language told them what he thought of them. A duel
—the most delightful in literature—was the immediate
result; then Gemma broke off her engagement with
the shopman and engaged herself to Sasine. But
before the young people can marry, Sasine will have
to return home and sell his property, for it has been
arranged they shall live at Frankfort. While considering how the sale may be well and speedily effected
he sees an enormously fat man walking in front of him,
whom he recognises as an old school-fellow. He
accosts him, and presently he learns that the fat man
is the husband of a very wealthy woman, and it also
transpires that she is buying property in the neighbourhood in which Sasine's land is situated. The husband
says he never interferes in his wife's business, but his
wife is now staying some dozen versts from Dresden,
if Sasine wishes he will drive him over, and he can
negotiate the affair at his leisure. Sasine is received by
many servants, and is shown through great staircases
and graceful saloons. The fat man's wife is a beautiful
woman, but she is evidently of common origin; there
is in her beauty, the French would put it, *quelque chose
de populacier*, and her vicious, animal-like sensuality is
indicated by the frequent dilation of the thin nostril
and the clenching of the little teeth. She will not tell
Sasine at once if she will buy his property. She cannot
tell him before three or four days. The game of
seduction is played out at the theatre and in a riding
excursion in the mountains. Sasine writes to Gemma
imploring forgiveness, and leaves Frankfort for Paris

with this almost vulgar siren. The husband interferes
in nothing. She married him as she hires her lackeys,
and he is content so long as he eats and drinks his fill.
His gluttony is beautifully indicated in the drive from
Dresden : " Polozoff, as if stupefied, swayed slightly, a
" cigar between his lips ; he spoke but little, and did not
" look out of the window once. The different views of
" the country did not interest him ; he even declared that
" scenery bored him to death. Nor did Sasine talk much,
" nor did he admire the landscape ; his mind was too
" full of other things. He was absorbed in thought. At
" every stage Polozoff added up his bills : he calculated
" the time, and rewarded the postilions little or much
" according to the zeal they had displayed. When they
" had accomplished half the journey he took two oranges
" from the provision basket, chose the better, and gave
" the other to Sasine." The reader has followed the
story ? The fat man is the pander to his wife's caprices ;
he is bringing a very young and a very handsome man
to her. See how full of imagination and delicacy is the
first scene, and imagine what it would have been in
less dexterous hands ! Sasine has washed and dressed
himself, and has come down to the prince's apartments,
for Polozoff is a prince. " He found that prince seated
" in the most luxurious velvet arm-chair in the middle
" of a splendid salon. Sasine's phlegmatic friend had
" found time to take a bath, and to return attired in a
" sumptuous satin dressing-gown ; a red fez cap covered
" his head. Sasine approached, and examined him for
" some time. Polozoff remained immovable, like an
" idol ; he did not even turn his face to look at him ; he
" did not frown ; he did not hear a sound ; he was a
" spectacle really full of solemnity. After having admired
" him for nearly two minutes, Sasine was about to break
" this irritating silence, when suddenly the door of the
" adjoining room opened, and on the threshold there

"appeared a young and beautiful woman, in a white
"silk dress trimmed with black lace, diamonds on her
"arms and throat.   It was Marie Nicolaievna herself.
"Her thick brown hair fell on both sides, plaited but
"not pinned up.

"XXXIV.

"'Ah!' said she, with a half-confused, half-mocking
"smile, seizing quickly the end of the tresses, and fixing
"Sasine with her grey, luminous eyes, 'Pardon me, I did
"not know you were already here.'

"'Sasine, Dmitri Pavlovich, a school friend,' said
"Polozoff, without rising, and not even looking at Sasine,
"whom he was satisfied to indicate with his finger.

"'Yes, I know; you have spoken to me about
"Monsieur.   Charmed to make your acquaintance; but
"listen, Hippolyte Sidorovich (Polozoff); I wanted to
"ask you—my lady's maid is so clumsy——'

"'You want me to do your hair?'

"'Yes, yes, I beg of you. Pardon me,' she said
"again, with the same smile, and addressing Sasine with
"a slight inclination of the head.

"She turned quickly on her heel and disappeared,
"leaving behind her a harmonious and fugitive impres-
"sion of a charming neck, admirable shoulders, and a
"ravishing waist."

Now I say I cannot conceive of anything better
done than this; a difficulty is mastered absolutely,
triumphantly; a physical and mental impression is
given equally; and so well are they contrasted that
each enforces the other, and both blend and are but
one picture.

These are things that the artist sees better than
the public, *des questions de métier*, but very interesting
to those who would look behind the scenes and understand a little of the art of fiction.   It is by such little

touches that we judge our *confrères;* our approbation is won not by the big drum parts, or the violin solo which captivates the public, but by a little bit of— shall I call it instrumentation? that is to say, the sound of a certain sentiment at a certain moment; the introduction of physical phenomena, used either in alternate or combined effect with the theme of suffering or joy which the characters are uttering. Flaubert's work is full of these devices, but they are too apparent; they are forced down our throats as if with a steel fork. In Turgueneff they are so subtle that they do not weary, and they keep their place in the picture. Flaubert reminds me of Mr Holman Hunt, that is to say, his faults remind me of those so religiously and so implacably perpetrated by Mr Hunt.

Fathers and Sons is considered by many to be Turgueneff's best book, but although fully alive to the fact that it contains Bazaroff, his most thorough and most vital creation, I must profess myself adverse to this opinion. The book is wanting in those simple lines which are the characteristics of the best fiction—So-and-so did so-and-so; such a thing happened, therefore the result was . . . It will be urged that notably *Vanity Fair* is not composed in accordance with this theory of composition. Without in the least professing to have invented a definition that will include all good stories, I will say that although *Vanity Fair* is not composed on one set of simple lines, it is composed on sets of simple lines—the Crawley, the Sedley, the Osborne, and the Sharp; and these sets of lines are placed in such juxtaposition with each other that the picture balances just as the parts of an elaborate decoration balance and unite. This is what the different parts of *Fathers and Sons* do not do, and we remember little of the book except Bazaroff. But he is a real creation, not a modernization of some

Shakespearean or classical conception, but an absolutely
new and absolutely distinct addition made to our
knowledge of life. There are moments when we are
not sure that we have not seen Bazaroff, that he was
not once one of our intimate friends. Very often we
think of him as we might of some tutor, some adviser,
and we dream of him as a possible character for a novel
or play. Who among the many who have thought of
turning the troubles of Ireland to literary account
has not thought of an Irish Bazaroff? Looking over a
photograph album we say "he is like Bazaroff"; in a
word, Bazaroff is the concrete image of a section of
human thought. To evoke a soul so vital and so
knowable is the ultimate result of genius. None but
the greatest have achieved this, even they only rarely:
Turgueneff never before, never afterwards.

I have been at some pains to show that this writer's
special power seems to be in his skill of laying bare,
not the body, but rather the nerve of an emotion or
passion, and in indicating that which is most individual
and constitutional in a character. Of this there is a
very admirable instance in the novel under notice, so
admirable that I cannot refrain from giving it. Bazaroff,
this savage, cynical, and hard-minded student, who
scorns the romance of love and believes in nothing
but the natural sciences, falls in love with Madame
Odentsoff. He is attracted by her elegance and refinement, and she by his savagery and rudeness. It is
necessary to show why she will not marry Bazaroff
should he propose to her. After a couple of pages of
abstract analysis Turgueneff thus crystallises the
analysis and gives it in the form of an image. "Often
"in the morning as she came warm and weak from her
"perfumed bath it came upon her to muse on the vanities
"of life, on its sadness, its troubles, its labours. . . .
"A sudden daring then animated her heart; she was

"conscious that noble aspirations were awakening in
"her, but an open window allowed a cold breeze to flow
"into the room, and, trembling, Madame Odentsoff com-
"plained; it was with difficulty she suppressed a move-
"ment of anger, and at that moment she cared for
"nothing but that that horrid wind should cease."
Turgueneff continues the analysis, but when employing
this method it is his habit to conclude with a second
image, and over the page we find the following suggestive passage: "'What a strange man the doctor
"(Bazaroff) is,' she repeated to herself as she thought
"of him. She stretched herself in bed, smiled, and
"passed her arms over her head; then, allowing her
"eyes to wander over a page or two of a stupid French
"novel, she let the book slip and fell asleep, white,
"pure, and cold, in her perfumed bed."

But Turgueneff's most complete work, the best
synthesis of his talents, is after all *Virgin Soil.* You
find there the same subtleties, and the story is clear,
precise, and absolute. The theme is at once eternal
and modern, and is instinct with all the choral music
of fate. For it is certain that in all complex civilisa-
tions there will come a time when a reaction more or
less violent will make itself felt, and man—man who
has ceased to believe in a future life—will long for a
more simple state, will cry out against the nerve-suffering
of his life, will strive to go back to the original stock.
For the illustration of this theme Turgueneff takes a
young man, a sort of Russian Hamlet, who, although
he is mortally ashamed of his weakness, cannot refrain
from writing verses. We are shown this young man,
Nejdanof, for a moment amid the Nihilists, then he
is offered employment as a tutor to a little boy in the
house of a rich man. There he meets two people who
decide the way of his life: a young girl and a poor
landed proprietor who believe in the regeneration of the

masses. In indicating the magnetism of idea Turgueneff is, as may be surmised, at his best, and it is impossible to imagine anything better in its way than the manner in which he shows us how Nejdanof is drawn toward Marianne and afterwards towards Markelof, and although in both, idea is the primary cause of the effect, yet we are made to feel in one the fibrous affinities of sex, and how they determine that the first call shall be passed from man to woman, and then it is repeated and passed on from man to man. And what makes it still more subtle is that the young people do not really love each other; there is no bond of flesh between them. They are watched and harassed by a jealous woman, and this makes it necessary that they should play at lovers. They escape together. The subtlety of their relations to each other in the factory, where they have taken refuge, is beyond all praise, and the conclusion is as perfect as if Balzac or Shakespeare had conceived it. It is this Markelof who believes that the time has arrived for action; he preaches revolution to his beloved peasants, and he is bound hand and foot and delivered up to the enemy by them. Nejdanof strives to continue the propagation of the faith by distributing pamphlets among the peasants. His account of the reception his efforts meet with is pitiful enough: one peasant cannot read, another won't listen, another threatens, another asks stupid and sottish questions; he is out of touch with them; he cannot make them understand; and he returns defeated, overcome with a hideous sensation of his own uselessness and the futility of all human effort. He has ceased to believe; he confesses his loss of faith to the woman he has run away with, who has united her destiny with his. She is an heroic soul; there is more stuff in her than him; she does not flinch; she will marry him if he wishes it; she believes in the ultimate success of the cause. But he cannot marry

her ; he does not desire her, nor even life ; as he puts
it, "*Je n'ai pas su me simplifier.*"

Virgin Soil will hold its own in any selection
that may be made of novels dealing with human
thought, but it is not until we come to the short
stories that we find Turgueneff standing quite alone,
towering above all competitors. The analytical novel
is distinctly a product of Western invention, but
the *conte* is Eastern in its origin, and has never been
handled by us as forcibly as by its inventors ; and it is
therefore natural in dealing with Russian literature to
expect him who is most thoroughly Tartar to write the
best *contes*. This is my answer to those who assert
that Turgueneff was a Frenchified Russian, and that
you must go to Tolstoy or Gogol for the genius of the
Slav. What have we, or what has France, that can
be for one moment compared with *A Sportsman's
Sketches* or the volume entitled *Strange Tales*? In
these stories the genius of Turgueneff is seen in its
original splendour. They sometimes consist of no
more than three or four pages, sometimes they extend
to sixty or seventy ; and in reading them the *littérateur*
is conscious of something absolutely new ; they are
absolutely new in form as in matter, nor can they be
traced back to any root ; and if an analogy must be
drawn to convey some idea of their character, I will
say that they remind me of *The Thousand and One
Nights*, so very Oriental are they in their abruptness
and freedom of psychology. I would select *A
Gentleman of the Steppes* as being especially representative of this quality ; *A Lear of the Steppes* is
another ; *Toc Toc* another. From the first line the
narrative rushes forth ; there is no hesitation, there is
no stop, nor is the reader warned of what is going to
happen. This is not necessary, for so perfectly are
the events chosen that they follow without jostling or

discord, and as each comes into the reader's mind he is surprised at once by its naturalness and unexpectedness. The illusion is complete; it is just, as the phrase goes, like life itself. And what is perhaps still more marvellous is that a mere narrative, I will say a bare narrative, should possess the same intellectual charms as the psychological novel. Flaubert attempted and achieved this in *Un Cœur Simple*, but the execution is hard and laborious, like a painting by Holman Hunt, and the artist's intention is unpleasantly obvious from the first; but Turgueneff's execution is light, facile, and yet certain, even as that of a landscape by Corot.

After praising, it is usual for a critic to execute a change of front as adroitly as he can and covertly attack; this is done with the best intentions, the pretext being that the reader must be shown both sides of the picture. What is unfortunate in this method is, that it pre-supposes that the writer under discussion would have been a greater writer if his temperament and instincts were altered so as to conform more closely to the critic's ideal. It is easy to see that this is nonsense, but at the same time it is impossible to admit that perfection has been attained. This dilemma seems to me to arise solely from a misinterpretation of the word *fault*, which is popularly supposed to be a moral stain that a little good-will will remove as turpentine will remove grease from a cloth coat. This is not so. What are critically known as the faults of great artists are the absence of certain qualities occasioned by the abnormal presence of other qualities. If the statement of an artist's merit was sufficiently precise it should not be wholly impossible to arrive *à priori* at a very fair opinion of what must be wanting in him; so if the critic makes it manifest that an author is infinitely subtle, it is reasonable to presume that he is never grossly vigorous or highly coloured : if his style is quaint and *rococo*, it is certain that he is often vague, wordy, and affected. Let the critic not inveigh against excess ; let him remember rather that anything carried to excess is genius : Rabelais and Swift are supremely gross ; Shelley is supremely spiritual ; Turgueneff is supremely subtle — subtle even to the exclusion of almost every other quality. Never, except in the case of Bazaroff, did he create broadly and boldly. His characters speak and act with absolute naturalness, but they are natural rather as Gainsborough is natural than as Rembrandt and Balzac. He is careful never to intrude his personality, to warm his work with the light and fire of his soul. You look in vain for any sudden lights and personal shadows, for any richness of colour. He is neither Titian nor Turner, and yet his characters are real—they are so real that they teach only as life teaches ; they puzzle as life puzzles ; they perplex even as a Terburg perplexes. He would show you a face, and he would not stoop to impress you by the exaggeration of a single feature ; a little, a very little, human passion seen carefully, seen at a curious, but not too curious, angle, will do. A married woman who intervenes and destroys the happiness of a young couple is a favourite theme. Not having married himself, and not having found life all happiness, the only possible conclusion is that he bungled his life by not marrying. A strain of the interference of the married woman runs through all his books. You cannot say if he regrets the society of the time of Alexander I., or prefers that of Alexander II., but he must tell of his own suffering soul.

The impersonality of the artist is the vainest of delusions ; Flaubert dreamed of it all his life, but *Madame Bovary*, with the little pessimistic flip at the end of every paragraph, is the most personal of books. Turgueneff attained absolute impersonality of diction ; but that which had influenced his life he put forward prominently in his books, and had Turgueneff's talent been less subtle, he would surely have drifted on the commonplace in dealing with such a time-worn theme, for he attempted no rearrangement of the dry bones —his imagination clothed them merely with new and splendid raiment. I have no personal knowledge on this point, but I should say, judging from certain internal indications, that he borrowed his stories, and that, so far as their structure was concerned, he left them very much as he found them. *Smoke*, I should say, was based upon the author's personal reminiscence ; *Torrents of Spring* upon a story that was told to him ; three stories out of the four in the volume entitled *Strange Tales*, viz., *A Strange Tale*, *A Lear of the Steppes*, and *Toc Toc*, were, I should say, certainly written from information arrived at either through conversation or the public press. I will add to this list the greater part of *A Sportsman's Sketches*, notably *A Gentleman of the Steppes*. A footnote tells us that the second part of this story was composed several years after the first. Now the first part I feel sure was a personal experience, the second an anecdote that was related to him, in which he saw instantly the completion of what he had left as a fragment. I also believe in the impotency of Turgueneff to evolve a human soul out of his inner consciousness, and that for the same reasons as obliged him to have recourse to adventitious assistance in the composition of his stories. He was obliged in his drawing of character to confine himself to the direct and absolute delineation of his friends and acquaintances. Nor do I feel sure that he always even understood his model. Bazaroff's characteristics were so strongly marked that he could not fail to perceive what was

eternal in him.   And Bazaroff, who should have belonged
to Balzac, embarrassed Turgueneff, for he was obliged
to fit him into an original story, and this is how I
account for the fact that *Fathers and Sons* alone among
Turgueneff's novels is a series of scenes held together
by the personality of the leading character.   I fail to
perceive any difference between Litvinof and Sasine,
the two young men in *Smoke* and *Torrents of Spring*,
they might be passed from one novel to the other without
the plot being affected or the reader's psychological
sense being disturbed.   And this last book will serve
for excellent illustration of what was said of Turgueneff's
illuminative rather than creative imagination.   For,
unlike *Smoke*, which consists solely of the hero's love of
the married woman, *Torrents of Spring* is made up
equally of Sasine's passion for the two women.   The
scene in the box at the theatre is as fine as it could
be.   I like the scene on horseback less.   A more
powerful imagination—let us say Balzac—would have
said the point here is first to differentiate between the
young man's love of the married woman and the young
girl; secondly, to show that nothing is lost in nature.
Shakespeare does not fail to do this in *Romeo and Juliet*.
Rosalind is not a married woman.   The Elizabethan
poet always avoided adultery, and pointedly.   But to
whom shall we compare Turgueneff?   Miss Austen's
charm is too special, too peculiar to herself.   Balzac's
genius lies in his universality, Miss Austen's in her
parochialism; the former was infinitely daring in
attempting almost everything, the latter is infinitely
daring in attempting almost nothing, and if the reader
can imagine a beautifully cultivated islet lying somewhere between the philosophic realism of Balzac and
the maiden-lady realism of Miss Austen, he will have
gone far to see Turgueneff as I see him.

Our author's verbal execution is all that now remains

to us to consider, and here I can only speak from hearsay. Turgueneff is considered by Russians as one of their greatest prose-writers, if not indeed their very greatest. I only know him through a French translation; those published by Hetzel et Cie. strike me as almost brilliant, certainly adequate.

His anonymous translator did not, it is true, do for him what Hugo did for Shakespeare, what Baudelaire did for Poe; the style does not precisely attract attention; it is straightforward and in no way deformed; it bears, I should think, the same relation to the original as a pleasant-faced housemaid does to a refined and beautiful mistress.

E

MY IMPRESSIONS OF ZOLA

M ANET had persuaded me to go to the *bal de l'Assommoir* dressed as a Parisian workman, for he enjoyed incongruities, and the blouse and the casquette, with my appearance and my accent, appealed to his imagination. "There is no Frenchman living in London who occupies the same position as you do in Paris," he said, and I pondered over his words as I followed him through *tout Paris* assembled at the Elysée Montmartre, for the ball given in honour of the play that was being performed at the Ambigu. "But I must introduce you to Zola. There he is," he said pointing to a thickly built, massive man in evening clothes for, as Manet said, a serious writer cannot be expected to put on fancy dress.

Zola bowed and passed on, chilling us a little; Manet would have liked to watch him struggling into a new acquaintanceship, and we walked on together conscious of our failure, myself thinking how pleasant it would have been to have gone with them into a corner, and talked art for half an hour, "and what a wonderful memory it would have been!" I thought, and begged Manet a few minutes later to come with me in search of Zola. But he was nowhere to be found.

"He must have gone home," I said, and Manet answered: "It doesn't matter. You'll find him at home at Mèdan any day you like to go there."

For one reason or another it was not till some

months later that I summoned courage and took the train at the Gare St Lazare. There is no station at Mèdan, the nearest station is — (the curious are referred to the time table for I have forgotten the name of it) — and Mèdan is a village known only to peasants, about a mile and a half from the station. Some chance had led Zola there, and being in want of a country residence he had purchased a cottage from one of the peasants, which he had just finished building into a sort of castle; an ugly place it seemed to me, a great red brick wall with a small door in it through which I was taken into the house, and left waiting in the billiard room.

It was not Zola that came down to me, but Madame Zola. She had forgotten me, though I had met her at Manet's studio, and it was only after many tedious explanations that she somewhat reluctantly led me through the house, up many staircases of polished oak, narrow and steep. On the wall of the last little flight there were Japanese prints depicting furious fornications; a rather blatant announcement, I thought of naturalism—but they were forgotten quickly, for in a few seconds I should be in the master's presence. She opened a door and left me, and I found myself in a place as large as the studio of an Academician, lighted by a skylight and a huge window. For a moment or two I lost my way among the massive furniture, and it was not until I passed a lectern that I discovered the master on a sofa by a window correcting proofs.

He did not rise to meet me, but contented himself with untucking his fat leg and motioning with his hand to a seat. His manner was terribly aloof and cold, and my embarrassment increased, for suddenly I remembered I had heard that Zola was never long in doubt as to whether he was talking to a fool or a man of wit, and that at the end of a minute a fool was dismissed peremptorily. "And he has discovered me to be a fool though I haven't said a word." I glanced at the terrible master who lay on the sofa, his glasses on his nose, reading me, divining the commonplace remarks that I was trying to conjure up. "If Homer and Shakespeare were suddenly introduced they would have to begin with remarks about the weather or the pleasure each had taken in the other's work" I said to myself, "and if this man would only give me as much rope as he would to Shakespeare or Homer I might think of something more interesting than the compliments that I am gabbling."

Zola was not then what he is now, a gracious, kindly man in the habit of receiving every one who chooses to call on him, and answering all sorts of questions. He was then the iconoclast, the idol-breaker, a bear that cursed the universe, and bade all comers begone. All the same his writings exhaled a certain large-heartedness and sympathy, and I had always felt while reading his weekly article in *The Voltaire* that we were intended to understand each other. I had imagined that when I went to see him he would come forward, his hands extended in benevolent gesture, taking me at once into his confidence. This Buddha lying on the sofa, fixing his glasses from time to time on his short, strangely square-cut nose, was in such strange conflict with my dream that I could hardly believe that this could be my Zola in those terrible moments during which I tried to improvise compliments. Not one had produced the faintest impression, no more than water flowing over a block of granite, and feverishly I sought for a subject of conversation, something, no matter what, that might interest him.

The power that the circulating libraries exercised on literature occupied my mind a good deal at that time, and I hurried to the subject, seizing the first transitional phrase.

"The position of the novelist in England is that of a slave," I said, "for books are not bought in England, but hired."

"But if a man writes a book that interests the public, the public will find it."

"The public will find it in time no doubt," I answered, "but the man may starve in the interval."

"Yes, he may; and your difficulty is no small one, a middle-man always between you and your public."

"Ah, he's beginning to see I'm not such a fool after all," I said to myself, and as soon as I had explained the power that their monopoly gave to Mudie and Smith I deflected the conversation dexterously from the practical to the moral question, dropping some disparaging remarks about Puritanism as an artistic influence. Zola, who had been waking for some time out of his slumber, was now wholly awake.

"What you say," the great man said, "is extremely interesting. I have written an article on the influence of Protestantism on art; it will appear in to-morrow's *Figaro*, and I make this statement, that Protestantism has never produced great art. Milton is the one Protestant writer. The Elizabethans, Shakespeare, and Jonson lived before Protestantism had taken hold of the national spirit, the genius of the nation, and so on."

The conversation then became friendly and pleasant. Zola asked me about George Eliot; which did I think was her best book? What French writer was she most like? Though I felt I was risking my newly-acquired reputation, I had to admit that I could think of no one to compare her with. The conversation paused a moment, and to my surprise and pleasure Zola began to tell me about the novel he was writing. We must have talked for three-quarters of an hour, and then, fearing to outstay my welcome, I bade the master good-bye. He took me downstairs, vivacious all the time, and asked me to come to see him again. Then I knew I had made a friend. "I have made a friend," I repeated to myself as the carriage rolled through the flat, green French country, my eyes noting the mystery of the long low horizon, the poplars pointing to the first stars. A train shrieked across the solitude. "I have made a friend," I repeated to myself as I listened to the distant rattle, and as the rattle died away in faint echoes, absorbed one by one in the dusky night of the long low plain I said: "Yes, he is the very man I had imagined from reading his articles. A clear, well-balanced mind, a sympathetic nature, passionate in his convictions, loyal to his opinions. A little rough-ness at first; possibly what I mistook for roughness was mere shyness; besides it cannot be amusing to be told to your face that you are a great writer. I shouldn't like it myself."

Years passed. I had written many books. *A Mummer's Wife* had been translated into French; it had been published in *The Voltaire* and the *Vie Populaire*. Charpentier was about to issue it in book form, and Zola had promised to write a preface. The *Confessions of a Young Man* was appearing in *La Revue Independante*, and the report had gone abroad that the next instalment would contain a scathing attack on *La Terre*. I wrote to Zola saying that this was not true, and proposing to spend Monday with him. "On Monday morning you will receive the new number of the *Review*, and we shall be able to discuss the matter at breakfast." I knew that the number con-tained—well, some frivolous remarks about naturalism; these I hoped to be able to explain away. But I did not feel quite at ease, so I called on my way for the

faithful Alexis—bulky Alexis's placid temperament
would serve as a buffer when the discussion became
strained. However happily it might end there could
hardly fail to be moments when—— I don't think
I finished the sentence at the time; I will not seek
to do so now.

Our walk lay by the river shimmering like watered
silk between green banks full of the lush of June,
and beyond them the green French country seemed
to rejoice in the sunshine like a living creature. We
sauntered, talking about our books, and I took exquisite
pleasure in the poplars growing so tall and straight
out of the plain, and the white clouds hanging between
the trees. And when remembrances of Zola interrupted
my reveries I told Alexis exactly what I had written,
and the dear fellow assured me that Zola could not
take offence at such light criticism.

"Yes, Alexis, but you always say what is agreeable
to hear."

As before, Zola was lying on the sofa by the window
and after a few words of greeting, he said:

"I'm afraid, my dear friend, that I shall not be able
to write the preface. You have made it impossible for
me to do so."

The phrases I had used when subjected to a close
critical examination proved more difficult of explanation
than I had anticipated. The discussion was painful,
and the breakfast bell was a welcome relief. "It's over
at last," I said to myself; but to my horror instead
of answering my thought the master said:

"We are going down to breakfast now, but after
breakfast we will go into the matter thoroughly; I
will read the passages aloud to you."

"Good Heavens!" I thought, "I wish I hadn't
come."

After breakfast Zola, Alexis, and myself walked in

the garden talking of indifferent things for an hour
or more.   Then Zola said:

"We will now go upstairs."   He led the way, and
I followed, feeling very much as I used to feel at
school when ordered a flogging.   The master lay on
the sofa; I took a small chair; he said: "You'll be
more comfortable in a larger one."

The passages were already marked, and they were
read to me in a low and deliberate voice.   I listened,
thinking what was the best defence to set up; Zola
commented on every fresh sarcasm.

"How can I write your preface after that?   I want
to, you know, but I ask you how can I?   Listen!"

"Don't you see, my dear friend, that that book
is not my real opinion about life and things, but
rather an attempt to reduce to words the fugitive
imaginings of my mind, its intimate workings, its
shifting colours?   Has it never come to you to think
differently about things?   To find your mind in a
ferment of contradiction?"

"No," he said, "I do not change my opinions easily.
There is Alexis" (he was indeed there, round as a
barrel with the inevitable cigar between his teeth); "I
have known Alexis these five and twenty years, and I
think of him to-day exactly as I always thought of
him.   With me an opinion is like a heavy piece of
furniture; it is moved with difficulty."

"But," I said, "the passages you have just read are
from a chapter entitled 'La Synthèse de la Nouvelle
Athenes' . . . and must be taken as an expression
of the opinions of the various *ratés* who assemble there."

"I will admit that as a legitimate defence, but
you see the opinions expressed in the café coincide
exactly with those which you express yourself in
an earlier part of the book."

I had to fall back on the original defence, that a

man changes, contradictory thinking should not be taken for the opinions which he holds by and abides by.

"How often do we hear Christians make jokes against Christianity?" I thought the argument specious, but Zola did not notice it. He continued reading:

"After what you have written about Goncourt," he said, "you never can go to his house again."

"I don't want to; he isn't a friend."

"The disciples, the childish vanity, the *bric-à-brac*, even the accusation of making copy out of his brother's corpse, *tout est là, rien ne manque*. What you say of me is nothing compared with what you say of Goncourt." I hastened to concur in this opinion, but Zola was not to be wheedled. "No, my dear friend," he said gravely and sadly, "you don't call your book *Memoirs d'un Jeune Anglais* you say *Confessions d'un Jeune Anglais*, and when we use the word Confessions we mean that at last we are going to tell the truth. I have gone through these pages calling attention to the expressions used, not because I am angry, but because I want to convince you that you have made it impossible for me to write the preface to your *Mummer's Wife*. What you think of me does not affect me, no, I won't say that; we are old friends. What you say about me does affect me, I mean that nothing that you can say can affect my position. . . . You admit in your book that you owe your first inspiration to me. I am proud that this is so, and thank you for saying it. I am sorry you have changed your opinions; after all it is the eternal law — children devour their fathers. I make no complaint. Nature has willed it so."

He spoke these words sadly as he walked across the room. The twilight was gathering, the great furniture loomed up like shadows. There were tears in my eyes. Never did I feel so distinct a sensation of my inferiority; the man was great in his simplicity. "The man is greater than his books," I said to myself, "and that is a great deal, for he has written some very fine books."

I have told the story of these two meetings with some levity, but I was deeply moved at the time, and I am troubled even now, for is it always right to wear one's heart on one's sleeve, and to publish one's opinions as they come up in one's mind? Or is it better to look upon one's opinions as heavy pieces of furniture that are moved with difficulty. Alexis had devoted months to the correction of the translation that Charpentier was about to issue, and looked to Zola's preface to recoup himself for the labour he had spent upon the book, and a few casual words of mine had wrecked these hopes. He did not reproach me with having cost him some monetary losses; he merely said, "*C'est Charpentier que va boire un bouillon. Mille francs de corrections.*" The grey-green country stretched out before us, flat and dim—a dark mass of trees in front of us, a poplar striking out of the long plain. Alexis lectured me as we walked through the solitary country, but I did not listen. All the while I thought of Zola's last words as he bade me good-bye. "I hope you understand that our personal relations are the same as they always were, only you have made it impossible for me to write the preface."

At this time Zola was a fat man; soon after he became a thin one. By abstaining from drink at his meals he reduced his weight thirty-six French pounds in two months. He seems to have accepted Balzac's maxim, that the elegance of life exists mainly in the waist. As his waist narrowed his manner of life became more expansive. No longer is he the recluse of Mèdan; he has added a tower to his country house —with what intention I never fully understood—and he lives in a spacious mansion in the Rue de Bruxelles, which he has furnished with oak carvings, tapestries, portraits of archbishops and wrought-iron railings. A plaster cast of the Venus de Milo stands on the balustrade that encircles the staircase. The house seems to reveal a large coarse mind, a sort of coarsely woven net through whose meshes all live things escape, and that brings to shore only a quantity of *débris*. " From the *Rue de Lafayette*," I said. Why should he consider it incumbent upon him to collect these things? Great artists need not be learned in *bric - à - brac*. Manet lived all his life amid red plush furniture; and I am not sure that I should have spoken of Zola's furniture (has it not been described by reporters and reproduced in photography in every illustrated periodical?) if it had not been that with the acquisition of a waist and much general *bric-à-brac* a definite mental change has come upon Zola. I once heard him say he was going to give a ball. I don't think he ever carried the project into execution. However this may be, his house has, for the last three years, been open to visitors, and he has answered the ten thousand heterogeneous questions that the eleven hundred and fifty-seven interviewers have put to him with unfailing urbanity, and I am bound to admit, with extraordinary common-sense.

His mind is not as intense or penetrating as Tourguèneff's, but it looks with admirable lucidity over a wide surface, and he can answer the most foolish questions reasonably. An elderly lady's apple-cart has been upset in the Place Cliche, and a reporter calls on Zola for his opinion. He says that he has no precise information on the subject of apples, but he believes that apple-growing is a very large industry in the north of France. If the apple sellers of Mont-martre are prevented from exposing their wares for sale, the liberty of the individual is called into question, and a very large and important industry is possibly affected. At the same time the streets cannot—and so on. But even these platitudes he will relieve with some touch of rare common-sense. This touch I have left out, it is the incommunicable secret of his genius. But if any reader of this article should desire to hear Zola talk, I will recommend him to a book called *Enquête Litteraire* by Jules Huret. Huret's interview with Zola is an astonishing piece of literature. In this interview we perceive, as we should in a long intercourse with Zola himself, that his genius is but the triumph and apotheosis of common-sense. For his genius is wingless, it never rises towards the stars ; it maintains itself at what I may term the level of superior mediocrity, and it is with him always, on small as on great occasions. Take his answer to an interviewer who called on him at the Savoy Hotel. Zola had arrived late the night before, and had only just got out of bed. The question was : "What are your impressions of London?" The answer was : "My first impression of London was an excellent appetite. The train was late, and we didn't dine until nine o'clock, but we dined excellently well." Is it possible to answer a foolish question more sensibly?

I said just now that Zola's vision of life was not so intense, penetrating, or subtle as Tourguèneff's. It is radically different. Zola's mind is patriarchal ; he is an old-world hero, a patriarch belated in the nineteenth century. Not Abraham himself encamped amid his flocks, herds, and a numerous servitude saw or thought more simply than he does. There are hackney carriages, washerwomen, and *châssepots* in the *Rougon Macquart* series, but these are merely adventitious attractions which affect in no way the general character of the work. Hugo is said to be the last of the old-world

poets; but the real difference between Zola and Hugo is
that one can, and the other cannot, write verse. Take
from Hugo his genius of versification and you would
get the novelist. He would have produced a set of
novels very similar to the *Rougon Macquart* series. It
would have been in twenty volumes, possibly in more,
and would have sold as largely. Robbed of his versification, Hugo would have accepted the hackney carriages
and the washerwomen. He could not have done otherwise, and both men saw life from the outside, and their
tendency was to exaggerate the outside. All the same
the hypothetical work would have differed from the
Rougon Macquart. Hugo was more naturally an artist
than Zola. His imagination was rarer, but it was not
more powerful nor more fecund. Zola's imagination
is one of the most extraordinary that ever found
expression in literature. Think, you who have read
the twenty volumes, of the hundreds of places he has
shown you and familiarised you with, even as you
are familiar with the room you live in. Can you not
see incestuous Renée dreaming in her yellow boudoir,
or feverishly flung on the skins under the malign shade
of tropical plants in the great conservatory? Are not
the market - places in your mind — the roofs for ever
silhouetting against the pale sky? The smell of the
fish and the hundred colours of the fish; the vaults
where the children roll amid the feathers? And the
scene where they chop the pigeons' heads, disputing
how many so-and-so can bleed in an hour? And how
intimately conscious we are of the great garden of the
Paradou and the adorable death of Albine, who dies
asphyxiated by the flowers with which she has filled
the room; the enumeration of the flowers, the evocation
of an orchestra of scents, for every scent recalls the
sound of an instrument, and the last phrase—"Albine
dies in a supreme hiccup of flowers"—how wonderful!

And the modes of life, the trees, the various ways
in which the human animal gains his livelihood!
Do we not all remember the gold chain-makers in
L'Assommoir and the vestment makers in *Le Rêve*?
In *Au Bonheur des Dames* the work of every employé
is explained ; the phenomena of each passing hour is
revealed to us. *Germinal* is full of every detail of
miner life, the ropes, the pulleys, the furnaces, the
trucks, the horses. But I must stay my pen or this
article will degenerate into a mere catalogue.

But has Zola furnished these extraordinary evocations
of the externals of human life with human souls? Has
he created characters that will not suffer by comparison with Balzac's? Zola's evocation of souls is
slight, nearly always fragmentary and shadowy. A
soul haunts in Gervaise, and Coupeau, too, has a soul,
and through the numberless pages a few shades flit
vaguely recognisable as human souls. That is all.
In the line of souls Gervaise is his greatest achievement,
and that is why I place *L'Assommoir* above all his
other books. There are other reasons. When he wrote
L'Assommoir Zola was more than he ever was before,
and certainly more than he ever was since, a pupil of
Flaubert. The book is written entirely in Flaubert's
manner, the short sentences relieved by the pictorial
epithet. The old masters thought that originality was
found in individual feeling and seeing rather than in
mannerism, and as I share their opinion I think that
it is regrettable that Zola did not continue to write
in the style in which he produced his finest book.
But the style became too laborious for him just as
pre-Raphaelism became too laborious for Sir John
Millais, and after *L'Assommoir* his style became looser,
and with every fresh book he seems more and
more inclined to abandon himself to the ease of
redundant expression. There are fine pages even in

his worst books, but so far as my personal taste and
interest are engaged in his work I would choose to
have revised editions of his early works rather than
the new novels he contemplates writing — *Lourdes*,
Paris, *Rome*, etc.

Revised editions of Zola's works! How easily one
drops into talking nonsense. His method of novel-
writing does not admit of revision. As well might we
ask the editor of a daily paper for concentration of
expression in leading articles, dramatic notes, and
reports of boat races. During the last ten or a
dozen years a striking resemblance has grown up
between the Zola novel and the popular newspaper.
The novel and the newspaper seem to me to stand
on the same footing; the intention of both is the
same, and the means employed are the same. It
is true that Zola's reports on the Franco-German
war are better done than the reports of the war
correspondent of the *Daily Telegraph*. It is also true
that the scenery at the "Lyceum" is better painted
than the scenery at the "Surrey," but that is hardly a
reason for confusing a set taken from *Much Ado about
Nothing* with the pictures of Turner, Constable, and
Wilson, and we find a like difference between the
battle pieces in *War and Peace* and those in *La Débâcle*—
a difference not of degree but a difference of kind.
Zola's novel is practically the daily paper. He has
discovered a formula that suits the average man as
well as the *Daily Telegraph* or the *Petit Journal*, and
he chooses his subjects, not in obedience to an artistic
instinct, but in accordance with public taste. Three
hundred thousand pilgrims go to Lourdes yearly.
Every pilgrim is a certain reader, and the afflicted in
all countries are interested in the question. Between
belief and unbelief he will steer a middle course just
as he steered a middle course between France and

Prussia. I heard him boast, without ever perceiving the enormous artistic significance of what he was saying, that he had written a French novel on the war without giving Prussia cause for offence. I take it that the sublime impartiality of the true artist is very different from the mock impartiality of the journalist who wants to get up a controversy. The true artist sees life as God sees it, without prejudice; life is for him—I think the phrase is Flaubert's—*une hallucination à transporter.*

Zola told me that he had gone into calculation, and allowing for a fortnight's holidays at Christmas, *Lourdes* would take him seven months to write. Five hundred pages in seven months! Tolstoy took six years to write *Anna Karenina,* ten to write *War and Peace;* Flaubert took seventeen years to write *La Tentation de St Antoine,* eight or nine to write *L'Education Sentimental;* and seven or eight translators are already at work on *Lourdes*; it will appear in the *New York Herald,* and Mr Bennet has paid a thousand pounds for the serial rights. But adequate information regarding the various forms and languages in which this book will appear would be the subject of an article on bibliography. Suffice it to say here that it will bring Zola something like four thousand pounds before it reaches Charpentier in book form; it will then be read by everybody except men of letters—but their number is so small that the abstention will not materially affect the sale. If the book does not sell three hundred thousand copies it is a failure, and if the book on the Russian Alliance which will follow does not sell half a million it will be a failure. Did any great writer ever see literature from this point of view before?

The idea of conquest seems inherent in Zola. Five and twenty years ago he wrote a book called *Le Conquête de Plassans.* The idea of conquest cropped up again in *L'Oeuvre*, and this time it was Paris that was conquered. And now it seems that Zola meditates the conquest of the world. He came to England at the head of an army of journalists; rockets were let off at the Crystal Palace, and trumpets were blown in his honour at the Mansion House. He will probably proceed on a similar mission to St Petersburg (it has already been spoken of); he may even visit America. Why not? There are sixty millions in the United States, who through the medium of translation, may read the *Rougon Macquart*! The newspapers reported that Madame Zola, astonished at the length of our London suburbs, said: "This is a town that would suit you, Emile." Every house represented to her a possible sale of a novel, Charpentier edition, three francs fifty. If Zola were told that a *concierge* had not heard his name he would feel discouraged. An enquiry would be set on foot, and if a *concierge's* guild could be discovered he would arrange to address a meeting. He looks upon all men who do not read his novels as lost. Lost to what? Ah, that I cannot say; not to art, for the quality of his writing does not seem to concern him any more than the quality of the things he buys. The carved woodwork and the iron railings may not be finely wrought, but they photograph all right, and every interviewer is received and every sightseer — Chinese, Peruvians, Esquimaux—all and sundry are granted audience, and the afternoon passes in talking of how books may be best put on the market.

Some translation of his works must appear in every dialect, and to discover one not yet reduced to written characters, and to arrange that the first work printed in it should be a translation of the *Rougon Macquart* series would be fame indeed. M. Bruneau comes in with the score of the music he has just written for one of the novels, and the gentleman from Paraguay

jumps up and proposes to do the opera into the
language spoken in his country ; the Thibetian might
do the same.   Bruneau and Zola put their heads
together.   Hurrah ! another outlet has been discovered,
and the terms of the contract are discussed.   Only
the other day in an article on the lyrical drama, after
coupling Wagner and Bruneau together, Zola explained
that he would create a lyrical drama with human
characters ; and when he has done this "the colossal
Wagner will grow pale on the high pedestal of his
symbols."   Zola believes that young French composers
have not written great music because their libretti are
not sufficiently human.   In a word, he imagines himself
writing various libretti to which the young French
composers will add a little music as cream is added
to *méringues*.   Well, if a man will talk on all subjects
the time will come when he will talk nonsense.   I
am afraid that time has come for Zola !

The desire of gold for its own sake is comprehensible
in a way ; but Zola has no love of money, he has
squandered all he made on vulgar decoration and
absurd architecture.   The pleasures of life bore him
exceedingly, so he says ; but I am afraid that he has
not acquainted himself with them.   Of the pleasures of
Art he is equally ignorant.   His youth was beset
with difficulties sufficient, be it admitted to his credit,
to conquer all but the most resolute.   He wrote for four
hours every morning at a novel, and every afternoon he
wrote an article for a newspaper, and those who have
felt the pressure of a weekly article, while engaged on
a work of the imagination, will appreciate the severity
of the ordeal that Zola bore for many years unflinch-
ingly.   He had little time for reflection or study,
and was only able to catch the few ideas abroad
in his day as they passed him.   He read his contemporaries, Flaubert, Goncourt, Daudet, and to obtain

a platform whence he might preach his doctrine he read Balzac and Hugo; but with the heart of French literature, with Montaigne, St Simon, and La Bruyère it may be doubted if his knowledge is more than rudimentary. The influence of Manet and Flaubert and Goncourt persuaded him that he was interested in the external world, and we hailed *L'Assommoir* as a masterpiece, for we wished to group ourselves round some great writer. We hugged the belief that, set free from pecuniary anxieties, he would read, think, travel, and refrain from constant production, giving three or four years to the composition and the writing of each book. We believed that he would cultivate refinement of thought, and refinement of literary expression. But Zola was not naturally an artist. Instead of the books becoming more and more beautiful, they have become larger, looser, and uglier, and they serve no purpose whatsoever, except to find money for the purchase of cock-eyed saints on gold backgrounds.

Alas! the ridiculous towers of Mèdan! Alas! the arrival of translators from Paraguay! Alas! the blowing of trumpets before the Lord Mayor of London in honour of *La Terre, La Débâcle, L'Argent*, and *Docteur Pascal!*

And, three times, alas, for are we not now menaced by a novel on Lourdes, on Rome, and on Paris? In these novels he will re-write everything that he has written before. His friends will drop away from him; he will be left alone; his excellent cigars will fail to attract us, and smoking bad ones in the café we shall regret his life and his works, and the mistake we made; and when the café closes we shall stand on the edge of the pavement wondering what the end will be. One of us will say, it will probably be Huysmanns: "In *Le Ventre de Paris* there is a pork butcher who, after having worked ten hours a day all his life is found dead sitting before a table *son nez dans le boudin.*"

"And you think," I shall say, "that he will just drop from sheer exhaustion over his writing table *son nez dans le boudin ?* "

Huysmanns will not answer, he will remember that Zola is the friend of his life. The little group will separate, and wending my way to my little flat in the Rue de la Tour des Dames, I shall think of Zola as a striking instance of the insanity of common-sense.

A GREAT POET

I WRITE about a poet whose verse, whose name, and whose life are unknown in England—of one who even in his own country is known only to the *élite*—of one who, although he has published beautiful books for more than a quarter of a century, remains to this day unhonoured and unrecognised by the general reading public in the most distinguished literary centre in the world—in Paris. His name is Verlaine, and standing to-day on the last verge of life he sees glory rising out of the chasm beneath him. And when he steps into the chasm, the faint light that now gilds the last rocks and peaks of life will ascend into those heavens out of which no light sets. In the meantime, he lives in poverty, if not in absolute hunger.

It is true that real talent may be passed by, but sooner or later it is recognised. The one invincible thing is a good book. It may be doubted if the world contains a single good unknown poem. If a man were to write a good sonnet and drop it in the middle of the Sahara, the fate that has watched over good poetry through so many centuries would catch it up, and carry it somehow into common repute. How, then, is it that Verlaine is unknown? I answer that just as there are many ways of being "stonebroke," so there are many ways of being unknown. No man, however great, is known to everybody, and no man, however solitary, is known to nobody.

Among men of letters Verlaine is as well known as
Victor Hugo; to the occasional reader his name is as
unknown as that of the *concierge* over the way, or the
cocher turning the corner of the street. And this,
because the general reading public cares little for
poetry? No. But because Verlaine is of all men
of genius I have ever met the least fitted to defend
himself in the battle of life. He is able for nothing
except the occasional writing of beautiful verses. And
verses that have no other characteristic than beauty
may be said to be an almost unsaleable commodity.
His instincts are neither patriotic nor popular, but
entirely æsthetical—the religious emotion of a monk
painting the joys of heaven above the dim altar, and
the sensuousness of the same monk delineating the tall
adolescent angel. He loves language and every
cadence the French language may inflect haunts in his
ear. So natural and instinctive is the music of his
verse that it often seems no more than the melancholy
inarticulate voice which nature speaks, penetrating and
profound by reason of its vagueness and utterness.

> " O triste, triste, était mon âme,
>   A cause, à cause d'une femme.
>
> " Je ne me suis pas consolé
>   Bien que mon cœur s'en soit allé,
>
> " Bien que mon cœur, bien que mon âme,
>   Eussent fui loin de cette femme.
>
> " Je ne me suis pas consolé,
>   Bien que mon cœur s'en soit allé,
>
> " Et mon cœur, mon cœur trop sensible
>   Dit à mon âme : Est-il possible,
>
> " Est-il possible—le fût-il,—
>   Ce fier exil, ce triste exil ?

" Mon âme dit à mon cœur : Sais-je,
   Moi-même, que nous veut ce piège

" D'être présents bien qu'exilés,
   Encore que loin en allés ? "

Is not this plaintive as water gurgling underground
and sad as reeds sighing in eventide? Verlaine is
exclusively a poet, and may leave for no moment the
immortality of his verse for the daily bread of prose.
His rhythms become disintegrated in prose, his thoughts
—gentle reveries—die in the looseness of prose.

But besides the disadvantage of being entirely and
exclusively a poet, the disorder of his private life has
reckoned heavily against Verlaine. For many years
hardly any newspaper dared to print his name ; only
the ephemeral reviews that the ardour of enthusiasts
called into existence for a season published his verse.
He has lived the prey of strange passions that have
ruined and dishonoured him. He has been in prison,
and has lived many years in exile, sometimes gaining a
precarious livelihood as a French teacher in English
schools. Of late years sickness has not left him ; from
hospital to hospital he has dragged a pitiful body,
and when discharged partly cured he has found shelter
only in distant quarters of the town, among the working
folk that herd together, *dans le quartier du Temple*.

I once saw Verlaine. I shall not forget the glare
of the bald prominent forehead (*une tête glabre*), the
cavernous eyes, the *macabre* expression of burnt-out lust
smouldering upon his face. He had promised a friend
of mine, a young enthusiast *décadent et symboliste*, a
sonnet on Parsifal for his review. The sonnet had not
arrived, and the review was going to press. Nothing for
it but to start in search of Verlaine. My friend asked
me to accompany him. I raised objections. First, I
did not care about knowing him ; secondly, I was not

inclined for the trip. My objections were overruled. My friend said : " In ten years hence, when he is dead, you will regret that you did not see him. You had better take advantage of this occasion, another may not occur ; he will probably not last out a couple of years." I recognised the validity of the argument, and away we went. We got into an omnibus and then we got into a tram. Then we took a cab, and I believe we had to take another tram. We passed factories and canals, and at one moment I thought we were going to take the boat. We at last penetrated into a dim and eccentric region which I had never heard of before ; we traversed curious streets, inhabited apparently by people who in dressing never got further than *camisoles* and shirt sleeves ; we penetrated musty-smelling and clamorous courtyards, in which lingered Balzacian *concierges* ; we climbed slippery stair-cases upon which doors stood wide open, emitting odours and permitting occasional views of domestic life —a man in his shirt hammering a boot, a woman, presumably a mother, wiping a baby. The address ! I give it for the sake of local colour : "C'est là-bas, là-bas, là-bas—à la Bastille, mais plus loin, rue Moreau, cour Saint-François, 6, Hôtel du Midi."

In a dark corner, at the end of a narrow passage situated at the top of the last flight of stairs, we discovered a door, knocked, entered, and saw the terrible forehead, bald and prominent, under a filthy nightcap ; a nightshirt full of the grease of the bed covered his shoulders ; a stained and discoloured pair of trousers were hitched up somehow about his waist. He was drinking wine at sixteen sous the litre. He told us that he had just come out of the hospital ; that his leg was better, but it still gave him a great deal of pain. He pointed to it. We looked away.

He said he was writing the sonnet, and promised that we should have it on the morrow. Then, in the grossest language, he told us of the abominations he had included in the sonnet; and seeing that our visit would prove neither pleasant nor profitable, we took our leave as soon as we could. But I remember one thing that seems characteristic. Speaking of a career for his son, whom he had not seen for twenty years, he said he regretted he had not brought him up as a *garçon de café*, avowing his belief that he could imagine no trade more advantageous than that of a *garçon de café*.

In speaking of Verlaine, in my book *Confessions of a Young Man*, I spoke of his devotional poems as being the result of poetic calculations; their originality I said was attained, as Edgar Poe puts it, negatively rather than affirmatively. Perhaps this is not quite clear. In one of his essays Edgar Poe says that no one is original by temperament; that we become original by a deliberate effort of reason, by desiring originality, and declining to write in this way and that way, because these methods have been appropriated by other writers, and not because they are unnatural to us. When I wrote the *Confessions* I was only slightly acquainted with Verlaine's later work, and being at a loss to reconcile beautiful, pitiful pleas for pardon addressed to Jesus Christ and His Holy Mother with the well-known disorder of his life, I hastily concluded that Verlaine was a striking exemplification of Poe's theory of originality and how it may be acquired. I have since discovered that I was mistaken. Nature is more subtle than our logic, even more subtle than Poe's. Verlaine believes in the Roman Catholic Church as earnestly as the Pope himself, but in Verlaine there is only belief—practice is wholly wanting in him. Nor do I think he ever quite realises how he lives or how he writes. For, after having given us an abominable description in abominable language of the sonnet he was pondering, after having sent my poor friend away in despair,

Verlaine sent him that most divinely beautiful sonnet
which I quote in the book already referred to. It is a
pleasure to quote it again :—

> " Parsifal a vaincu les Filles, leur gentil
>   Babil et la luxure amusante—et sa pente
>   Vers la Chair de garçon vierge que cela tente
>   D'aimer les seins légers et ce gentil babil.
>
> " Il a vaincu la Femme belle, au cœur subtil,
>   Étalant ses bras frais et sa gorge excitante ;
>   Il a vaincu l'Enfer et rentre sous la tente
>   Avec un lourd trophée à son bras puéril.
>
> " Avec la lance qui perça le Flanc suprême !
>   Il a guéri le roi, le voici roi lui-même
>   Et prêtre du très saint Trésor essentiel.
>
> " En robe d'or il adore, gloire et symbole,
>   Le vase pur où resplendit le sang réel.
>   —Et, ô ces voix d'enfants chantant dans la coupole ! "

At first it would seem that these verses had been
laboriously hammered out and cautiously filed. The
false rhyme so exquisitely placed in the middle of the
twelfth line, the total suppression of the cæsura, with the
sixth syllable falling upon the first syllable of *adore*,
the daring originality of following up this verse with
another constructed, so far as the cæsura is concerned,
in exactly the same manner, and the hiatus in the last
line, seem to announce premeditated art ; but I am convinced that this is not so. I feel sure that these strange
cadences are an integral part of the man's ear, and are
as spontaneous and unconscious as the thought. In
Verlaine, mental and corporeal life are distinct and
separable things working almost unconsciously of each
other. Nevertheless, these verses, although found in his
last volume, *Amour*, are in a measure a survival, a
recrudescence of the complex forms of *Les Fêtes*

Galantes; for as Verlaine's art developed it grew simpler, until it reached the colloquial naturalness of Wordsworth. For instance, that more than beautiful poem *A la gare d'Auteuil*, beginning :

> "Ame, te souvient-il, au fond du paradis,
> De la gare d'Auteuil et des trains de jadis
> T'amenant chaque jour, venus de La Chapelle?"

and ending with the strange enchantment of the line :

> "Mon pauvre enfant, ta voix dans le Bois de Boulogne!"

How simple and yet how subtle is the music of this poem—music that had lain for centuries dormant in the French language, and this music that some dead singer should have sung sounds strange in modern speech.

In considering Verlaine's claims to high poetic fame we are more concerned with his last two volumes, *Sagesse* and *Amour*, than with the earlier ones, beautiful though they all most certainly are. For it is in *Sagesse* and *Amour* that we are most fully treated to the astonishing spectacle of a man writing purely devotional poetry while leading notoriously a more than profligate life. In the Middle Ages, when faith in God was firmer than it is now, it was not infrequent to find the devout Christian saying prayers in the morning and committing murder and robbery in the afternoon or evening. Villon is a case in point, and between Verlaine and Villon there is some analogy. In both lives there were terms of isolation from the world, though for different reasons; and to find the seed whence sprang the devotional verses of Verlaine, I look in vain through French poetry until I happen across Villon's Ballade to his Mother. Unconsciously and without suspicion of plagiarism, Verlaine has elaborated that beautiful poem into many volumes, and were Villon unknown to me and I were shown the refrain of the ballade in question : *" Dans cette foi je veux vivre et mourir,"* I would stake my very existence that it was a line of Verlaine's, and probably to be found in *Sagesse.* But it must be remembered that in this ballade Villon is not speaking in his own person, but in that of his aged mother ; and the note of complete humility which we find in this ballade is absent in nearly all his other poems, as it is absent in the poems of all other poets. Some poets write to tell how well women have loved them, others seek to record their exploits in the battle or the hunting-field, others desire to convince the reader of their excessive erudition ; all show pride more or less hidden on some point, and they write with the object of acquainting the world with their excellence or their peculiarity in this or that respect ; but I am not aware of any other poet except Verlaine who has written solely to tell how weak, helpless, and undistinguished he is in all ways and things. Nowhere do we find a trace of personal pride ; even his afflictions he relates gently and without bitterness. He is in his books what the poor old woman is in Villon's ballade. She goes into the church to pray : in the painted windows she sees saints in heaven playing lyres, sinners in hell being boiled. She is only a poor, ignorant Christian woman, utterly unlearned ; she knows only that one vision gives her pleasure, the other gives her pain, and in that faith she wishes to live and die. Verlaine in his poetry is no more than the poor woman of the ballade. He is a poor Christian, devoid of riches and all distinction, who believes and hopes to find grace hereafter with his sovereign Lord and Master.

The whole man—his poetry, his life, his literary success, and his failure—is contained in an all-embracing sense of his own unworthiness ; he keeps it continually

TWO UNKNOWN POETS

HAVE not all young men of the last quarter of this century come within the magnetism of the name of Shelley? Have not all at some time felt that the pale ethereal poet was walking by them, that he was their friend? Have we not all experienced the nympholepsy of La Pompadour? Have not many more young men sighed at her feet in this generation than in the brief years which she surrendered to a king's caprice? We all have surely been touched with the love and knowledge of the body and soul of one that the earth is over, we all have surely at some time felt ourselves mysteriously interested in a name, a name in whose syllables there is evocation, a name around which hangs some suggestive story, a name that some fortunate description has awakened into life. Is there one among us so common that he has never felt intimately qualified to know men and women that death, distance, or the multifarious accidents and barriers of life have irreparably separated him from?

And the two young poets of whom I am going to speak have always attracted me. My sympathies were engaged by the strange and sad stories which surround them, and were confirmed by the personal talent manifested in all they wrote. Their names?—Arthur Rimbaud and Jules Laforgue, names for the first time printed in an English newspaper. But it is not infrequent for me to introduce French genius to the few among us who are willing to allow themselves to be interested in artistic work. It was I who introduced that adorable poet, Paul Verlaine, to English readers; it was I who wrote first about that ineffable book, *A Rebours*, the value of which has since been so copiously acknowledged. Possibly the same success will attend my present adventure, and in a season the plagiarist and his pursuers will make riot amid the tender beauties of *Le Miracle des Roses*, *L'Imitation de Notre Dame la Lune*, and *Les Premières Communions*. Be this as it may, I concern myself with my sensations of these strange poets, whose talents and whose tragic ends have interested me so singularly. The poet that death has nipped in the first blossom of his talent, the girl that dies in her bridal month, the first poems, the first kisses, my soul goes out to one as to the other. And I know that I should have proved singularly capable of understanding that young Bohemian who came to Paris composing beautiful verses when he was fifteen, and who in a few years anticipated in some half-dozen prophetic poems all the poetic revolution of the last twenty years. Truly it was but the promise of May, and the blossoms fell before the fruit had begun. The blossoms fell, but those who love beautiful French verses have treasured them: *La Saison en Enfer*, *Le Bateau Ivre*, *Les Premières Communions*, *La Mort des petits Poux*—strange titles, strange as the poems, strange as the life of the poet—the miraculous boy who came to Paris when he was fifteen, with such a poem as *Le Bateau Ivre* in his pocket — that extraordinary boy who has fled from civilisation, and whose brief life is involved in legend and mystery, fantastic and impenetrable. We know that it befell him to meet Verlaine almost immediately after his arrival; how or where there are no means of discovering. It is certain, however, that Verlaine was the hourly companion of the younger poet for some years, and it is therefore impossible not to speculate sometimes how much the genius of the poet who has since realised his æstheticism depended on the genius of him who made formal renunciation of the laurel wreath. Rumour has busied itself with this friendship, but little is known — one fact only, and that is written on the sky of palest legend in letters of blood. It is known that one night, in a house of ill-repute in Brussels, in some drunken quarrel that had suddenly sprung up between them, Rimbaud was stabbed by Verlaine. For this crime Verlaine spent two years at Mons. Rimbaud was taken to the hospital, where, after lingering some weeks between life and death, he eventually recovered. The poets only met once again. The account we have of this meeting rings strange and hollow as an old-world story. For the story is that in the years that had divided them Rimbaud had learnt to understand the immediate necessity of repentance, and it was only in the vain slight hope of inducing his friend to follow him into a purer life that he consented to see him again. But Verlaine's hour of grace had not yet come, and he sought to dissuade the young disciple from his resolve to abandon the vain glory of art, and consecrate his life to the redemption of his soul. But Rimbaud closed his eyes and ears to allurements and temptations, bade Verlaine farewell, and left Europe to immure himself for ever in a Christian convent on the shores of the Red Sea ; and where it stands on a rocky promontory, he has been seen digging the soil for the grace of God.

The mediævalism of this strange story has always had a singular fascination for me. I have dreamed the meeting of the poets at Stuttgart in many an unwritten poem, and I have seen in many a picture, the desolate convent and the single figure digging in the eastern

G

twilight. The story is singularly romantic, especially when looked at in the light of Verlaine's subsequent conversion and the beauty of his religious poems— poems that take you back to the simple unquestioning faith of mediæval Christianity. Verlaine's genius has quite lately come to be accepted even by the general reader, and we are sure, though poor and afflicted with bodily ill, that he stands on the verge of glory; but of Rimbaud few know anything. The now Christian monk, the whilom scorner of all law, human and divine, left the poetic revolution to be achieved by Verlaine, and all that remains of this Marlowe of 1870 are a few poems and a few fragments; but these are sufficient to show that he carried in his heart all the riches of a great poet. To prove decisively that my words are not vain exaggerations, I need only quote *Les Premières Communions*, or *La Mort des petits Poux*. But I have no wish to prove anything. My object is rather to convey a sensation of this strange boy, and I cannot make more sure of doing this than by quoting a sonnet (never, I believe, before published), written between fifteen and sixteen, before Rimbaud came to Paris:

MA BOHÈME

(*Fantaisie*)

" Je m'en allais, les poings dans mes poches crevées ;
Mon paletot aussi devenait idéal ;
J'allais sous le ciel, Muse ! et j'étais ton féal ;
Oh ! là, là ! que d'amours splendides j'ai rêvées.
Mon unique culotte avait un large trou.
Petit-Poucet rêveur, j'égrenais dans ma course
Des rimes.   Mon auberge était à la grande Ourse
Mes étoiles au ciel avaient un doux frou-frou.

" Et je les écoutais assis au bord des routes,
Des bon soirs de Septembre où je sentais des gouttes
De rosée à mon front comme un vin de vigneur ;
Où, rimant au milieu des ombres fantastiques,
Comme des lyres, je tirai les élastiques
De mes souliers blessés, un pied près de mon cœur."

Did a child ever write such verse before? I think not. But I have now to try, in a few English words, to give a sensation of the delicious talent of Jules Laforgue— delicious, delicate, and evanescent as French pastry. Can I help you to see this Watteau de café-concert? I will ask you to think of the beauty of a moth fluttering in the soft twilight of a summer month. Touch it not, lest you destroy the delicate dust of its wings. I hold it on my forefinger now, examine the beautiful markings. *L'Imitation de Notre Dame la Lune*, *Fleurs de Bonne Volonté*, *Les Moralités Légendaires*, *Le Miracle des Roses*, etc. Is there not in these titles something like genius? and is it possible that any one not touched with genius could have invented *L'Imitation de Notre Dame la Lune*? I have called Laforgue a Watteau de café-concert because his imagination was as fanciful as that painter's, and because he adopted in his style the familiarity of the café-concert, transforming, raising it by the enchantment of his genius. What I am writing should in truth be delivered in a literary academy with closed doors. But do not gather up your skirts, for in the end I may be able to leave on this page some faint shadow of my beautiful moth. Here is a little poem which appears to me to be wholly exquisite, and scintillant with French grace :—

" Mon Sort est orphelin, les vêpres ont tu leurs cloches. . . .
  Et ces pianos ritournellent, jamais las ! . . .
  Oh ! monter, leur expliquer mon apostolat !
  Oh ! du moins, leur tourner les pages, être là,
  Les consoler ! (J'ai des consolations plein les poches) . . .

" Les pianos se sont clos. Un seul, en grand deuil, s'obstine . . .
  Oh ! qui que tu sois, sœur ! à genoux, à tâtons,
  Baiser le bas de ta robe dans l'abandon ! . . .
  Pourvu qu'après, tu me chasses, disant : ' Pardon !
  'Pardon, m'sieu, mais j'en aime un autre, et suis sa cousine.

"Oh ! que je suis bien infortuné sur cette Terre ! . . .
  Et puis si malheureux de ne pas être Ailleurs !
  Ailleurs, loin de ce savant siècle batailleur. . . .
  C'est là que je m'créerai un petit intérieur,
  Avec Une dont, comme de Moi, Tout n'a que faire.

" Une maigre qui me parlait,
Les yeux hallucinés de Gloires virginales,
De rendre l'âme, sans scandale,
Dans un flacon de sels anglais. . .

" Une qui me fit oublier
Mon art et ses rançons d'absurdes saturnales,
En attisant, gauche vestale,
L'Aurore dans mes oreillers. . . .

" Et que son regard
Sublime
Comme ma rime
Ne permit pas le moindre doute à cet égard."

Hard to understand? I admit it, but how winning
and how unlike anybody! Isn't it strange that the
beginning and the end of French poetry are almost
incomprehensible—Ronsard and Laforgue? And his
prose is as exquisite, and as wilful; and his titles!
Le Miracle des Roses!

" Jamais, jamais, jamais cette petite ville d'eaux ne
" s'en douta, avec son inculte conseil Municipal délégué
" par les montagnards rapaces et nullement opéra
" comique malgré leur costume.

" Ah, que tout n'est-il opéra comique! . . . Que tout
" n'évolue-t-il en mesure sur cette valse anglaise, *Myosotis*,
" qu'on entendait cette année-là (moi navré dans les
" coins) au Casino, valse si décemment mélancolique, si
" ésotériquement dernier, derniers beaux jours! . . .
" (Cette valse, ah! si je pouvais en inoculer d'un mot
" le sentiment avant de vous laisser entrer dans cette
" histoire!)—O gants jamais rajeunies par les benzines!
" O brillant et mélancolique va et vien de ces existences!
" O apparence de bonheur si pardonnable! O beautés
" qui veilleront dans les dentelles noires, au coin du
" feu, sans comprendre la conduite des fils viveurs et
" muselés qu'elles mirent au monde avec une si chaste
" mélancolie! . . .

" Petite ville, petite ville de mon cœur."

I think that even these, the first twenty lines of *Le Miracle des Roses*, testify a style, full of grace and fancy, and incurably his own.   Nor can I easily imagine anything more wilful than his evocation of this watering-place, and the story sketched with crow-quill pen and mauve ink—the story of the consumptive Ruth, dying amid tea-roses, the blood-red roses that she loves having been forbidden her.   Nor can we help being doubly attracted to this story when we consider its significance and its foretelling of the poet's own end.   For if Rimbaud's fulgurant verses correspond to the passions that forced him to fly from life and hide his soul in a convent, Laforgue's fancies harmonise equally with the facts of his blameless and sad existence, so sad and so little.   We know that he was reader to the Empress of Germany—happy indeed was the selection ; and we envy more than the bauble of her wealth the hours she passed with Laforgue.   One winter's day in Berlin, Jules saw a girl skating as none ever skated before—the grace of the waist, the flowing boa, and the feet lifted beneath the dark skirt, filled him with happiness.   The beautiful skater was an English girl. I hardly remember the name, but I know that it recalled Annabel Lee, as, indeed, the story of this love recalls a tale by Edgar Poe.   He resigned his place as reader to the Empress and married ; and he and the beautiful English girl came to Paris in the hope that literature would yield them a living.   But Laforgue's genius was of the kind that wins the sympathy of the elect, and instead of making his living with his pen Jules grew more and more consumptive.   I have heard that the young couple lived in a poor apartment—two or three rooms—and that the beautiful English girl, now stricken with the dreadful malady, passed between the rooms with *tisanes*.   Friends climbed the high stairs to see them on Thursday evenings ; a few admirers attended

Jules's funeral, and published the volume he left in his desk, *Les Moralités Légendaires*; the girl died soon after —two or three months. How did she live during the brief interval, where is she buried? Nobody knows. Yet I have a very separate and complete sensation of these two little lives. I was their friend although I never saw them, and I shall not forget them, though I never visit their forgotten graves, nor shall I cease to cherish *L'Imitation de Notre Dame la Lune* and *Les Fleurs de Bonne Volonté*, though the ordinary readers of verse allow these books to lie in the limbo of embryonic things.

LE REVERS D'UN GRAND HOMME

AN interesting article might be written on the part accident or luck plays in the composition of works of art. Edgar Poe did not take the initial accidents of inspiration into consideration when, in the *Philosophy of Composition*, he told how he wrote *The Raven*. But his was a mind that would have seen the oversight had it been pointed out, and would have confessed that in the strain and stress of other thoughts, this, the very corner-stone of the theory he was constructing, had escaped him. To supply a deficiency in our analytical literature, I will suggest that some writer should take his best-known book and tell the tale of the luck that followed him in the composition of it, showing thereby how the book would never have attained the form in which it exists, had it not been for the adventitious aids of special circumstances. Waiting the advent of this modest essayist, I will say that two things are necessary for the success of every enterprise—the chance and the man ; a book is no exception to this law. A paragraph in a newspaper, a word dropped in conversation, the sight of a special landscape in a special light, a moment of *ennui* or of joy, it is such things as these that dictate the first idea of a book. Philosphically, of course, there is no such thing as chance ; but, accepting the word in its everyday meaning, who can say that chance has not a large share in the creation of a work of art ? To-day the artistic mind is healthy, and fit for fecundation, but the breeze sets from the wrong quarter, and no pollen comes to fertilize it ; to-morrow the mind is indisposed, unready to receive, or may be the pollen that the breeze brings is not of prime vigour; the fecundation is, nevertheless, accomplished, and the process of cerebral gestation begins.

The value, therefore, of the incentive chance is, surely, incalculable. When the rich thought falls into the rich furrow, each reinforces the other, and every day the writer finds his field growing more luxuriously and flowering in unexpected places. But alack the hour ! when the thin thought falls into the furrow; rich though the soil be, it exhausts itself in vain efforts to infuse life and health into the seed—a short, scant harvesting is the inevitable crop.

What writer, as he turns his thoughts over, has not longed for the kindling word, for the incentive suggestion ? Sometimes it lies for months forgotten in the fallow of the mind, sometimes for years ; then, and only then, a tiny shoot appears. With what joy it is hailed, and how soon it grows and spreads ! What writer, as he restlessly throws aside thoughts dry as withered leaves, has not basely envied another writer his subject, or regretted that some dramatic event, divorce, or suicide, now in progress through the newspapers, was not whispered to him as he walked home some evening, or sat brooding over the fire listening to the chirping of thoughts he is weary of?

Such regret laid fast hold of me when I had read a few pages of that extraordinary book lately published by Messrs. Fisher Unwin, *The Letters of the Duke of Wellington to Miss J*. "Oh, what a subject for a novel," I cried. "Why did not some angel or demon whisper it to me ? " Here is the subject : Miss J., a young lady of

marked religious tendency of mind, succeeded in con-
verting a hardened criminal who had been convicted of
murder, and was awaiting the death sentence. The
man had resisted the efforts of the Protestant and
Catholic clergymen; but the influence of Miss J. produced such an effect on him that he confessed his guilt,
and "professed repentance and conversion."

The result of this success convinced Miss J. that she
had been called to do great work. Scanning the
horizon of life from her little lodging in Kensington,
she espied the Duke of Wellington, and decided that
he would suit her purpose very well indeed. Miss J.
was one of those women who believe that they are
born to influence the destinies of great men; and
Miss J. was more qualified for the task of influencing
the Duke than she knew, and this is paying a high
tribute to Miss J.'s modesty, for she was a beautiful
girl. The first letter of a correspondence which lasted
over seventeen years, the editor says, is unfortunately
missing, and Miss J. gives no extracts from it in her
diary. The editor is right; the absence of this letter
is regrettable, for it would have settled whether the
Duke knew that his correspondent was a beautiful girl
of twenty, and not an elderly lady of fifty. A most
important fact, this, as all who receive letters in their
public capacity will testify. After the series of letters,
" I understand you and you understand me, let's go under
the willows and weep," he who has found a skinny
spinster of fifty, extending to him a sisterly hand,
will take care to make sure of the fair incognita's
age and personal appearance before he risks himself in
another adventure. That Miss J.'s first letter, notwithstanding the nauseating religious phraseology it was
most assuredly couched in, did convey some slight
inkling of the charms that awaited his Grace, should
he come to see her, I think there is little room to doubt.

The biblical cant in which she must have wrapped up this necessary bit of worldliness must remain a matter of conjecture.

Technically, the hypocrite is one who is conscious that he is passing himself off upon others for what he is not, by means of moral disguisements. But in actual life no such being exists. Hypocrites are not distinctly conscious of their hypocrisy; otherwise they would deceive no one. Miss J. was undoubtedly a religious woman; at the same time she must have used religion as a cloak under which she might advantageously ensnare the Duke into a promise of marriage, or, at least, procure a compromising letter from him. In England, self-deception is a common vice; it is found growing plentifully in nearly all places, especially in the shadow of pulpits and news-paper offices. In the case of Miss J., the dividing line between truth and untruth is so faint as to be practically indefinable; yet we are sensible that it is there, just as we are sensible of the horizon's line, although we cannot follow it through the mid-day mist and glitter of the sea.

The Duke having been assured, as I beg leave to suggest, that his correspondent was young and fair, replied with alacrity. "He regrets that he will be "detained at Walmer Castle for more than a fortnight, "but suggests that Miss J. should write informing him if "she would be then in town?" A meeting was arranged and it took place in the back-parlour. Miss J. armed herself with a large Bible; but in spite of the weapon, the Duke seized her hand, exclaiming, "How I love you— "how I love you!" On being questioned by Miss J., concerning who had caused him to feel thus towards her, he replied, "God Almighty." The account of this strange interview is taken from Miss J.'s diary. "During "the next visit from the Duke," Miss J. writes, "the

"Duke, speaking of his feeling for me, exclaimed,
"'This must be for life!' twice over successively. He
"then asked me if I felt sufficient for him to be with him
"a whole life, to which I replied, 'If it be the will of
"God.' I observed much excitement about him, and,
"in a very hurried manner, he told me he was going
"on a visit to the King." She did not see the Duke
again for some time; and in the meantime reflection
led Miss J. to suspect the propriety of these visits,
and she wrote him her usual long pietistic rigmarole,
interlarded with scriptural quotations, out of which
I pick the following, as being indicative of the Duke's
desires:—"I cannot place myself in the power of one
"who, however honourable and noble, seems occasionally
"to forget that he is confided in by a being," etc. Then
again, "That you should think of me, notwithstanding
"your occasional forgetfulness, with any other than the
"most honourable feelings is, of course, as impossible as,"
etc. To this missive the Duke answered: "My dear
"Miss J.,—I have received your letter and enclosures.
"I beg to remind you of what I said to you the second
"day that I saw you; and, if you recollect it, you will
"not be surprised at my telling you that I entirely
"concur in the intention which you have communicated
"to me."

We know all about the critics who will not impute
evil motives, and who are sure that the world is not
half so bad as some people would try to make it
out to be; but surely every man of the world must
smile as he reads the Duke's letter, and reading the
wealth of meaning that lies locked between the lines
he will roar with laughter, remembering the celebrated
"Fanny! publish and be damned." But although
the Duke was willing to let the woman go, the
woman was by no means inclined to let the
Duke go, and for seventeen years she continued to

bombard him with pietistic letters, tracts, Bibles, etc.
She was Exeter Hall in epitome.   The efforts the
poor man made to rid himself of his tormentor, the
patience with which he bore with her, the time he
devoted to reading her letters, and to answering them,
cannot be described.   Quarrels, because the Duke had
not signed his name in full.   Quarrels, because the
Duke had not sealed the letter with his own seal.
Marvellous, indeed, the picture that these letters
create of the man with his name wide in the world
standing, as it were, under the very eye of Europe,
and this poor crazy woman, receding out of all sight
and hearing, becoming day by day more and more
like a forgotten tract on a forgotten shelf.   It is pitiful
as life ; it is as real as life.   What a subject for a
novel !   But in a novel you want proportion, you
want *crescendo*, and in these letters there is neither.

I said that I regretted that some one had not
whispered the theme to me as one suitable for a
novel.   But is it suitable for artistic treatment ?   We
can only find out by inquiring how those novelists who
would be drawn towards such a theme, would treat it.
Mr Henry James would probably leave the story
exactly as it is.   The Duke would make some absent-
minded advances, which in an absent - minded way
would be repelled, or I should say avoided, slurred
over.   Then the flirtation would drift into vague and
undetermined efforts on the part of the Duke to shake
himself free, and on the death of the Duke the lady
would return to Boston.   Zola would probably allow
the Duke to become the lady's love.   The remorse
of the lady would be indicated by lavish descriptions
of the cathedrals she visited.   Finally, the Duke would
tire of her ; Miss J. would follow him through his
dissipations, distributing tracts as she went.   The

book would end by the description of the Duke's
funeral, interwoven with the description of the violent
cold in the head that prevented the lady attending
the ceremony. . . . She sat on the Kensington hearth-
rug on a narrow cane-bottomed chair, her knees pressed
forward almost against the bars of the grate. "Susan,
give me another pocket-handkerchief!" "There are no
more, mam, I gave you the last one ten minutes ago."
Daudet would describe the Duke dying in Miss J.'s
house, and the various subterfuges resorted to by the
family to close Miss J.'s mouth.

Guy de Maupassant would show the Duke tiring of
the homilies with which this religious maniac's bedroom
was ever garlanded. Maupassant would re-introduce
H., the young man whom Miss J. had rejected because
"he had never known a new birth into righteousness."
The Duke would approve of the marriage of the young
couple; in a quiet suburban chapel he would give her
away, not forgetting, however, to settle a handsome
fortune upon her and her husband and their heirs
for ever.

I think this is the way the subject should be treated.
Miss J. would succeed in entangling the Duke
sufficiently to make it imperative that he should
marry her; for it would be pleasing to show the
glory of Waterloo fading in the ridicule that would
follow and fasten on the absurd marriage; above all
it would be delightful to determine how far this lady's
religion was true, by testing it in the crucible of court
life, and the book should be called *Le Revers d'un
Grand Homme*.

Fighting over again the battle of Waterloo in the
back-parlour would be a glorious possibility, one that
Balzac might have been able to realise. Given the
subject, he would have recreated it, building it strangely
by the sheer edge of some blind abyss, and even when

night was darkest some spires, like tiny fingers, would be seen pointing to the stars. He would have made of it something terrible and something pitiful, but he, too, would have recoiled from the subject had he been shown the letters, knowing well that their relentless truth was beyond his painting. Nature appears in this book in all her shocking nakedness, in all her crudity. Not Balzac, nor Thackeray, nor Stendhal, nor yet any one has done what is done here; and I am as astonished as a painter in the fifteenth century would have been at a photograph. But Art is always something more and something less than Nature, and none but the fool will enter into a competition where defeat is inevitable. In these letters the characters of the Duke and Miss J. are painted with that complete and vivid truth which is not Art but Nature, and Nature is not the end and aim of Art—she is, at most, the means to an end. In the representation of any object, an accident of light, a sentiment, a touch that reveals the artist's soul is necessary. But in this book the Duke and Miss J. are shown to us as in a mirror.

You see an astute statesman and a religious hypocrite, and he and she bore you exactly as such persons would bore you in real life, one by interminable streams of pietistic exhortations, the other by solemn care to say nothing that might not be printed in the newspaper next morning.

AN ACTRESS OF THE EIGHTEENTH CENTURY

SOME four or five years ago M. Goncourt announced his intention to refrain from writing any more novels. He has kept his word, and has since confined himself to extracting from his diary such passages as he judges may be published during his lifetime, and to completing the series of historical studies of the actresses of the eighteenth century, which he began years ago in conjunction with his brother. He has lately published the biography of Mlle. Clairon, "by means of her secret and intimate correspondence, by the aid of the divulgations of the police reports on her private life." His object has been, he says, "to reconstruct the character of the illustrious *tragédienne* and pseudo-German Princess in all its crude reality, and the material routine of her existence." M. Goncourt has done miraculously well what he set himself to do. I doubt indeed if he has ever written a better book, and I do not except those he wrote in conjunction with his brother, nor do I attempt to differentiate between his novels and his historical studies. His biography of Mlle. Clairon has interested me exactly as his novels have interested me, only perhaps in the biography the charm is more enveloping and more naturally seductive. I have never read a book with greater interest. My knowledge of life has been definitely increased, and at this moment I know no one so intensely and so completely as Mlle. Clairon.

Greater praise I cannot give, and out of the innumerable accidents and countless passions with which her life was shaken I select for the purpose of this article these three or four.

When Mlle. Clairon was a child, her mother, a work-woman, who could not afford to pay any one to look after her, often left her under the guardianship of lock and key in the bedroom. To pass the time, the child used to climb on a chair and look into a room opposite where an actress was engaged in rehearsing her part. She watched the actress closely, studying her gestures, and practising them when she had finished; and her industrious and persistent mimicry was of such value to the child that her mother agreed to allow her to attend school. Her manner of coming in, going out, and sitting down was entirely changed, her little body took new graces, her intelligence developed. But her secret weighed heavily upon her, and she confessed it all to a man who used to come to the house and who treated her less harshly than the others. He told her that the actress was Mlle. Dangeville, explained to her what was the Comédie Française, and finally obtained permission from her mother to take her to see a performance of *Le Comte d'Essex et les Folies Amoureuses.* What passed within her on that evening Clairon was never able to tell very clearly. She re-membered only that she could not utter a word, and her absorption was so great that her mother was about to turn her away when she returned home. *Allez-vous coucher, grosse bête!* She fled to her bed, but instead of going to sleep, she spent the entire night in turning over and over in her little brain what she had heard declaimed on the stage, and next day the stupefaction was great among the frequenters of that house at hearing the child repeat more than two hundred verses from the tragedy and two-thirds of the little play.

But this effort of memory was nothing compared to her assimilation of the manner of every actor, the *grasseyement* of Grandval, the stuttering of Poisson, the regulated mimicry of Mlle. Dangeville. Henceforth, notwithstanding all the abuse and blows her mother showered upon her, she refused to learn to sew, finding, even then, in her little dramatic soul one of those tragic phrases, one of those *claironades* which, in after years, she made such frequent use of, crying, as she drove back her childish tears, "Kill me, you had better do so, for if you don't I shall be an actress." And nothing could force Clairon to give up her vocation, and her mother seeing that she was losing her health, was obliged to give way, and Clairon joined, soon after, the Italian Comedy, and was given instruction in writing, in dancing, in the Italian language. She was hardly fourteen when she made her first appearance.

Love adventures naturally began soon after. In her *Mémoires* she is very silent regarding those early years, years of poverty and low vice; but the police reports of which M. Goncourt speaks, and from which he gives some astonishing citations are more explicit. Her lovers seem to have been of all kinds, and as numerous as the sand on the shore. At Gand, my lord the Duke of Marlborough offered her an immense fortune, which, however, for patriotic reasons she declined to accept. There were captains and colonels, there were authors and *abbés*; like the lady in Congreve's comedy, lovers were to her like curl-papers, she made them as fast as she pleased, and then if she pleased she made more. It is not, however, until we find her established in Paris a great actress, creating the leading parts in all the great tragedies of her time, that any lover appears upon whom she bestowed any more than the favour of a passing caprice. Sometimes her lovers were rich, sometimes poor; sometimes she ruined them, oftener it must be confessed they ruined her. And the end of all these leave-takings were poverty and trouble. And the letters written about this time have for refrain: *Je suis sans le sol*. And at every moment she was obliged to have recourse to her friends and her former lovers. Looking over her life I find three love stories which represent especially well the three most usual phases of her character, and these stories seem to me to be not only typical of the woman, but of life itself. The first of these three lovers was Marmontel, a young and fashionable author, whose tragedies were played constantly at the Comédie Française. According to him, Clairon was a mistress full of vivacity, gaiety, and all the characteristics of an amiable naturalness without admixture of any caprice, having but the one desire to make her lover happy.

But at the end of a few months of this love which was to last for ever, she said to Marmontel, who was supping with her at a friend's house:—"'N'y venez-"pas ce soir, vous seriez mal à votre aise; le bailli de "Fleury doit y souper, et il me ramène.' 'J'en suis "connu,' lui répondait naïvement Marmontel, 'il voudra "bien me ramener aussi.' 'Non, il n'aura qu'un vis-à-"vis.' Marmontel à ce mot devinait tout, et laissait "voir sa surprise sur la figure. 'Est-il bien vrai, parlez-"vous serieusement?' 'Oui, je suis folle quelquefois, "mais je ne serai jamais fausse.'" A few days after Marmontel received a letter from Clairon asking him to come and see her on a matter of importance. He went, and the matter of importance was that she liked him far better than le bailli de Fleury, and begged to be reinstated in his affections. This Marmontel refused; but when his next piece was read at the Comédie, to the astonishment of the actors

and even of Clairon, he gave the principal part to
Mlle. Clairon. A quarter of an hour after, she arrived
at his house, accompanied by a friend : " Take it,
sir," she said, speaking as she would on the stage
and throwing the MS. at his feet. " I cannot accept
the part without the author, for both belong to me."
Marmontel explained that he belonged to her as a
friend, and that any other sentiment only made them
unhappy. " He is right," cried Clairon ; " my folly
" makes us both miserable. Come then, my friend, and
" dine at your friend's house."

On this amorous *liaison*, so gallantly broken off by
mutual agreement, during the course of the rehearsals
of the Aristomène there was founded a friendship
which lasted for thirty years unshadowed by a single
cloud.

It is difficult to imagine anything more deliciously
eighteenth century than this anecdote. But more
deeply human is the story of the actress's love for
Larive. Larive was a young actor in whom Clairon
took the warmest interest, and her correspondence
with him shows the actress amid her daily occupations.
We see her starting to *promener son importance au
Bois de Boulogne*, we learn that her sprained arm is
better, and that her cook has left her. It is Clairon
who looks after the money of the young actor ; and
she tells him never to deprive himself of any real
necessary, for to do so narrows the heart ; and
throughout these gossiping letters a slight moral tone
prevails, the grave words of a father or of a loving
mother. Sometimes she upbraids him, but she is
quick to beg forgiveness for a harsh word addressed
to the spoilt child of her heart. He sends her every
new part he plays, and she instructs and advises him ;
nor does she fear to open the chapter entitled Women ;
indeed she returns to it often. Caprices she will permit

him, but begs of him to beware of any serious attach-
ment. And always behind a mask of pure affection
we find ourself in the presence of the passion of an
old woman for a young man. A warm and sensual
tenderness penetrates these letters. Nor do I know
anything more strangely dramatic than those written
when Larive began to think of marriage—those dolorous
cries with which she tells him that she will not be
able to see him again. "Good-bye, be happy; this
"is the only consolation I ask from you, and whatever
"may happen to me you will always serve to remind
"me of the instability of human things. I said yesterday
"that I counted on you as on myself, that you would
"be the delight of my life, and to-day I am forced to
"tell you that we are lost to one another for ever."

The third lover who left his mark on her life was
the Comte de Valbelle. This *liaison* lasted for nineteen
years—it is true with the help of a certain number of
coadjutors. In the first years of their *liaison*, the
Comte had very little money, and to gratify his taste
for good living, Clairon was frequently obliged to sell
all that was not absolutely necessary, and live in
the greatest poverty. Thousands of women have done
this; but there is, to my mind, something strangely
grand and noble in the passion for a memory which
allows a woman to write to a lover—and, mind you,
to a lover who had left her—in reply to a letter
saying that although he had four thousand a year,
he had not twenty-five louis to lend to *une amie*: "I
"shall be glad to send you fifty louis if you want them;
"I have them, and if I hadn't them I would sell all I
"have, as I have done before, so that I might give
"them to you." A few weeks after she sold her
jewellery, her furniture, her wardrobe, all she had,
so that she might lend him the money he wanted.
"I forgive you the misfortunes you have caused me,

"and I beg of you to cherish my memory. . . . Tears
"prevent me from seeing what I am writing. Adieu,
"Val."

In writing of this strange woman, so multiple and
so diverse, and yet single-natured when you come to
study, and through study to understand her, I have
addressed myself entirely to the human, I will say
the fleshly side of her character; but it is necessary
now that I should allude, even if I can do no more,
to that splendid intellectual nature which made her
Mlle. Clairon, and which is her claim upon the consideration of posterity.   Her intellect was as passionate
as her flesh, and we know how that was attuned to
all emotions. The woman was strung with passion,
and vibrated all her life like a harp in the wind. Like
her physical nature her intellectual nature was passion,
yes, truly, she was as passionate in her art as she
was in her loves. Life came to her in two great
passions — love of art and love of man; she
sacrificed all else for these, and occasion never came
in her life when she found herself obliged to choose
between them. Space is wanting to tell of her life-
long rivalry with Mlle. Dumesnil. Suffice it to say
that these two actresses disputed the dramatic sceptre
at the Comédie Française for many a year. One was
the first *tragédienne* that dared to *speak* on the stage,
the other remained in the empyrean of the old-fashioned
grandiloquent tragedy, the *tragédienne* of thunder and
lightning. One with a more modern talent, newer,
more prescient of the future; the other with perhaps
more genius. It must, however, be remembered that
if Mlle. Dumesnil was the first to *speak* on the stage,
Mlle. Clairon was the first to appear on the stage
without *paniers*. It is to her that we owe the reform
in theatrical costume, and it was she who inaugurated

the first movement in the direction of local colour. No space remains to me to speak again of her letter of farewell to the Comte de Valbelle, of her life at the Margrave's Court, of how she was supplanted in the affections of the Margrave by Lady Craven, and how, after seventeen years of absence, she was obliged to return to France. Still I would not close this article without saying a word on the old age of Clairon.

M. Goncourt says: "An old age of passions badly "calmed, of resentments unappeased, without any soften-"ing of the heart, without charity in the soul. Never "in Clairon a pretty regret for the past, one of those "smiling melancholy moods of the aged sinner, as in "the case of Sophie Arnold; never a gentle and witty "mocking at the suffering of the body." . . . I think that M. Goncourt judges the character that he has created, or, should I say, evoked from the past somewhat harshly. The strange passionate woman whom we have seen as a disobedient child refusing to learn to sew, whom we have seen at the little supper parties in the Rue Bussy and the great supper parties in Racine's old apartment, whom we have seen as the illustrious *tragédienne* of the Comédie Française creating all the leading parts in Voltaire's greatest plays, whom we have seen a sort of German Princess at the Margrave's Court, and whom we now see sitting alone, deserted by all in her solitary house at Issy, I confess, affects me differently. Yes, I am inclined to judge her more lightly. I am inclined to think of her kindly, even when she writes to a would-be visitor describing her wrinkles and her want of teeth in exaggerated terms, obviously because she would not have him too deeply shocked at her appearance. This terrible sensibility, this passion for life that years could not quench, is not wholly unsympathetic to me.

It attracts me, and when I find the old woman, now eighty years of age, writing: "I know I am eighty, "but my heart is between five-and-twenty and thirty," I am filled with wonder and admiration for the vital energy that could find such words after so many years of passion and adventure, and having regard for her great love of life it seems to me impossible to withhold from her our forgiveness and love.

MUMMER - WORSHIP

AN actor is one who repeats a portion of a story invented by another. You can teach a child to act, but you can teach no child to paint pictures, to model statues, or to write prose, [poetry, or music; acting is therefore the lowest of the arts, if it is an art at all, and makes slender demands on the intelligence of the individual exercising it; but this age, being one mainly concerned with facile amusement and parade, reverences the actor above all other beings, and has, by some prodigy that cannot be explained by us succeeded, or almost succeeded in abstracting him from the playwright, upon whom he should feed in the manner of a parasite, and endowing him with a separate existence—of necessity ephemeral, but which by dint of gaudy upholstery and various millinery has been prolonged beyond due limits and still continues. We of the nineteenth century have witnessed this, and things even stranger and more wonderful, and we bear testimony to them. For according to ancient books and traditions, the actor and actress of past times—those times when Congreve and Wycherley lived —may be compared to a careless lad and wench who, having tired of the ties of home and ways of respectability, threw off galling restraint and roved, after their own hearts' fashion, on the outskirts of society, telling poetry to the joyous who, like them, cared little for beads, ashes, and repentance. Such manner of dramatic

life found favour up to the close of the last century
and did not fall into complete desuetude until about
twenty years ago. Then a great and drastic change
came; the mummer grew ashamed of his hose and
longed for a silk hat, a villa, and above all a visit
from the parson. Nothing is more touching than the
shame that suddenly came upon mummers, male and
female; and now, in full fig, that is to say in a villa,
in a silk hat, and with the cards of the parson and
his wife in their hands, they lay claim to our sympathies
and demand our household affections. Their women
assure us that they are excellent mothers and have
not known the joys of lovers; the men invite us to
their club, and speak of aristocratic connections. So
the mummer has changed his garb and name; he is
now the actor, and wears a silk hat. Can the leopard
change his spots or the Ethiopian his skin? The
modern mummer sits on the lawn outside his villa in
St John's Wood; his boys play beneath the leafage;
his wife, a portly lady on the verge of forty-five and
society, tells you of the many acts of Christian charity
she is performing and of the luncheon parties to which
she has been asked. His house is full of letters from
eminent people, cuttings from newspapers, and portraits
of himself and his wife, for as he was civilised (up or
down, which is it?), his vanity has grown as weed
never grew before: it overtops all things human, and
puts forth religious blossom.

Genius and respectability for the actor, genius and
virtue for the actress, is the cry from the modern
stage. Grant us this and we'll be still. He who has
met the young actress in a Bayswater drawing-
room has heard her say, "Why shouldn't a girl
be virtuous on the stage as well as elsewhere . . .
and a great deal more so too?" And the young
lady's aphorism finds echo in the newspapers. It

would be vain to seek for the John and Paul of
the new gospel. So numerous are they that their
individualities have been lost, and suffice it for the
purpose of this article to say, its apostles are everywhere. The Word is preached, miracles are recorded,
and in that Jordan, the Roman Church, the black
are made white, and turned bleating into society's fold.
Every day the strength of the movement calls new
preachers into existence, and we must needs seek
sermons in skirts and prayer in the wings. Five years
have not passed since we heard for the first time that
a favourite actress nursed her children, read prayers,
and gave tea and tracts to naughty chorus girls. A
favourite American actress has improved upon the
Englishwoman's initiative, inasmuch as the details concerning her private life which are offered for our
delectation are of a more refined nature. When the
first rumour of her refusal of the Duke's hand had
been adequately contradicted, we were informed that
she went to church every Sunday, and lived a holy
and retired life with her mother, and latterly it has
transpired that she will never marry: virtue is not
enough for this young lady, she must have the sacred-
ness of the vestal; and so a corner - stone of the
convent has been added to the Church of the Drama.
And as a Lyceum tragedy is burlesqued at the Gaiety,
so did *danseuses* and others burlesque the moral tone
that came from Wellington Street, and we have had
to listen to persistent asseverations of virtue from
notorious "professional" ladies who accept presents
of jewellery and sup with the young dogs of the town.
The trade in stage virtue waxes fast and furious, and
it seems not unlikely that signs of it will soon be put
over theatrical doors.

Mummers interrupt our path in life — their virtue,

their beauty, their successes, their books—for lately they have taken to writing books; books about what? about themselves. There is but one subject of interest to the mummer, and, like his clothes, his talk, and his virtue, his books excite the curiosity of the public. We have had five editions of the Bancroft *Memoirs*— two bulky volumes of five hundred pages each. Mr Toole's *Memoirs* are promised, Mr Grossmith's [1] have appeared, and Mr Corney Grain's are announced; and the daily press, letting pass the rarest prose and verse without a word (I believe no notice appeared of Mr Pater's *Imaginary Portraits* in the *Telegraph*, the *Standard*, or the *Chronicle*), eagerly gives up dozens of columns to praise and quotation of the stupid anecdotes that any one who has held or played in a theatre chooses to write out. And when not engaged in compiling the stories of their virtuous and successful lives, the mummers discuss their social grievances in the evening papers. What is the social status of the actor? is argued as passionately as a frontier question of European importance. Mr Grossmith writes to the duke, before he consents to accept ten pounds to sing a couple of songs, to ask if he will be received as a guest. . . . Or was it that the duke wrote to Mr Grossmith and asked how he would like to be received? Be this as it may, something went wrong, and Mr Grossmith declares that he scored over the duke by taking a countess down to supper. Neither doctors, lawyers, nor dentists stipulate how they are to be received when they attend. And it will seem to many that when a gentleman accepts a fee for singing in a drawing-room he would prove his blue blood better by declining to consider himself in the light of an ordinary guest than by afterwards discussing his claim to be received on an equal footing with those

[1] *A Society Clown*, by George Grossmith.

whose presence was not paid for. It would also be well if, on retiring from the stage and entering society, actresses would refrain a little, not criticise too severely the morals of the ladies around them, and not wonder in stage whispers why Mrs So-and-so is received.

I know how easily the present may be depreciated by comparing it with a past that time has hallowed and the imagination must needs idealise, knowing it only in its noblest aspects; but facile, common, and unjust as the expedient generally is, it seems to me impossible to consider the state of our drawing-rooms without glancing at those that preceded them. I will attempt no description of an eighteenth-century *salon* —a mention of Mr Orchardson's picture will bring my reader's thoughts to the desired point. Such representation of the eighteenth century, even when we have exaggerated what time has taken of ugliness, and allowed for what the imagination lends of beauty must be admitted as proof that our manners have declined out of all reckoning. We should have looked in vain for mummers in the *salon* of Madame Récamier, and it is to the honour of ladies of old time that we do not find them ostentatiously love - making with inferiors. Love then spread his wings in court phrase and political intrigue; now he is a vulgar parrot that speaks by rote and screams before the foot - lights. He who thinks society has lost nothing of dignity and elegance must call to mind Mr Orchardson's picture as he walks into a London drawing - room. Here is a specimen of a modern *salon* in a fashionable house wherein the mummer has gained a footing. Look with me at the company. First, some young Jews whose long locks do not conceal their Whitechapel origin. One is at the piano. The eyes of many middle-aged ladies are fixed on him; he ogles them in turn; on his especial patrons he lets a single glance fall; he strikes a chord with his right hand; he lets his left drop by his side and utters the last note. The song is done, the middle-aged ladies remove their eyes and sigh with admiration. His place is taken by a girl of wild and unsettled look. Her dress is loud, her hair is perhaps touched with dye; she plays and sings, acts and recites, and is said to make a great deal of money. She is always engaged to a young mummer, and she is now playing the accompaniment for her future husband. Like the others, he is exceedingly lovely, and everywhere you hear of his loveliness. When he gives a concert the hall is filled with women mute with delight or talking incoherently. Will any one assert that this is not true, and, being true, that it is not decadence? The individual standing in the doorway left the army some years ago; there is still a look of the officer in his mild face—a face made mild by long association with folly, vanity, and caprice. As usual, he is waiting for his wife; as usual, she stands at a little distance in the middle of the room, talking of herself. She explains that she is a popular favourite, and how, in the event of not getting an engagement, she will give another *matinée*. How much money has the poor man spent on *matinées*, on tours, on seasons at the Opéra Comique, the Globe, the Olympic, the Strand? There are always people in his house, principally dramatic authors—unkempt dramatic authors from the Strand; erudite and melancholy dramatic authors from Oxford; foolish and foppish dramatic authors from Mayfair. They read plays after breakfast, after lunch, and after dinner, and the readings are only interrupted by fashionable men who come from the clubs and make up parties to go to the theatre. The poor husband sits on the stairs with his only child on his knees; the child says, " When will mother come home, father ? "

The elderly man who sits talking to an old lady was stricken in early life with a hatred of dressing for dinner and afternoon calls, and to escape from what he hated he lived with an actress. His social experiment succeeded for a time, but as society became disorganised the lady succeeded in scrambling through some unguarded loopholes, and when she married her protector she determined to make up for lost time. No more loose jackets; no more smoking in the drawing-room; no more Bohemian friends, but society select and rare; and the little man has now to take in double doses what he hated—afternoon calls and formal conversations. He is not only obliged to dress every day for dinner, but he has to give entertainments in the open air—they give him violent colds ; afternoon calls interfere with politics, but every day you can see him crumpled up in his wife's vast carriage. The horses step out, her bosom stretches forth, and away they go to leave cards. Deluded little politician! Had he married a lady he would have escaped with half his present visiting, and might have been allowed to dispense occasionally with evening dress.

In the *salons* of the eighteenth century love was interwoven between literature and politics. Now our love passages twine round a criticism of acting—how So-and-so used to play the part walking up the stage with his hands in his pockets, whereas So-and-so used to play the part walking down the stage with his hands behind his back. "I want you," says the actor to his lady, "to come to the theatre to-night, for I have invented a new bit of 'business': while So-and-so is singing his sentimental song I pretend to have lost my tobacco pouch, and so that the public shan't get tired of it I intend to vary the 'business' next week by pretending that I have got a pebble in my shoe." Over

such points the season goes mad, falls prostrate and
licks the boots of mummerdom. Every prostration has
been performed, every servile contortion has been made ;
and these changed creatures, with hymn-books in their
hands and their pinchbeck virtue oozing through their
speech, come up every staircase shaking the dust of
their past careers from their garments.

For the last ten years the actor has not only
demanded acclamation for what he does, but he has
striven to obtain, and has succeeded in obtaining, praise
for what he is, thus emulating all priests and sacred
apes. He demands more than they : by right of his
office he claims intelligence as his inalienable right.
Even priests and sacred apes have refrained from this
last audacity. When I say the actor claims intelligence,
even genius, by right of his office, I do not mean that
the claim has ever been put into writing—in the form
of a deposition read before the Lord Mayor, who will
listen to depositions on all subjects—but by his attitude
of late years the actor has not only made, but has
maintained, his right to genius. Not only all he asked
has been conceded, but he has been encouraged to come
again and ask for more.

I pass without comment the banquets that have been
given to him on leaving for America, of the inordinate
use made of the telegraph - wire in proclaiming his
victories; it would hardly be to the point to speak of
the reporters who go to his ship when the anchor-chain
has run out, write of his health and his impressions in
endless columns, and style him "great chief." Let all
this be waived. So many have been treated in this
way, that such consideration and recognition is valued
little by them. So Mr Wyndham must have thought
when he planned his continental tour. "America,
what is it? At best a land of dollars. I will go
where there are Emperors—to Russia and Germany."

Our contention is a threefold one ; first, that acting is the lowest of the arts, if it be an art at all ; secondly, that the public has almost ceased to discriminate between bad and good acting, and will readily grant its suffrage and applause to any one who has been abundantly advertised, and can enforce his or her claim either by beauty or rank ; thirdly, that the actor is applauded not for what he does, but for what he is— that of late years the actor has been lifted out of his place, and that, in common with all things when out of their places, he is ridiculous and blocks the way. A plain account of Mr Wyndham's continental tour will fully prove these three indictments. Mr Wyndham is an actor who has played very well indeed in numberless adaptations of French farces, and his plea for seeking the suffrages of Emperors is that he was at school in Germany, and knows French as an educated Englishman knows it. Miss Mary Moore (the " leading lady " at the Criterion Theatre) tells the story of her qualifications for the tour in question in the *Evening News* of March 24 ; and it is worthy of repetition here, if only to show the slight preparation and training which are now necessary to gain a footing on the " boards."

" Well, I began my stage career at Bradford, in " Yorkshire, in the first touring company of ' The " Candidate,' sent out by Mr Wyndham. I went out " as understudy of Miss Eveson in the leading part of " ' Lady Dorothy.' At Bradford Miss Eveson was taken " ill, and I had to go on at very short notice. I need not " tell you how dreadfully nervous I was. It was a very " severe trial, but I managed to get through it. *It was* " *actually my first appearance on any stage. I had no* " *previous experience, even as an amateur.*"

The italics are mine ; I would ask those who think I have unjustly depreciated the art of acting in comparison with the other arts, to think if they can of a man painting a picture without "previous experience," or modelling a statue, or composing a sonata, or even playing a piano.

"When Miss Eveson returned to London I continued "with 'The Candidate' company, playing the leading "part all through the tour. . . . My first appearance in "London was at the Criterion Theatre, in October "1885. . . . One day I received a cablegram from "Mr Wyndham, asking me whether I would play 'Ada "Ingot' in German at Berlin in October. It was a "startling proposal, for we were already in the latter part "of August, and I had never kept up my familiarity with "the German language since my school-days. But I "made up my mind to do it if it were at all possible. . . . "*In order to get as much practice as possible in the foreign* "*tongue in which I had somewhat rashly undertaken to* "*play, I took my passage in the North German Lloyd* "*steamer 'Saal.'*"

The touching simplicity of this confession deserves italics. A new amateur goes to Germany and Russia to play in German and French, neither of which she is more than superficially acquainted with.

Only those who have lived ten years abroad and speak a foreign language with fluency and conversational correctness, and therefore know how skin-deep their knowledge of the language is, may appreciate at its full value the exquisite absurdities that this very English couple must have been guilty of. The newspapers told us that they were applauded and received floral tributes, but so would a band of Hottentots who came to Europe to flourish clubs; and no doubt Mr Wyndham and Miss Mary Moore will be applauded and will receive floral tributes if they go to Paris and play there in Russian; and I would advise them to do this, for Russia is all the fashion in Paris. The Parisians will nod their heads and say, *Que c'est charmant . . .*

I

quelle jolie langue . . . *harmonieuse*, etc. But to return
to their German tour. Telegrams came from Berlin,
Frankfort, Moscow, and St Petersburg, announcing
Mr Wyndham's and Miss Mary Moore's triumphant
success. Evidently the passage in the North German
steamer bore fruit, and I can imagine them preparing
their French by engaging ticket-collectors in discussion.
When they returned home there was more banqueting
and more floral tributes, and for a big bomb the
Chancellor of the Exchequer was invited to supper on
the stage of the Criterion Theatre, and he made a
speech. I regret that I cannot lay hands on a verbatim
report, but, in default, I give some lines of a description
of it which appeared in the *Era* :—

"Mr Charles Wyndham will need all his natural
"modesty to prevent his becoming intoxicated by his
"recent achievements. It was much to carry the flag
"of the British drama to Berlin ; it was more to win the
"admiration of Russian royalty ; but to get Mr Goschen
"to bear eloquent tribute to the actor's merits was,
"indeed, something remarkable. The Chancellor of the
"Exchequer is, as everybody knows, the embodiment of
"the practical. Stern, shrewd common-sense has always
"been his most striking characteristic. To find him the
"sympathetic and admiring laudator of the buoyant and
"volatile actor-manager who has recently returned to the
"Criterion Theatre with all his blushing honours thick
"upon him is, indeed, as Mr Coburn would say, 'a
"surprise.' Mr Wyndham has, indeed, been curiously
"fortunate in his connection with political magnates.
"It was at the Criterion Theatre, it will be remembered,
"that Mr Gladstone sat on the very evening when the
"fall of Khartoum was announced. Much political
"capital was made out of the circumstance ; and both
"parties had reason to be grateful to 'The Candidate'
"on this occasion. The Liberals must have been

"thankful for the much-needed relaxation afforded to
"their sorely harassed chief, whilst the Conservatives did
"not fail to make a vast amount of political capital out
"of the coincidence, comparing the 'grand old man' to
"Nero fiddling whilst Rome was in flames, with other
"pleasant parallels of a similar nature. And now a
"Chancellor of the Exchequer holds forth in polished
"terms at a banquet on the very Criterion stage, and
"sings the praises of the British drama of the day.
"Mr Goschen's knowledge of German theatrical taste
"enabled him confidently to pay a tribute to the reality
"of Mr Wyndham's success. After a pun, that Mr Toole
"might have envied, about 'Garrick on the Spree,' Mr
"Goschen went on to say that a new form of British
"competition was being carried into the heart of the
"German Empire. It was said, remarked Mr Goschen,
"that the Germans were pushing us hard in many
"directions; they were said to be depriving us of a
"portion of our trade; they were said to be our most
"formidable rivals in all quarters of the globe; but
"though German men-o'-war might plant the German
"flag in the Navigator Islands, Mr Wyndham had
"planted the Union Jack of Old England on the Court
"Theatre of Berlin. People had talked about the
"Pendjeh incident; but what was such an incident
"compared with the incident of 'David Garrick' acted
"on a Moscow stage? 'The Germans,' continued the
"Chancellor of the Exchequer, 'have long admired, with
"proper reverence, the splendid works of our great
"dramatists; but till lately they scorned the efforts of
"those who endeavoured to render them on the stage.'"

C'est gigantesque, as Flaubert used to say when some
more than natural enormity of the *bourgeoisie* was
brought under his notice. But we will not draw
attention to any particular sentence, either by italicisa-
tion or comment; each is a flawless gem of the rarest

human stupidity, and the whole forms the most perfect and complete diadem of nineteenth-century sottishness that we can call to mind.

It would seem therefore that our contention, namely, that our century delights more in parade and gross satisfactions than the centuries that immediately preceded it, and therefore accords worship to the mummer, less for what he does than by right of his mummerhood, is not a light paradox founded on fancy, but a solid truth resting on a substantial basis of fact.

Cruelty was the vice of the ancient, vanity is that of the modern world. Vanity is the last disease. To-day we all seek admiration—that is to say, admiration in its original sense of wonderment. It matters not at all to us if we obtain approbation—instinctively we eschew it, fearing all that might tend to diminish the sentiment of wonder which we eagerly strive to create. The stage therefore catches the great part of the attention of modern society. Painting, music, and poetry demand special talents—ability is required to compose even a bad opera, a bad epic, a bad picture—but any one can play Juliet and Hamlet badly ; besides, to compose even bad operas, epics, and pictures, solitude and long concentration of thought are needed, and with solitude and long concentration of thought the young ladies and young men of to-day will have nothing to do. Desiring parade and wonderment, they turn their eyes to the stage. Our generation has ceased to care for work ; we all want to live well, to enjoy life. In the lowest as well as the highest I note the same desire. Twenty years ago farm labourers were paid by the piece and they worked on till eight o'clock in the evening ; now they are paid by the week and they strike work at half-past five. This general inclination to take pleasure and ease is of course more acutely

marked in society than in the fields. Young sons
shrink from the counting - house and shudder when
Manitoba is mentioned. The arts offer them a
pretext for remaining at home. So the arts are
encumbered with young men and women. The most
intelligent and the least carnal go to literature, painting,
sculpture, and music; the stupid, the vain, and the
fleshly go to the stage. Not in vocation and original
impulse must we seek the reason of the thousands of
pictures that yearly line the walls of the public galleries
and the piles of novels that crowd the stalls of the
booksellers, but in vanity and idleness; and the dull-
witted, uneducated, over-dressed young men who speak
of being on or of going on the stage in Kensington and
Bayswater drawing-rooms, are too cowardly to enlist,
too lazy to face the hardships of colonial life. They
would pull plums out of the mummer's pie, but they
will not go into the kitchen where it is made and
baked. . . . The profession must be raised, elevated,
etc. If I except a couple of princesses and a duchess
in perspective, I know no young lady who has not at
one time or other expressed a regret that she was not
an actress. Women are quite as foolish and quite as
vain as men—which is saying a great deal—and they
desire the stage for the same reason as their brothers.
But for the young ladies there is at least an excuse:
now that we have a surplus female population it is clear
that all women cannot marry, they cannot enlist, nor
yet go out to the colonies and become domestic servants.
So they sigh after the stage. "What are we to do
with our daughters?" is a vital question. The young
ladies cry in chorus, "Put us on the stage, mamma;"
but mamma still hesitates, and the question is debated:
"Can Ethel, Harriet, and May sing in the chorus—not
in Mr Farnie's operas, but in Mr Gilbert's—and remain
as good and pure young ladies as if they had continued

to do crochet-work in the drawing-room at home?"
The parents oppose for a while their daughters' wishes,
but in their heart of hearts they think it would be
no bad thing if Ethel, Harriet, and May were to
earn each thirty shillings or two pounds a week. Such
is the "psychological moment" in Kensington and
Bayswater, and out of it come all the various hypocrisy,
subterfuge, and sophistry which we may read under
such headings as "Church and Stage," "Social Status
of the Actor," etc.

Ethel, Harriet, and May take lessons in elocution.
They assure their parents that to be taught to read
Shakespeare by Mrs A. is just the same as to be taught
to dance by Mrs B. At Mrs A.'s they make acquaintances, they invite their new friends to come to their
house, or they go to their new friends' houses, where
they make more acquaintances, all more or less con-
nected with the drama. If they are lucky, Ethel,
Harriet, and May are engaged at small salaries as
under-studies. They leave home at eleven in the
morning for rehearsal, and they spend several hours
wandering about in the twilight of the stage, or sitting
in the darkness of the wings. There are the dangers
of familiarity. The stage-manager calls them "dear,"
puts his arm round their shoulders, and walks across
the stage with them; and he is a bullying, blaspheming
fellow when he is at work, a coaxing, sensual fellow
when he is idling. "And how is she to-day?" he asks
Ethel. The young girl rebukes him, but she is laughed
at by her companions and told she is ruining her
chances. Harriet may feel faint: if so, she is led out
into the air by the young man standing next her, and
he presses her to drink a glass of wine. At rehearsal
the formality of introductions is dispensed with. A
friend of the manager arranges a lunch, and if our
young ladies refuse the invitations so graciously

extended to them they are looked upon with suspicion in the theatre. Bouquets and presents are left for them at the stage-door. In the dressing-rooms they meet all sorts and conditions of girls ; they have to dress in their company; they have to listen to their conversation, which is often sometimes more than a trifle coarse. They have not been on the stage a month, and already into what shadow has not home faded, with its familiar restraints, associations, and influences! At the end of the season Ethel, Harriet, and May go on tour. They are friendless, they are lonely and a little afraid ; and the instinct is inherent in woman to look to man for love and protection. Now a long railway journey, passed amid enervating conversations and card-playing, is over ; the girl is tired ; there is a rush for lodgings. " Come along, my dear," cries one of the principals ; " I'm going to the ' Hen and Chickens' ; you'll be able to get a room there." She spends months with this man for sole companion, sometimes living under the same roof with him. After having " knocked around " for ten years, and danced and sung in long clothes and short, and been loved much and often, Ethel returns to London, where she is sometimes engaged to play small parts at a salary of five pounds a week. Harriet married an actor ; she is now divorced. May ran away with a banker, who promised to marry her, but didn't ; she went to America ; she tried to "get" on the stage again ; now she is drinking herself to death. And as I have sketched it, so might the fate be of three young ladies taken from a Bayswater drawing-room, and turned into the dramatic profession to make their living ; I mean three average young ladies who, meaning to be good girls, might turn to the stage for the usual reasons — vanity, weariness of home, and ordinary love of change. I do not say adventure :

grant love of adventure, and you draw perilously near
vocation. The young lady who, wild with love of
adventure and masquerade, beats her wings against
the plate-glass window of her prison, and looks to the
dark doorway as the lark to the bright sky, will
possibly fight her way to the front. Nature has chosen
her for the battle of the footlights. The ranks of the
chorus will be better filled by those who enlist out of
inclination than by those who have been led by false
promises out of their way of life.

Far less than art or government is a philosophic idea
understood ; but how much suffering might be avoided
if the truth could become generally recognised and
acted upon, that no world can be wholly pure or
impure—that some proportion of vice, as well as virtue,
must find its way into human life! The entire removal
and abolition of either would mean death to the race.
Mr Lecky, in a magnificently eloquent passage, inspired
by a profound philosophy, has described the harlot as
the guardian angel of our wives and daughters. Our
every - day moralists would do well to master such
primary truths before they seek to subvert entirely the
present order of vice and virtue.

The stage was once a profession for the restless, the
frankly vicious—for those who sought any escape from
the platitude of their personality ; the stage is now
a means of enabling the refuse of society to satisfy
the flesh, and air much miserable vanity. Such change
has come. No change is more than superficial, and
dramatic art has not risen above the law that governs
human things. To-day the stage is as moral as it was
a hundred years ago—as much so and not one jot
more. The alliance between church and stage is a
subject wherewith the hypocritical may trade on the
eternal credulity of mankind ; the alliance between the
stage and society is unfortunately a reality, and I have

attempted to explain its genesis. The dramatic profession has been, is, and always must be, a profession for those to whom social restraints are irksome, and who would lead the life their instinct dictates. The ideal mother cannot be the great artist. The ancients knew this well, and did not waste time in striving to unite the cradle and the *chef-d'œuvre*. And since, in the eternal wisdom of things, we must find a place for vice as well as for virtue, for the Bohemian as well as the housewife, I believe that little will be gained by emptying the *coulisse* into the drawing-room, and the drawing-room into the *coulisse*. We have no belief in the amalgamation of classes, and still hold by the old distinctions. We do not prefer vice to virtue, or virtue to vice, but believe both, since both exist, to be necessary; and our morality consists mainly in striving to keep them apart and refraining from experimental mixing. Victor Hugo in his last book, *Choses Vues*, has a chapter entitled " Mlle. Georges." The great actress comes to see him in a moment of great distress, and he records her conversation :

"Voilà la vérité. Je suis dans la misère. J'ai pris
"mon courage et je suis allée chez Rachel, chez Mlle.
"Rachel, pour lui demander de jouer *Rodogune* avec moi
"à mon bénéfice. Elle ne m'a pas reçue, et m'a fait dire
"de lui écrire. Oh! par exemple, non! Je ne suis pas
"encore là. Je suis reine de théâtre comme elle, j'ai été
"une belle catin comme elle, et elle sera un jour une
"vieille pauvresse comme moi. Eh bien, je ne lui écrirai
"pas. Je ne lui demande pas l'aumône. Je ne ferai pas
"l'antichambre chez cette drôlesse! Mais elle ne se
"souvient pas qu'elle a été mendiante! Elle ne songe
"pas qu'elle le deviendra! Mendiante dans les cafés,
"M. Hugo; elle chantait et on lui jettait deux sous! C'est
"bon. Dans ce moment-ci elle joue chez Véron à un
"louis et elle gagne ou perd dix mille francs dans la nuit ;

"mais dans trente ans elle n'aura pas deux liards et elle
"ira dans la crotte avec des souliers éculés ! Dans trente
"ans elle ne s'appellera peut-être pas Rachel aussi bien
"que je m'appelle Georges. Elle trouvera une gamine
"qui aura du talent et qui lui marchera sur la tête et elle
"se couchera à plat ventre, voyez-vous. . . . Je dois dix
"francs à mon portier. J'ai été obligée de laisser vendre
"au Mont-de-Piété les boutons de diamant que je tenais
"de l'empereur. Je joue au théâtre Saint-Marcel, je joue
"aux Batignolles, je joue à la banlieue, je n'ai pas vingt-
"cinq sous pour payer mon fiacre. Et bien, non, je
"n'écrirai pas à Rachel, et je me jetterai à l'eau tout
"bonnement."

This seems to me truth—truth for yesterday, for
to-day, and for all time. Hypocrites will write about
the church and stage, and new devotees will fall before a
single shrine of shovel-hattedness and motley; young
ladies will think more than ever that the stage-door will
lead them from the irksomeness of *chaperons* to fame
and fortune, and Kensington matrons will incline a more
and more docile ear to that which they are now seeking
to believe—that their daughters may be virtuous
actresses ; the flame of mummer-worship will be blown
higher ; society will embrace the mummer, the mummer
will return the embrace more ardently ; we shall hear
of another queen of the boards who nurses her children,
and another who goes to church every Sunday ; many
strange things will come to pass, but such phases
of stage-life are ephemeral and circumstantial—gnats
on the surface of a well, and in the end the abiding and
important truth will be found unchanged at the bottom ;
and I have not found it more strikingly expressed than
in the words of the unfortunate Mlle. Georges.

OUR DRAMATISTS AND THEIR LITERATURE

WHEN we reproach our dramatists with the illiterate puerilities of their stories, they reply that the public will listen to nothing more sensible; and it is clear they hope we shall infer from this statement that they are capable of rising to very superior heights of fancy and imagination, and were not at all intended by nature to grovel; and then, bewailing their lot, they point with despairing glances to the trough full of guineas, and with leisured gait return to the unclean straw of melodrama and farce.

Our dramatists' apology for their foolish plays, and their plea for the genius that might have been theirs, but which lies a wreck submerged beneath the waves of popular taste, might have been allowed to pass with an incredulous smile for sole comment, if, by a series of unwise attempts to follow us into book literature, they had not proven that they are no better than we expected—third, fourth, and fifth-rate men of letters; and, as all our leading dramatists have written essays, novels, newspaper articles, and even poems, it seems to me that before examining their plays it would be well to cast our eyes over what they have produced when liberated from the thraldom of the public, the actor, the flare and tinsel of the stage, and the many various disadvantages they labour under. In their novels, their poems, and their essays, they should have found an escapement for

the genius which they so confidently assure us exists in
them. It is not possible to conceive that a man should
be capable of writing in the strictest form with thought
and eloquence and only capable of expressing the
most hackneyed commonplaces in easier forms of
composition. The converse is of course not true;
many have written excellent books and ridiculous
plays, but no one who has written great plays has
written foolishly when he wrote sonnets, poems, or
novels. And for these reasons, the validity of which
will not be questioned, we shall be able to determine the
exact measure of intelligence now in the service of the
stage by an examination of the book literature of our
dramatists.

Mr Gilbert has assumed a sort of headship of dramatic
authors, and in deference to that headship we will begin
with him. He has written a volume of comic poems;
and the little poems really deserve all the popularity they
have obtained, so prettily are they versified, and many
of them he has since elaborated into successful plays.
And the measure of his success has always been determined by the measure of his faithfulness to these ballads;
and if we examine them we find they contain in essence
the whole of his literary perceptions. Surely the veriest
tyro in criticism could detect the hand that wrote the
Bab Ballads in *Gretchen* and *Pygmalion and Galatea*.
Mr Gilbert has contributed short papers to the Christmas
annuals, but I am not aware of any that rose above
a seasonable piece of jocosity. His prose plays, with
the exception of two acts entitled *Sweethearts*, have
varied between mechanical inventions and profitless
commonplace; and after the production of the last
he thought it necessary to redeem his imperilled reputation by promising to confine his efforts for the future
to the fabrication of libretti for Sir Arthur Sullivan, an
art in which he pre-eminently excels.

Mr Burnand, the genial editor of *Punch*, has written *Happy Thoughts*, which ranks as high in English prose as the *Bab Ballads* do in English poetry, and in equal degree both works have contributed to the amusement of suburban drawing-rooms. Mr Burnand has published a number of parodies of Ouida's novels; the best known, I believe, is *Strapmore, by Weeder*. Also his parody of Hugh Conway's *Dark Days* fell in with some readers during the period of the popularity of the original. Unlike Mr Gilbert, Mr Burnand has never attempted serious work, and he would, I am sure, repudiate a proposal to judge his writings by any other standard than a desire to conform to the passing mood of a middle-class public. Similar judgment is applicable to the works of Mr George R. Sims. Indeed, his appeal to the intellectual habits of the middle classes is so frank and undisguised that no part of his work can be said to come within range of literary criticism. He provides certain fare, he calls it through the area railings, and the *Dagonet Ballads* are bought, sold, and consumed like necks of mutton and loaves of bread. If the "middles" like the *Dagonet Ballads*, they like them, and if they don't like them—well, they don't like them; but in neither case would the interference of a critic be justified. Lest this should seem like unrelieved bitterness, I will say that *Mary Jane's Memoirs* appear to me a good subject spoilt through inadequate treatment. It is realism in its naïvest form, but Mr Sims is not a realist because he writes about Mrs Three-doors-up, any more than Mr Buchanan is an idealist because he observes life badly.

Mr W. G. Wills has written, I believe, many novels, but as no slightest trace of them remains, their mediocrity may be assumed. Four or five years ago he published an epic, and it has gone the way of his novels.

Immediately the success of the *Silver King* was established, Mr Henry Arthur Jones wrote some long letters to the *Era* on dramatic writing, and he published in the *Nineteenth Century* an article on the union between the pulpit and the stage, or some similar theme. At the same time Mr Jones declared himself the sole author of the *Silver King*, and accused his collaborator, Mr Herman, of inability to write the simplest English sentence. He has since written other articles, all of which prove that he is more fitted for play-writing than for literature.

Mr Grundy has published a few short stories in the magazines, but they attracted no one's attention. Mr Hamilton and Mr Augustus Harris have occasionally contributed to the Christmas annuals ; and I have seen some slight verses of Mr Pinero's in similar publications, but they did not strike me as being anything more than those of a very minor poet. Mr Robert Buchanan is, past question, the most distinguished man of letters the stage can boast of, and Mr Robert Buchanan is a minor poet and a tenth-rate novelist. As a poet he was beyond all question outpaced by at least six men of his genera-tion—Mr Swinburne, Mr Rossetti, Mr Arnold, Mr William Morris, Mr Coventry Patmore, and Mr George Meredith ; and to be outpaced by half a dozen men of your own generation, not to speak of the two giants of the preceding generation, is complete extinguishment in poetry. In prose fiction, Mr Buchanan is either commonplace or ridiculous, and it is a matter of surprise how a man who can at times write such charming verse can at all times, and so unfailingly, write such execrable prose. His novels are clumsy and coarse imitations of Victor Hugo and Charles Reade. The best is *The Shadow of the Sword*; and it is so invertebrate, so lacking in backbone, that, notwithstanding some fine suggestions, no critic could accord it a higher place than

in the second class. *Foxglove Manor* and *The New Abelard* are, in thought and in style, below the level of the work that the average young lady novelist supplies to her publisher. It is, therefore, in accordance with my views of the relation of stage literature to literature proper that Mr Buchanan should have turned from the latter to the former.

I cannot recall the name of any other dramatic author who has dabbled to any appreciable extent in literature. The writers of comic operas and farces are men whose names are unknown beyond the stage-door and the play-bill—clerks from the Government offices, or the obscure contributors to obscure journals.

It must be granted that the relegation of the entire dramatic literature of an epoch to writers of the third and fourth class is a unique literary phenomenon. By the examination and study of such phenomena we may understand the dominant forces of our century, and learn in some measure whither the civilisation we are so proud of is tending. And it is difficult to find a test more just and more conclusive of the state of the popular mind than the open and spontaneous verdict expressed in a theatre. The poet and the novelist may sacrifice the present, but in the case of the dramatist such sacrifice is not possible, for his work hardly exists off the stage, and depends upon the temper of the public mind. The most successful play of the year contains therefore in a state of essence the sentiments and feelings agitating the multitude during its period of stage life; and by looking into the intellectual idiosyncrasies of some four or five representative plays may we not arrive at a very fair understanding of the normal comprehension of our epoch?

The most popular play produced in 1889 is without question *Sweet Lavender*. We are introduced to an

impecunious, drunken barrister, and with him is living a young man, who instead of reading law makes love to the laundress's daughter. (Laundress is Temple slang for charwoman.) The charwoman is represented as a person who, although she lives in the kitchen and washes dishes, is as a matter-of-fact a most refined person, and is endowed with such sentiments as would become the superior of a convent. Her daughter although she helps her mother in her duties of cleaning and scrubbing, wears white muslin dresses and large straw hats trimmed with wild-flowers, and talks with the ease and refinement that is expected from young ladies educated in a high-class boarding-school.

The young man is loved by his cousin, who in turn is loved by an American, who follows her, asking her to marry him; and, blind to all rebuffs, continues his courtship in a manner unparalleled in real life except perhaps by Mr Rouden. In the second act the uncle of the young man comes to town and finds his nephew engaged, not to his cousin as he thinks, but to the laundress's daughter; and the situation is still further complicated by the arrival of a telegram announcing a bank failure, which involves the uncle in complete ruin. Here it is necessary to remark that the complete ruin of the uncle is necessary for moral reasons, for it was he who seduced the laundress eighteen years ago. In the third act the ruined uncle and his relations come to live in the chambers of the impecunious barrister, and we find everybody sweeping and cleaning and cooking. The American is still proposing to the cousin, and he insists on following her in and out of the kitchen and helping her with her work. We are in the third act, and every one must be made happy. The impecunious barrister inherits fifty thousand pounds, and pays the ruined uncle's liabilities; the young lady consents to leave off loving her cousin and to marry the

crazy American, whom she really loved all the time; the ruined uncle marries the laundress; and the nephew marries her daughter. This is the story of a play which London has been going to see for nearly two years.

In *The Profligate* Mr Pinero had a better subject. A young woman, truly loved by a virtuous young man, prefers a profligate, and only begins to learn his past when her honeymoon is waxing to fulness. Thinking it was Mr Pinero's intention to show the disaster that must result when a man brings an amorous temperament into family life, I said: Should Mr Pinero have the strength to let his hero remain a profligate, this play will be the best since *The School for Scandal*. But his hero ceases to be a profligate at the end of the first act; and there is no relapse into vice. His regard for virtue is as intense as St Augustine's. It may have been Mr Pinero's intention to show how a vicious nature may be reformed by the beneficent influence of a pure woman. Then why did he choose the honeymoon for time and an Italian terrace for place?

It is probable that he meant no more than a play. The reconciliation of the wife to her husband, a concession made by Mr Pinero at the earnest request of Mr Hare, proves the actor to be a better dramatist than the dramatist. For were the profligate to shoot himself as originally intended by the author, the play would be shorn of all meaning and would fall into a mere collection of incidents. It was Mr Hare that saved Mr Pinero's play from shipwreck; he endowed it with its one idea—namely, that in the first stress of horror and disappointment caused by the discovery of her husband's past life, the young wife leaves him, but leaves him only to learn that no life exists for her apart from him. She forgives him, or, I should say, is reconciled to him, but her heart is full of

K

fear for the future; for she now knows that women attract him, as the magnet attracts steel.

Mr Pinero speaks the language of the stage with rare fluency; he is well armed with pointed repartee and various verbal excellence, and these qualities show him to the very best advantage in the opening acts. The presentation of the hero—his scorn for his virtuous friend, his easy admission that his marriage with the school-girl is inspired by *ennui* of facile loves, his careless assurances of reform—is not bad. And the second act deserves but few words of reproach. The change of the girl into woman—a blossom broken to flower in the warmth of the Tuscan night, and the seeming change in the profligate, whose heart is at least temporarily won by the beauty and the youth and gladness of his wife is commonplace but agreeably set forth.

It is unfortunate, however, that the maidservant whom the profligate seduced is not a mother, for a girl does not denounce her seducer unless he has made her a mother. We denounce those who have done us material injury; mental injuries are not spoken of, for we know instinctively they would not be understood. Then instead of a simple, pathetic explanation between the women interrupted by the profligate, his entrance into the tumult of his wife's grief, his explanation that the past concerns his wife not at all, his assurance that no matter whom she had married she would have encountered the same sin, that hers is the lot of all women, that her own father probably had a similar sin on his conscience before he married, we have a game at cross purposes, and the servant girl goes down-stairs crying, "Kill me, kill me, kill me!"

Perhaps Mr Pinero means that the girl cries for some one to kill her because, thinking the elder and not the younger man is the husband of her benefactor, she sees no harm in denouncing him as her seducer. If this is so,

Mr Pinero's ideas of dramatic climax do not stray beyond an ordinary stage misunderstanding. But if Mr Pinero had seen or had not turned from the true situation, so thrilling in its plain psychological truth, we should have had one of the finest plays of modern times. The scene I have indicated, written in simple words and spoken in simple tones, would have electrified the house. I can see men moving nervously in the stalls, avoiding each other's eyes.

I am drawn to sympathise with Mr Jones's talent because he desires the *new*. He is in touch with modern life and thought; he says almost what he wants to say, and he wants to say far more than any other dramatist, and having obtained a remarkable mastery over that most obstinate vehicle of literary expression—the stage, one that seems to rebel against all innovation—he introduces into his work far more personal observation of life than any other writer. What, then, is wanting to complete a very real talent? Taste: a vein of commonness degrades, if it does not wholly ruin his best work.

In his play of *Wealth* Mr Jones started with an excellent idea, one that Balzac might have welcomed. This is it. A man pursues without halting his passion for money-making, piling fortune upon fortune, until his brain weakens, and a thought begins to haunt him that he may die after all in the work-house. To develop a latent force into an active force an event is necessary, and it is in the invention of this event that the common side of Mr Jones's talent reveals itself. He can think of nothing better than to make the father turn his daughter out-of-doors because she refuses to marry the man he desires her to take. And this treatment of the subject Mr Jones has defended in the course of a long essay. It would seem that he has not learnt that it is not time nor repetition that

ages a story. Some themes are eternally young, others were always old—have never been young. A father sacrificing himself for his daughter is an example of a theme that never grows old ; a father turning his daughter out-of-doors because she denies his right to choose a husband for her is an example of a theme that was always old. The youth or the age of a theme is determined not by years, but by the amount of truth to human nature the theme represents. A father turning his daughter out-of-doors because she would contract a marriage which he, with his superior know-ledge of the world, foresees could not fail to lead her into unhappiness, would have been better, suggesting as it does a conflict between instinct and experience ; but that would be the basis for a new story, not the pivot on which a theme already chosen might be happily worked upon. Mr Jones required a pivot, and the pivot he chose was as common as the story he wished to tell was refined.

The same vein of commonness runs through *The Middleman.* Passing over all such crudities of execution as placing in the middleman's mouth the very argu-ments which the enemies of our system of labour and capital would have used against him, which he is supposed to speak unconsciously, I go straight to essentials. Mr Jones did not see that to satirise the middleman effectually, the middleman must triumph over the inventor ; if the fly kills the spider, it is clear that the spider is a subject if not for pity at least not for satire. Yet in the play it is the inventor who ruins the middleman, and this stupid blunder obviously deprives the play of all *raison d'être.* And he dramatises the theme of this play just as he dramatised the theme of his other play. True, that he does not make the middleman turn his son out-of-doors because he wants to marry the inventor's daughter ;

he stops on the brink of this precipice, but only to fling himself over another. The middleman's son seduces the inventor's daughter! It seems strange that Mr Jones could not think of something better, and how he could write the wholly stupid and irredeemably vulgar comic love-scenes that disfigure a really beautiful third act, is also a matter which tantalises the curiosity of the critic. It would seem that last acts are of necessity absurd, and many of the childishnesses of Mr Jones's last act are no doubt deliberate, and have been perpetrated with the view of securing a popular success, but the incident of the loan, when the successful inventor offers to lend the ruined middleman "a fiver," and in the middleman's house, out of which the inventor is about to expel him, is an example of that vein of commonness which pollutes Mr Jones's best aspirations.

I was in Paris when *Judah* was produced, and shall not easily forget the stupor of astonishment with which I read Mr Clement Scott's article in the *Daily Telegraph*. I remembered how easily a generous emotional nature may be led out of all critical judgment and calm discrimination by the febrile agitation and excitement always on the move during the first performance of a new play, and how this hysterical abandonment of critical reason is fomented in the red pepper hours of spontaneous composition in a printing-office. Even then, I could not reconcile Mr Scott's extraordinary eulogies with what I knew of Mr Jones's talent, and the expansion I believed it to be capable of in fortunate circumstances. I read of "literature," "the redemption of the stage," "originality," "genius." I read in amazement that George Eliot had done nothing better than the dissenting clergyman in *Judah*. And when I returned to London I went at once to the Shaftesbury Theatre to see the play that had turned the heads of the London critics, transforming them one and all into a pack of yelping urchins, a little drunk with the sunlight, a little unduly excited with tea and " caike." But although I could not see *Judah* in the light in which the critics saw it, it seemed to me useless to drop critical salt into any one's jam-pot. Let the treat, I said, go on to the end unembittered with any salt of doubt. There will be plenty of time for my little pinch when all the happiness is over.

The subject of the play is good, but so are all the subjects of Mr Jones's plays. A nobleman's daughter is dying of consumption, all remedies have been tried and have failed. But a girl is said to be working miracles in the neighbourhood, and in the decline of hope from the natural sciences he is tempted to ask aid from this itinerant dealer in the supernatural. His guests, who are eminent scientists, endeavour to dissuade him, and one undertakes to prove that the girl is no more than a vulgar charlatan. This is the root of Mr Jones's subject, and it seems to me to be difficult to imagine one more beautiful or more human, or one more characteristic of the mind of the nineteenth century. But only in his primary ideas is Mr Jones original : the moment he moves to develop a first notion he degrades it, and the first movement of his mind in this instance was to associate the miracle-monger with a dissenting clergyman. True it is that a clergyman comes well into the subject, but the girl should have met him in the nobleman's house ; for the whole beauty and originality of the subject lay in the unprotected entrance of the girl into the midst of her natural enemies, the scientists. Daniel among the lions ! Henceforth every step Mr Jones takes in his story is a step in the wrong direction. The girl does not believe in herself, and pretends to fast only to procure belief in her supernatural powers ; with duplicity and not with faith does she enter the battle. And her imposture would have been proved if the clergyman who loves her did not give false testimony in her favour. The play then resolves itself into a discussion regarding the sin of lying. The clergyman makes a full confession, the girl confesses too, and they both declare their intention of sailing for foreign shores and living happily for ever afterwards. And while the lovers are publicly denouncing themselves, the poor consumptive child who has placed her faith in the miracle girl is juggled out of the room, and we are asked to take no further interest in her.

But is it impossible that a mad fanatic who believes she possesses supernatural powers should be able to induce belief in others even to the point of curing them of mortal maladies? The secret of life still escapes our ardent research, the mysteries of hypnotism and auto-suggestion have not yet been fully unravelled. And why should not a maid with faith for sole aim— faith, that weapon of the ancient world, be still able to refute and confute the incredulities of a band of semi-ignorant scientists? Science is still in its infancy, and the old world may win a last triumph over the new. And this new Joan might rise to the giddiest height and only fail and fall, when like the first Joan, she began to doubt, and deem that her mission was ended. And how such a story would recall the world's eternal stories, the ancient symbols of eternal truths!

I have tried to indicate on which side lay the great classical highway, but Mr Jones does not seem to me to walk firmly even in the by-path.

When the curtain went up for the second time disclosing a romantic castle with moat and ivied tower, I felt that the note was a false one ; and the act proceeded amid comic love-scenes, as good as and no better than a set of drawings by Du Maurier taken

from the pages of *Punch*, and the attempts to supply
the girl with food were puerile and far too suggestive
of conjuring. The difficulties and the paraphernalia of
ordeal had not been solved by the author, though his
solution had been accepted by the audience ; as for
the human side of the ordeal it was not even touched
upon, and when the curtain went down for the second
time the words that came into my mind were: "Le
ventre n'a pas crié et le cœur non plus." I missed
the brutality of the stomach. Every great writer
would have gone to the stomach of the starving girl
for originality, Shakespeare as well as Zola, Balzac
as well as Hugo, the execution in every case would
have been different, but the intention would have
been the same. And how splendid it would have
been to have exhibited the man with love upon his
lips and the girl with starvation in her stomach ! It
would have been the ideal and the real, heaven and
earth in their accustomed strife set facing one another
in the same scene—the two deepest instincts in man
striving for mastery, wound one within the other, an
epitome as it were of life itself. Had Mr Jones for a
single moment suspected how near he was to the
highest work, his play would, perhaps, never have
been produced, for it is hardly probable he could have
collected sufficient strength even dimly to sketch
what some great master, living in a great age, would
have set the seal of immortality upon. For Mr Jones
there was nothing in the scene but the more or less
successful attempts of a charlatan miracle-monger to
place meat lozenges where his daughter might find
them, and so deceive the science-labelled old gentlemen
who wander through the play.

There are many other points where Mr Jones fails.
He fails particularly to do what Mr Scott, overcome
in the nervous emotions of a first night, fondly imagined

he had done—namely, to develop the character of the dissenting clergyman. The Welsh minister who had fed his flocks on the hills, and had never dreamed of love, is wood from the first word he utters to the last, and never awakes for a single instant to life. I wanted the words that reveal the burning heart, the words that bring little shudderings into the flesh of the listeners, but I heard only vague hollow commonplace—"You are more beautiful than an angel." But it would be useless to discuss minor failings or minor beauties in a work in which the author has failed where it was imperative he should succeed.

I have heard dull and even stupid plays applauded at the Français, but a really low-class play would not be tolerated there, and I confess I was filled with shame at the attitude of the public on the production of *A Man's Shadow* at the Haymarket Theatre. It is not necessary that I should wade through every part of the story, it will suffice my purpose to say that *A Man's Shadow* is an adaptation of *Roger la Honte*, and when I say that *Roger la Honte* first appeared as *roman feuilleton* in *Le Petit Journal*, and was afterwards dramatised and produced at the Ambigu Comique, the reader will have no difficulty in divining how intimately the story must reek of the good *concierges* of Montmartre. That the Haymarket Theatre should have sunk to the level of the Ambigu Comique! Imagine a Surrey or Britannia drama, a dramatic arrangement of one of the serial publications in *Bow Bells* or the *London Journal*, being translated into French and produced at the Français or the Odéon! Imagine the audience of either of those theatres howling frantic applause and cheering the adapters at the end of the piece! Imagine a leading French actor — Coquelin, Delaunay, Mounet-Sully—

playing the principal part! The mind refuses to
entertain such impossible imaginings; but what is
impossible to imagine as happening in France has
befallen us in London. Hume did well to call us the
barbarians of the banks of the Thames.

Almost equally reprehensible is the entertainment
provided by Mr Irving at the Lyceum, and if it is
not so unpleasant it is only because fewer words
are spoken on the stage. For some time past the
tendency of Mr Irving's management has been in
the direction of pantomime. The production of *Faust*
(of the Irving *Faust*) was the first decisive step, and
the success of this experiment in witches and blue
devils showed him that the utmost licence would
be allowed in the substitution of scenery and his
own personality for the text of the author. Having
ascertained the debased state of the public mind, he
proceeded to speculate upon it, and in *The Dead Heart*
has approached marvellously near to pure pantomime.
One step nearer and even his well-fed critics would
have had to cry, halt! It would be interesting to
learn how many words are spoken on the stage during
the performance of the play as given at the Lyceum.
I should say not more than six or seven thousand;
of this I am certain, that the Lyceum text is not
a quarter the length of another play that occupies
the same time in representation.

The first scene is laid in a garden. There is of
course a lavish display of foliage and lanterns, and
there is a fountain with real water. Mr Bancroft
comes on and mumbles some incoherent and, as far
as I could judge, irrelevant remarks; then there is
an elaborate dance, and for ten minutes the audience
is entertained by an exhibition of dancing so elaborate
that the thought of a succession to Mr Turveydrop's

academy is irresistibly suggested. Then there is a front scene, and Mr Bancroft mumbles a few more irrelevant remarks until the scene is set behind. The third scene is Miss Terry's bedroom. She makes a few remarks concerning a scarf she is about to wear; a man enters by the window and declares his love. Mr Irving enters and declares his anger; he is arrested and sent to the Bastille. Surely not a thousand words are spoken in this act! The second act opens with the taking of the Bastille. There is a brass cannon and a heterogeneous crowd that howls and climbs upon barrels, etc.; great doors fall down, and then everybody dances, and the dance lasts several minutes. When the dance is done various prisoners are exhibited to the audience, very much as strange animals are exhibited in a show; eventually Mr Irving is brought out, and, in such crazed and dilapidated condition as seventeen years in a dungeon would produce, he lies down in front of the audience, moaning from time to time. Inconceivable as it may seem, he elects to lie there for several minutes, holding the attention of the audience by the help of occasional moans or grunts and furtive grimacing. I have long known that the actor secretly chafes against the author, who he believes robs him of a part of his triumph, but I did not think the press would have allowed such a childish manifestation of vanity to pass in silence.

The next scene is an apartment in a palace in which the Abbé Latour (Mr Bancroft) makes an incomprehensible declaration of love to the Comtesse de St Valéry (Miss Terry), and this is followed—stay, it is preceded—by some mysterious allusions to a debt which the Comtesse's son has contracted in a café of which the Abbé Latour is a part proprietor. But it is as like as not that I am wrong, so incoherently is the scene played, and I think written. A number of scenes follow, all very useful to prolong the piece, but absolutely unnecessary. There is no story to develop, but there is an incident; it is this. The Comtesse de St Valéry's son is condemned to death, and his mother beseeches Landry (Mr Irving) to save his life. To prolong the fourth act Landry sends for his old enemy, the Abbé Latour, who goes to the guillotine next morning and challenges him to a duel. The duel serves the same purpose as the dance in the first act, the taking of the Bastille in the second, it appeals to the vulgar appetite for stage realism, and it fills up the time. When the Abbé Latour has been killed, Mr Irving takes the place of the son of his old sweetheart, and mounts the scaffold with all the lights of apotheosis playing upon his face and hair.

Mr Irving is credited, and he takes credit, for having contributed to what we must call the development of artistic tastes. I confess I do not perceive very clearly how the production of such pieces as *The Dead Heart* can advance artistic taste. I do not deny that the taking of the Bastille is exciting, but so are a rat-hunt and a prize-fight, and I should say that a rat-hunt was a less depraving sight than a performance of the *The Dead Heart*. A rat-hunt is an appeal to our animal instinct pure and simple. We enjoy it, and have done with it, but stage realism corrupts our intelligence by easy satisfactions instead of stimulating the imagination, which should create all from the words of the poet.

Mr Irving understands better than any one the baseness of modern taste, and he appeals to it more flagrantly than any other manager. He was, of course, well within his right in appraising and selling his goods in the largest market, but I am acting well within my right when I attempt some criticism of the value of his supposed contributions to the development of dramatic art. He dresses out his theatre as Octave in *Au Bonheur des Dames* dressed out his shop ; he has invariably appealed, though never before so outrageously, to the sensual instincts rather than to the imagination. Others may praise him for this ; but I look back to those times when theatrical audiences did not require *real* fountains and *real* trees, and I cannot but believe that they who did not require these realities were gifted with a sense that is wanting in us.

Some months after the publication of this criticism of modern dramatic writing, the subject was reviewed by Mr Crawford in the pages of the same Review,[1] and the discussion was continued two months or more by the daily and weekly press. Mr Crawford's article strikes me as thoughtful and suggestive ; but it is sometimes contradictory, always uncertain and hesitating. As a man of cultivated literary taste, Mr Crawford does not fail to perceive that the plays produced in the London theatres are unsatisfactory ; he tries to determine why this is so ; but his criticism is no more than haphazard beating of coverts. He beats every possible bush, fluttering a quantity of sparrows ; now and then an owl flies out of a tangled growth of ivy ; but he does not seem to me to have started game anywhere.

The cause of deterioration of stage literature must be sought for far down in the constitution of modern society. The prevalence of the three-hundred-night run dams the current, and a free current is necessary for the development of every literature ; secondly, it forces the author to compose strange compounds of farce, comedy, drama, and sensationalism. Thirdly, it forbids all originality of thought and treatment, for

[1] *The Fortnightly.*

such might prove dangerous; mediocrity will alone find favour in the eyes of a million or so of people drawn from all classes of society. And the fact is significant that in the great French dramatic revival of 1830 plays did not run for more than forty or fifty nights; and in France, as in England, since the three-hundred-night run became an essential condition of success, dramatic literature has steadily declined. For some years I held to the belief that the real cause of the decline of dramatic literature was the three-hundred-night run: but while I still continue to regard it as an evil, my views have modified, and I am inclined to think that we must look still deeper.

The real cause for the decline of dramatic literature is cheap books. In the time of the Greeks there were no books; in the time of Shakespeare there were few books, and for stories the people had to go to the theatre. We, on the contrary, when we want stories, stay at home and read them — we go to the theatre for what we do not find in books — pretty faces, brilliant costumes, scenical display, and acting. The Elizabethans went to the theatre for fine language, and their dramatists wrote in verse, even if the subject were not poetic in itself, because verse lent itself more easily to declamation than prose; and as the art of declamation declined, so did the art of writing blank-verse plays. When the tail became an inconvenient appendage man lost his tail; but were man to take to living in trees again I have little doubt that in a hundred thousand years the rudiments of a tail would begin to show, and I have no doubt whatever that if newspapers and cheap books were suppressed, the art of declamation, and with it that of writing good blank verse, would again become popular. I do not argue that it would be well to sacrifice book-literature, were such a sacrifice possible, so that we might have a new poetic dramatic literature

I am merely minded to examine certain effects and to report upon the causes that produced them.

Perhaps it is possible to create artificially a dramatic literature. It would be pleasant to have a subventioned theatre which could afford to produce plays that in all likelihood would not run for three hundred nights, a theatre from which *le spectacle coupé* would not be entirely banished—for I regard as one of our greatest misfortunes that in the present ordering of things a one-act comedy finds every door shut against it. But the State-subventioned theatre is a dream so hopeless that it is not worth dreaming. Mr Crawford admits that this is so, and he flutters in the wake of various will-o'-the-wisps, considering many social changes that might do what a solid subvention of £10,000 a year would do. In one paragraph he imagines that when permission is granted to the music-halls to produce stage plays, and the "gods" are finally got rid of, a more critical state of things may come into fashion. I disagree with Mr Crawford. The coster is a better critic than the City clerk—a more intelligent and, above all, a less conventional critic. The coster and the man of genius are the only critics—one is self-educated, the other is uneducated. But the man who has been educated is a hopeless lump of conventionality, and is inaccessible to new ideas. Napoleon did not seek for generals among the middle classes; they would have come with ledgers in their hands and pens behind their ears. He went to the people, and there he found brains and swords; and were a new Othello to be produced to-morrow, the criticism the author would have to fear most would be that of the second-rate dramatic critic. The man of genius would applaud it at once, the coster would be equally prompt in his applause, but the man who has been educated would hiss the piece—no, he would not even do that; he would go away talking languid nonsense. To get rid of the "gods" would be fatal; they are what is most spontaneous and natural in our theatres.

Then Mr Crawford speaks of a movement which he says is now on foot for the establishment of a Théâtre Libre in London. Who is concerned in this movement? Who are the authors who will write for this theatre when it is established? Without giving any information on these points, Mr Crawford expresses vague belief that such a scheme might be of service, and in the next sentence he ventures to doubt if it could seriously affect the London stage? I agree with him; I do not think it could, for there are no plays to represent, except the conventional rubbish that has been refused because it is too conventional even to find favour with a manager. Literary adventure is not a characteristic of modern London.

Then there is no hope? Yes, I think there is. Although the State may never give £10,000 a year to support a literary theatre, it does not follow that a private individual may not do so. Men have committed suicide so that their names might appear in the papers; men have spent hundreds of thousands upon women who deceived them, and who bored them; men have wasted thousands on race-courses, on the conversion of the Brahmins, on many conceivable and many inconceivable follies. Why should a man not endow a theatre? There is no reason why he should not, except that it would be an uncommonly intelligent thing to do. This is, I admit, an almost unanswerable argument against the realisation of my ideal theatre. But while fostering vanity, civilisation curtails the means of gratifying it. War is becoming rarer, duelling is prohibited, the whole world has been discovered or soon will be, but vanity is daily seeking more uneasily than ever an outlet for its gratification, and no better outlet will ever offer itself than the endowment of a theatre. This being admitted we have only to imagine a millionaire slightly less stupid than his fellows saying, "For ten thousand a year, for perhaps five thousand, I can procure an immortality that time will not destroy, a most honourable and a most glorious immortality, and so cheap too—ten or five thousand a year! Why, on the turf that would only procure me a few years of dubious notoriety. I'll do it." Such is the psychological story of the subvention theatre which we shall soon possess.

It would be pleasant, but perhaps this would be too wild an expectation, to think of its founder as being sufficiently intelligent to realise the fact that the man who gives pleasure is as charitable as he who relieves suffering. Looked at in this light it would be equally meritorious to endow a theatre as a hospital; but the patron of the drama who will give us our national theatre and free us from the thraldom of farcical melodrama and melodramatic farces will not go deeply into the philosophy of the question; he will be attracted by the assurance of high renown while he lives, and a most durable immortality when he is dead. Everything happens, and sooner or latter this will happen; an endowed theatre is inherent in our civilisation, and, article, go forth and whisper thy Secret of Immortality!

L

NOTE ON "GHOSTS"

THE representations at the Théâtre Libre are but private theatricals. Private individuals subscribe a certain sum yearly for these entertainments, and once the doors are opened a thousand pounds would fail to procure you a seat. But M. Antoine is always anxious to oblige a *confrère*, and, although he expected that Ibsen's great play of *Ghosts* would draw an exceptionally large audience, he promised to do his best to find me a place, warning me, however, that a *strapontin d'orchestre* would be all that I might hope to receive. But we go to the Théâtre Libre to see fine plays and fine acting, not to digest a heavy dinner ; and we do not mind sitting for three hours in a dark corner on some small ledge that unhooks from the wall. A dark corner, deep hidden in a passage, and beyond this passage some ten feet of gallery ; and as the *ouvreuse* and the late comers are engaged in an unintermittent wrangle concerning umbrellas and overcoats until the clock strikes ten, you are apt to lose your temper, and declare a visit to the Théâtre Libre a useless suffering. Needless to say that the discussion relative to umbrellas, coats, and seats, is likely to reach its highest pitch exactly at the moment when it is indispensable that you should hear what is being said on the stage. In addition to all these disadvantages the accoustics of Le Théâtre des Menus Plaisirs are acknowledged to be lamentable, so you may conclude, and, indeed, you will conclude rightly, that I did not hear every single word of Ibsen's play. But M. Antoine will have a theatre of his own next year, and when we think what were the beginnings of Le Théâtre Libre—from what it sprung— we can but feel surprised that he has got in five years even so far as the Théâtre des Menus Plaisirs.

I was especially anxious to see the play of *Ghosts* acted, for I was anxious fully to test a certain conviction which, notwithstanding the many excellent arguments I have heard urged against it, I have never been able completely to abandon. Plays read to me exactly as they act—only better, and I find myself still unable to admit the possibility that a play that reads well should act badly ; when I say reads well, I mean reads well to him who follows each exit and entrance, seeing each part dovetail into the succeeding part, seeing all the parts in their relation to the entire play. No single passage or number of well - written passages would, I think, blind me to the inherent weakness of the play as a whole ; nor do I think that the representation would reveal an incongruity in character or situation that I had not already discovered, and the well-known fact that actors are so often absurdly, incomprehensibly wrong in their judgment of plays, I can only explain by supposing them to be deficient in those higher imaginative faculties which enable us to see through the mere print every gesture of the characters involved in the action of the story.

Céard, with whom I discussed the question, whether plays acted as they read, while waiting for *Ghosts* to begin, said that he did not think it would act as well as *Nora*. *Ghosts* had seemed to him vague and un- determined in the reading, but when the third act was over I heard his voice in the tumult of praise con- gratulating Antoine. He confessed that he had mis- judged the play ; the dimness and vagueness that he feared in the reading had in the representation been changed into firmest outline.

Antoine was wonderful in the part of Osvalt. The nervous irritation of the sick man was faultlessly rendered. When he tells his mother of the warnings of the French doctor, at the moment he loses his temper at her interruptions—she seeks not to hear the fearful tale — Antoine, identifying himself with the simple truth sought by Ibsen, by voice and gesture, casts upon the scene so terrible a light, so strange an air of truth, that the drama seemed to be passing not before our eyes, but deep down in our hearts in a way we had never felt before. "Listen to me, mother. I insist upon your listening to me," he says, querulous already with incipient disease. And when the end of the first acts comes, when the mother, hearing the servant-girl cry out, goes to the door, and seeing the son kissing the girl, cries, "Ghosts, ghosts!" what shall I say, what praise shall we bestow upon a situation so supremely awful, so shockingly true?

Owing to many new disputes, or violent continuations of former disputes, concerning cloaks and umbrellas, and seats which had been taken possession of during temporary absences or *strapontins* which should exist, but did not exist or could not be found, I heard even less of the second act than I had done of the first; the entire discourse of the workman with the wooden leg was lost to me. During the third act there was less wrangling, and I heard nearly all. And in that half-hour I lived through a year's emotion. It was terrible when Osvalt came in smoking, and, puffing at his pipe, and with an air of familiar contentment, he tells his mother how much he likes the maid-servant, and how he always wishes her to be near him. The maid-servant is there. He calls to her, and the distracted mother is forced to

reveal the secret — the maid - servant is his half-sister.
And the scene is simple in its dire and doleful humanity.
Even the servant - girl recognises that the fatal taint
inherited from their common father has descended on her.
She upbraids Mrs Avling (Osvalt's mother) for having
brought her up as a servant, and tossing her head, and
looking bitterly at the champagne, she says: "mais
cela ne m'empêchera pas de boire du champagne avec
les gens comme il faut." Mrs Avling asks her where
she is going, and she answers significantly that she
knows of a house where she will be welcome. *Mrs
Avling*: "Regina, you are going to your ruin."
Regina: "Oh, stuff!" (She goes out pushing violently
through the swing doors.) Then comes the awful, the
drastic, the overwhelming scene of the play, and most
assuredly nothing finer was ever written by man or
god. Its blank simplicity strikes upon the brain, until
the brain reels, even as poor Osvalt's brain is reeling.

In the last moments of his sanity, before darkness
comes upon him, he calls his mother to him, and mother
and son sit side by side talking. Talking of what?
Of the father whom he never knew, but who has nevertheless laid upon him the irreparable fate of idiocy,
idiocy that even at that moment is creeping upon him,
and will overtake him as night overtakes the day. The
mother calls upon him to cherish his father's memory,
and the boy answers not in tragic phrases, but in
words so simple and so true, that listening, the
heart turns to ice. And all the while they talk the
dreaded malady is creeping upon him. Night is closing,
and in the last moments of the twilight of the brain
Osvalt shows his mother the poison, and tells her that
he will not live helpless as a little child that must be
dressed and fed. It is true she will always look after
him. But she may die before him, he may fall into
the hands of strangers. The doctors have told him he

may live for years. The mother answers : " I, who gave you life ! " " A nice kind of life it was that you gave me, and now you shall have it back again." Startled by some incoherency in his speech, she calls in terror to him. The scream rescues him for a moment out of the night that is deepening in his brain, that is approaching blackness, and for a few moments more he speaks reasonably.

The sun has risen, the world is bright with the dawn. Mrs Avling draws the curtains, letting the sunlight into the room. But Osvalt still sits with his back to the light, now mumbling in toneless voice, " The sun, the sun." Mrs Avling stares at him in speechless terror, her hands twisted in her hair, and he still mumbles, " The sun, the sun."

The tragedy of fate Ibsen has taken out of the empyrean of Olympus and hexameters, substituting the empyrean of science, and in the simple language of a plain Norwegian household, we learn that though there be no gods to govern us, nature, vast and unknown, for ever dumb to our appeal, holds us in thrall.

Out of the story the characters evolve themselves sufficiently ; they are not forced into any sharp visibleness ; we are merely in the presence of a mother and son ; it is the idea that Ibsen seeks to express, and not special types from which the idea may be deduced ; the art of Ibsen is rather that of Sophocles than that of Balzac (the exact opposite to what is generally understood, but that, of course) ; the mother and son could not be defined more sharply without loss to the play. But what shall be said of the parson ? I do not think that any one could utter a word in praise, or even in mild defence, of this dreary old bore, who spoils so far as it is possible the first and second acts with such intolerable sermonising as would empty any nonconformist church. I make no exception either in favour of Mr Ibsen or Mr Archer; neither could find a reasonable word to say in defence of this parson. Considered as *the* parson, he is an effigy, wooden in Ibsen's most wooden manner; but what is wanted is not *the* parson, but *a* parson, hard and cold if you will, but with a vein of geniality in him, not much — too loud a note would jar the harmony of the picture. Ibsen was a clever man, and he knew that what was wanted was not an Abbé Constantin, "the practical dramatist" would have rushed an Abbé Constantin into the play, sure of finding in him "sympathetic relief"; the humanisation of the stern figure that the play demanded was not an easy task, but it was just such a one as the highest genius would have asserted itself in.

Mlle. Barny was excellent as the mother, and the other parts (there are only five characters in the play) were sufficiently well filled. Paris artistic and literary was in the stalls and boxes, and since the memorable night when Tolstoï's *Puissance des Ténèbres* was given, the Théâtre Libre has not won a triumph either so deep or so pronounced. An evening at the Théâtre Libre is now looked forward to with the keenest interest, and instead of there being too few subscribers, Antoine is obliged to refuse subscriptions until he can get a larger theatre. Why have we not a Théâtre Libre? Surely there should be no difficulty in finding a thousand persons interested in art and letters willing to subscribe five pounds a year for twelve representations of twelve interesting plays. I think such a number of enthusiasts exist in London. The innumerable articles which appear in the daily, the weekly, and monthly press on the London stage prove the existence of much vague discontent, and that this discontent will take definite shape sooner or later seems more than possible.

THEATRE LIBRE

AN idea, that is to say, a general law deduced from the observation and the comprehension of natural phenomena, is seldom, if ever, the exclusive honour of one discoverer; the idea is often declared simultaneously in several countries by several individuals having no acquaintance with each other, or knowledge of the direction in which their thoughts have been travelling. To offer illustrations of this would be vain; half-a-dozen must have already risen up in the mind of every reader. Still, so far as the actual publication of the idea is concerned, there must always be a first, and I think there can be no doubt that it would be easy for me to establish my claim to having been the first to introduce the discussion now waging in review and newspaper, regarding the present condition of the stage. My article, entitled "Our Dramatists," published in the *Fortnightly*, first drew attention; but I had expressed myself on the subject many years before, and the arguments of later writers are little more than the development of certain ideas vented by me. Even so far back as 1884, I wrote an article in another paper, since dead, in which I attributed the decline of dramatic writing to the three-hundred-night runs. I explained at some length of what a piece must consist that could draw crowded houses for such a space of time, how it forbade all experimentation, the risk being too great. Turning to history, I called attention to the fact that dramatic literatures arose when new plays were produced in rapid succession. In England, in 1600, plays ran for ten or twelve nights; in France, in 1830, plays ran for thirty or forty nights; but since long runs have obtained possession of the French stage the art of writing plays has steadily declined.

The article entitled "Our Dramatists" was too violently conceived and vehemently written to produce fruitful discussion; but when the sullen anger it occasioned had worn itself away, many were moved to consider for themselves the question I had thrown into the arena, and Mr Crawford's intelligent and suggestive article has resulted in the provocation of so much discussion that it would seem we are within measurable distance of realising our hope—the founding of a theatre which, by producing some thirty or forty new plays every year, will allow us to say what we have to say, and in the form which is natural and peculiar to us. Mr Beerbohm Tree and Mr Jones will tell us all they know about the artistic advantages and disadvantages of the actor-manager system in the next *Fortnightly*. Mr Tree will be, I know, all for Art and the Artist. I shall have no fault to find with any of his theories, only to regret that his practice does not more closely coincide with them. Mr Jones will—well, we shall see what he has to say. In the meantime it will be interesting whilst these two distinguished men continue to tempt and tantalise the public with ingenious conjecture and fanciful dream, to hear what has been done in France towards opening the theatrical ways, hitherto so strictly barred, to literature, and towards freeing the drama from the fetters of convention and prejudice. Since we have arrived within measurable distance of the time when an English Théâtre Libre will open its doors to a play written on the new lines, since it has been more than hinted that the man is now among us who will organise the new theatre, it will be surely well for his encouragement and instruction, and for the encouragement and instruction of those who may support him, to furnish some exact information concerning the period of adversity through which the Théâtre Libre has passed, and the splendid future into which it is now about to enter.

Before me lies a square book bound in red paper. It bears for sole inscription the words : Le Théâtre Libre. The copy on my table is probably the only one in England. Antoine has just issued the book for private circulation among his subscribers. The book is exceedingly explicit, and could not fail to interest any one concerned in the redemption of the drama. Here are the passages which especially attracted my attention.

"It is hardly three years since the first performance "was given in the Théâtre Libre.

"The founder of the Théâtre Libre had never acted "in public ; in the beginning of 1887 he was then an "employé in the gas company at a salary of about "£30 a year, one of a modest circle of amateurs who "occupied their leisure time in acting the ordinary "stock pieces. One day he advised his comrades to "produce the unacted plays of young and unknown "authors, so that they might hold out to the Press "an inducement to attend their performances.

"This advice was accepted, and the performance of "30th of March 1887 bore the simple inscription : ' Le "Théâtre Libre.' It took place in the *passage* de "l'Elysée des Beaux - Arts, and four one - act pieces "were played, one of which, *Jacques Damour*, was "immediately accepted by the management of the "Odéon.

" The expenses of this evening were defrayed by the
" subscriptions of friends, principally out of Antoine's
" monthly salary; he fixed the date for the 30th
" because it coincided (as did that of the second repre-
" sentation fixed for the 30th of the following May)
" with the payment of the employés of the gas
" company.

" After the evening of March 30th money was not
" forthcoming, and the second performance could not
" take place till the end of May. It comprised
" *La Nuit Bergamasque*, by Emile Bergerat, and *En*
" *Famille*, by Oscar Méténier.

" The second performance not only exhausted the
" funds of the newly-founded theatre, but it was impos-
" sible to appeal again to the generosity of the first
" subscribers, and a heavy debt, amounting to some
" £10 or £12, seemed to close all hope of any further
" performances.

" It was then that Antoine conceived the idea of
" having recourse to the world of fashion for annual
" subscriptions which would secure the continued exist-
" ence of his project. To succeed it was necessary that
" he should be able to offer an entire season's programmes,
" seven or eight performances. And so, that he might
" devote himself exclusively to his idea, Antoine resigned
" his place in the gas company at the end of July,
" without considering the possibility of failure, in the
" single hope of bringing his project to successful
" issue."

From the following letter an idea can be formed
of the difficulties, the obstacles, the deceptions and
heart-breaks that he met with. It would have discouraged most young men, and it was sent to him
by one of the highest and most influential journalists
of the time in answer to a letter begging for the
aid of the notoriety of his name.

Here are two or three passages :—

"You think that ten lines from me will extract from
"the cash-boxes the 8,000 francs you require.

"I will tell you first that the question of Le Théâtre
"Libre does not enter within my province. Vitu is
"at the *Figaro* to write on such subjects.

"I add *that the public is not very much interested
"in your laudable enterprise. Free theatre or no free
"theatre, what does it matter?* The public will remain
"deaf to your appeal, and will not subscribe a penny.

"The question is to find seventy or eighty people
"who will give a hundred francs each—managers, fashion-
"able writers, and perhaps a few journalists. If such
"a movement in favour of the Théâtre Libre should
"arise all will go well; *but I cannot and will not take
"any initiative.*—ALBERT WOLFF."

Nevertheless, in October 1887, the Théâtre Libre
commenced its first season with 3,500 francs subscribed,
from which it was necessary to deduct about 1,000 francs
of debts; for it had been found necessary to hire and
furnish the premises in the Rue Blanche so that regular
rehearsals might be assured for the works in preparation. The rehearsals of the first performance took place
in a public-house in the Rue Lepie, those of the second
in an unoccupied flat in the Rue Breda, lent by a
concierge who was a theatrical fanatic. To save the
postage, friends offered to deliver the invitations. The
performance was an immense success, — too successful, for the proprietor of the little theatre in the
Passage de l'Elysée des Beaux-Arts, fearing that so
great a crowd endangered his fixtures, the strength
of which seemed doubtful, gave Antoine notice to quit
on the following day. It became therefore necessary to
seek another theatre, and the penniless Antoine sought
admission in all the little outlying theatres. He was
driven even as far as Montparnasse. When the season

was over, Antoine, who had to collect eleven thousand francs, found himself face to face with a serious and troubling deficit, and a theatre in a more central situation became a matter of absolute necessity. But to tell the story of all the obstacles that Antoine met with would take too long; let us remember that the Théâtre Libre was in the end able to take up its quarters in the Théâtre des Menus Plaisirs, and that Antoine signed an agreement with the manager which assured his enterprise against all further eventualities.

The subscription for the second season realised 40,000 francs, and this has enabled Antoine to produce his plays with suitable scenery and to pay his actors and actresses. The theatre is packed from floor to ceiling at every performance. Every day Antoine receives numbers of subscriptions which he cannot accept. In 1889 he tried for the Vaudeville, the Porte St Martin and the Ambigu, but meeting with insurmountable obstacles he is obliged to take advantage of the clauses in his present agreement which allow him to remain some months longer in the Menus Plaisirs.

THE RESULTS ATTAINED

In the tentative performances of March and May, '87, eight new acts; in the season of '87-'88, thirty-seven; in the season '88-'89, forty; in the season of '89-'90, forty; total, 125 new acts in three years. Thirty authors whose plays had never been acted before, fourteen authors who had only been acted once before. On the programme of the Théâtre Libre will be found the following names: MM. Aubanel, Théodore de Banville, Emile Bergerat, Leon Cladel, Duranty, Edmond et Jules de Goncourt, Henrik Ibsen, Catulle Mendès, Comte Léon Tolstoi, Ivan Turgueneff, Verga, Emile Zola.

WHY THE THEATRE LIBRE HAS SUCCEEDED

First, the indifference of the public to plays that are always the same. The dramatic output is limited to a dozen or fifteen writers who go from theatre to theatre, monopolising the bill and serving up always the same mixture dissimulated by a change of label. Each one has his mark, all tolerably alike by the way, each rewrites the same play a little worse every time, for age intervenes, and the hand grows heavier. Managers, however, do not tire of offering to the public these fruits of decrepitude, but the public, disgusted, turn from them and pass on.

ANOTHER REASON, THE HIGH PRICE OF PLACES

By a constant upward tendency, the illogic of which is surprising, by a strange reversal of that social transformation in progress beneath our eyes, when "the cheapest market" has become within the last fifty years the universal law, when the price of newspapers has constantly diminished, when the means of transport have become easier and less expensive, when trade has ingeniously contrived to make and sell its productions for less and less money, when one can go from Bercy to Auteuil for three sous, and can cross France for a few louis, the theatres, setting themselves against an irresistible force, have raised their prices, and to this extent, that now a stall costs three times more than it did forty years ago, a private box is unprocurable, and unless you are very rich you are obliged to climb up to the second or third galleries, wedge yourself into a place where you are as badly seated as on the top of an omnibus, plus the heat and minus the pleasure of the street.

The result of such a state of things is that, unless by

virtue of a free pass,—that vice which avaricious and unwise managers have called into existence, which they have complacently developed, and to which they attribute their misfortunes,—unless by virtue of a free pass, the theatre which was in other times within the reach of all pockets, has become a luxury, has reduced its supporters, diminished its receipts as it raised its prices, and driven the great paying public to the music halls.

Another reason for the decline of the theatre is the disorganisation of theatrical companies. The first thing that the interpretation of a play demands, a quality so essential that it can dispense with all others, is *l'ensemble*, a condition without which a literary work is mutilated and disfigured *as a musical work would be if the musicians did not play in tune*. Managers have substituted a star system for the system of *l'ensemble*, and about a favourite actor or actress we find a number of "sticks," whose ignorance and stupidity serve to bring the star into prominence.

These are the principal evils which we must seek to abolish. The reforms that have become necessary are:—*New pieces, comfortable places, low prices, and an ensemble in the interpretation.*

ON THE NECESSITY OF AN ENGLISH THEATRE LIBRE

IT must be clear to all of us that there are plays which, although they would not draw large audiences for the space of a year, would prove highly interesting to the three or four thousand people who are more or less directly interested in literature and new artistic manifestations. It is these three or four thousand people who call for a Théâtre Libre, a small minority tired of conventional plays, good and bad, that is to say, of all the plays now being performed in the London theatres. It is, therefore, evident that if it is no part of the intention of the manager of the Théâtre Libre to produce the class of play which we see in the London theatres, it is still less his intention to produce the class of play which is heard at *matinées*. Then what kind of play do you wish to produce? Plays which a manager of a regular theatre will not produce, not because they are bad, but because he thinks there is no money in them. What kind of plays are these? Plays in which the characters, although true to nature, are known as "sympathetic characters," plays in which there are no comic love-scenes—plays that contain no comic relief—plays that deal with religious and moral problems in such ways as would not command the instantaneous and unanimous approval of a large audience drawn from all classes of society—plays in

which there is no love-interest, plays composed entirely
of male or entirely of female characters, etc. You see
the list is a long one, do not ask me to complete it,
try to think it out for yourself; by doing so you
will bring yourself into sympathy with and learn to
understand my project.   It was by producing such
plays that Antoine succeeded, and it is necessary to
understand, once and for all, that it is as imperative
for an English as for a French Théâtre Libre to refuse
good conventional plays as bad ones. It behoves the
founder of the new theatre to understand this clearly
and definitely, beyond subterfuge, equivocation, or
evasion, nor can he even take the first step towards
the realisation of our project until he has mastered
this elementary truth.

Society will not subscribe for the performance of
plays, the representation of which must of necessity
be inferior to that of the plays performed in the regular
theatres, unless the plays are different from any plays to
be witnessed elsewhere. To get the *fine fleur* of society,
literature and art, the Théâtre Libre must offer a
supremacy of sensation — the strange, the unknown
the unexpected. The plays need not be great plays
—great plays are out of question—they need only
be plays with something in them ; even though that
something is not always deeper than the charm which
we find in a piece of *bric-à-brac,* or a piece of old
china. "You want to set up a dramatic curiosity shop,"
cries a cynical reader. An epigram is not an argument,
and I repeat, that to justify its existence as much here
as in Paris, a Théâtre Libre would have to devote
itself exclusively to the representation of unconventional plays. What proportion the *bizarre* would
take in our programme it would be useless to conjecture, but it is certain that the most absolute
eclecticism should prevail, and that no preference be

M

given to one form of art more than to another. That the play should be *rare* is the first and almost the only qualification necessary to secure for it right of representation.

But are *rare* plays written in England? Ah, now we come to the point on which the question turns. . . . The money question presents no difficulties. A hundred to a hundred and fifty subscribers at five pounds would be easy to obtain. For seven hundred and fifty pounds it would be possible to give ten performances—a year's programme; for of course during August and September no performances would be possible. About finding the money I really do not think there would be any difficulty, if a full year's programme, and perhaps something over, were forthcoming. In half an hour I could myself find twenty subscribers, and while writing this very line ten more names have come into my mind. But to find even five subscribers it will be necessary to show a year's programme, ten, twelve, fifteen, twenty unconventional plays. I confess that the prospect frightens me not a little.

Mr Tree says that he reads (perhaps, for after all life is short, it would be more correct to say informs himself concerning) all plays that are sent to him, and that he never meets anything except ineffectual attempts to write conventional plays. It may be doubted whether Mr Tree would dare to produce an unconventional play if he had one, but I am sure he is capable of recognising and admiring original work when he sees it, and when he says he never receives it, I am sure he does not. Nor is corroborative evidence wanting. Mr Archer tells me that out of the many plays that have been sent to him only two proved to be even passable attempts to write good conventional plays. And Mr Archer has seen all the plays that have been produced in London for the last ten years, and as he puts it: "I have never met with any play at "a *matinée* that aimed at anything higher than an "attempt to write a conventional play, never did I meet "among these any of those curious literary experiments "in dramatic writings which Antoine produces in the "Théâtre Libre. Now as we know that *matinées* are "almost invariably paid for by the author, we have to "fall back on either of two alternatives: That no one "attempts to write unconventional plays in England, or "that those who do have no money to produce them. "The unconventional plays cannot always be written by "those who have not and cannot obtain money." After leaving Mr Archer I consulted another friend. He said: "I have read an immense number of plays for "Wilson Barrett; I have met two or three that I asked "him to read, but not because I thought them either "interesting or novel, but because I thought with a bit of "pulling together they might do to make money with. "*I never met a play that was literary either in conception "or in language.*"

Does it follow then that it would be useless to found a Théâtre Libre in London? I think not. True it is that my optimism does not carry me into the belief that the creation of the demand would instantly pro-duce a new dramatic æstheticism and a crop ripening at hand—the three acts, the five acts, and the one acts calling to us to gather them; nor do I propose to set translators to work on Antoine's published stock. We want an English Théâtre Libre, not a translated Théâtre Libre. But Antoine himself has not relied entirely on France for plays, he has turned to Norway and to Russia; and if we can find a dozen or fifteen plays, half of which are English, we might make a start. I propose that we neither demand nor seek anything further than one year's programme, that is to say, sufficient dramatic matter for ten performances.

If we succeed in this there will be cause for congratulation.

First let us consider what we have got, and then whither we may go to get more. We have got, and it is certain that we had better begin with, *The Dominion of Darkness*, by Tolstoi. We have got *Ghosts* by Ibsen, and I suggest that *La Mort du Duc d'Enghien*, and *Jacques Damour*, by Léon Hennique, likewise *En Famille*, by Oscar Méténier be translated;—for the moment I cannot say what other plays I would choose from Antoine's *répertoire*, nor does it matter. There are plenty that are admirable. It is not until we come to the English plays that we experience any difficulty. Frank Danby has spoken to me of an adaptation of *A Babe in Bohemia*, and with the scenes in the Salvation Army this would be of the very highest interest; indeed, it would be exactly the kind of play that we want. Of all Michael Field's works what I most admire is *William Rufus*. It is many years since I read it, but I cannot think without a thrill of those splendid forest scenes. I see the endless colonnades touched with the setting light. I hear miles and miles of silence broken at last by the sound of a distant chase, and then comes the startled deer and then the swish of the arrow. I cannot say now whether it would be possible to act this play, but it would surely not be impossible to induce the talented authoress to rearrange her work so as to bring it within the scope of the unconventional stage. It is so long since I have read *Chastelard*, that it is impossible for me to say if I think it could or could not be acted. Shelley's *Cenci* has been tried; and little would be gained by trying it again.

The young man who undertakes to carry the scheme through will have to go to Mr George Meredith, and ask him if he has a play, and if he has not, Mr Meredith might be induced to dramatise a very beautiful story that he published some years ago in the *New Quarterly Magazine*. Mr Hardy should be applied to, and he might consent to write, not a play that could be played by Mr and Mrs Kendal, but unconventional scenes of the sordid avarice and crime that lurks among sheepfolds and hayfields as well as a city's slums and by-ways. Mr Stevenson and Mr Henley have written some plays in collaboration; I have heard of one,—I think it is called *Beau Austin*. The title is attractive. I have not read the play, and it may be no more than an ineffectual attempt to write a Haymarket piece. But we want neither effective nor ineffective Haymarket plays. The question is whether Mr Henley will write an unconventional play, whether he can write an unconventional play; for strange as it may seem, it is nevertheless true that the moment we sit down to write dialogue we become changed beings, and the most original are at once possessed by comic relief, and happy endings. But if Mr Henley could write as unconventionally in dialogue as he can in verse! Ah, if he would give us something like his hospital poems; if he would take Mr Stevenson's *A Night with Villon* and turn it into a one-act play in three scenes. First scene in the thieves' kitchen, the murder, etc., exactly as in the story; second scene, a front scene, Villon in the street finding the two coins exactly as in the story; third scene in the old baron's chambers, with that marvellous dialogue between the baron and the poet; and the play ending exactly as the story ends on the departure of Villon. These are the plays that we want for the Théâtre Libre. Were I the founder of the Théâtre Libre, I would apply to all the novelists: gold is found in the most unexpected places. I would apply also to some two or three dramatists. For instance, I would go to Mr Pinero and to Mr Grundy. I would ask them if they had anything to say on the moral and ethical problems of the day. I would say to Mr Grundy : "You have, I know, odd views on the religious and ethical questions of our day ; will you forget Le Théâtre de Monsieur Scribe and give us your views in dramatic form?" I would press Mr Jones to say that he is haunted with an idea which he cannot use on the regular stage.

You must see now, I think, that the possibility of getting seven or eight unconventional English plays does not seem so hopeless as it did at the end of the paragraph in which I related my conversation with Mr Archer. Mr Archer is a little gloomy, a little disposed to throw cold water, but let the scheme be once put into shape and I am sure he will be one of the most enthusiastic supporters of the new theatre. There are a hundred other questions to be gone into, but I have said enough to bring the project to a head if it be really in the air.

The composition of the programme for the first year is the first thing to do. When we have arranged a satisfactory programme we shall be able to ask for subscriptions. I avoid discussion anent actors and actors ; this is a delicate question but not one I think that presents any special difficulties. The first thing to do is to get the plays. Regarding the theatre, the present time is most propitious. The Novelty has been unoccupied for months, I might say for years ; it would suit us as well as any theatre in London, and no doubt the proprietors would be delighted to let us have the theatre ; for if our ten performances proved fairly successful, we should double the value of their property.

Our hundred and fifty or two hundred subscribers would include all that is rare among the intelligence and fashion of London, and our monthly performance would be celebrated in the press even as the annual exhibitions at Burlington House or the State Balls at Buckingham Palace.

MEISSONIER AND THE SALON JULIAN

IN 1868 M. Julian founded an academy of painting in the Passage des Panoramas, in the very rooms in which the illustrious Markouski had taught two generations how to dance. A few biographical and personal details will be of interest concerning a man who, in the opinion of many competent judges, has done much to popularise and improve French art; who, in the opinion of an equal number of competent judges, has done much to degrade and destroy it ; who to-day is the most notorious and powerful personage in the Paris art world, whose studies are in every quarter of the town, almost as numerous as *brasseries*, whose pupils, in the past and present, are numbered by thousands, fear and hatred of whom have occasioned irreparable schism in La Société des Artistes Français, dividing it in twain, one half remaining at the Salon under the presidency of M. Bouguereau, the other half following M. Meissonier to the Champ de Mars, there to found another society, La Société Nationale des Beaux-Arts.

M. Julian was once a shepherd in the south of France. In his native village he established a reputation for extraordinary strength and artistic capacity. He had thrown every young man within twenty miles in the wrestling contests, and he had astonished every one by the skill he showed in drawing. For a time his fate hung in the balance. A great wrestler or a great painter, which was he to be? The village decided that he was

to be a painter and sent him to Paris. The young
provincial walked about and wondered, read Balzac,
dreamed, studied at the Beaux-Arts. But his artistic
talents were slight, and a certain *succès de scandale*
gained in *Le Salon des Refusés* for a picture depicting
the last scene in *Rolla* did not help him in the least
towards selling his work. It is curious to note that in the
same salon, *Les Salon des Refusés*, Manet and Whistler
laid the foundation-stones of their future reputations.
But the public could not then distinguish between the
Rolla, by Julian, the *Le Déjeuner sur l'Herbe*, by Manet,
and the *Femme en Blanc*, by Whistler. All three pictures
provoked an equal amount of sarcasm in the press, and
an equal amount of laughter among the sightseers.
Two of the three painters had genius, and were able to
continue their art and conquer the public; the third,
a subtle, crafty southerner, whose peasant blood had
been but warmed in the sacred fire, found himself forced
to seek a livelihood in artistic commercialism. His
student days were over, he could expect nothing more
either from his village or his parents, the time had come
when he must support himself. But how? At some
time all who have sought a livelihood in art have been
asked this question; and never, I believe, was it put
more pitilessly than to Julian. Too proud to return
home, confess failure, and take up his crook, Julian said
No—the word reverberating in his brain as he questioned
his garret walls, for his eyes fell only upon the coarse
and crude art from which, notwithstanding his very real
intelligence, he could not escape. He examined it
in despair; and the iron of a despairing conviction
forced him to admit that the struggle was hopeless.
We may only work in conjunction with nature; none
may war against her successfully; and the wise man
is he who judges if nature's opposition to his desire
is real or only apparent; if it is real he abandons

the battle. But Julian possessed just sufficient talent
to obscure the truth, even to the point of rendering any
certain reading of it an impossibility. There is the *Rolla*,
truly not a bad piece of painting. The naked flanks
and back are full of colour, the drawing is hard and
coarse, but, *ma foi, c'est assez crâne.*

Is not an insufficient talent the most cruel of all
temptations? Julian could not surrender his cherished
hope, and yet he could not improve upon his *Rolla.*
Worse still, the creative faculty withered in poverty
and privation ; he did not exhibit again for two
years, he was forgotten, it became harder than ever
to obtain a meal, and his thoughts turned swiftly,
surveying every horizon. Julian used to tell us stories
of those days, making us feel how implacable nature had
told, not the whole truth at once, but bit by bit in her
own cruel fashion, and how she urged him at the same
time to seek by other means the sweets of life for which
his southern nature craved. He told us how suddenly,
through some dreams of the old days, of the luminous
south, of the great wrestling contests, the thought
struck him that Paris knew nothing of these sports, and
that to grasp a fortune securely, he had only to bring
the champions Cœur de Lion, Œil de Bœuf, Bras de
Fer, to Paris, and show the Parisians the splendid
Lutte Romaine. Hardly was the thought conceived
than it was put into execution. A capitalist was found,
and a light wooden circus was run up on a piece of
waste ground somewhere between the Rue Lafitte and
the Rue Chateaudun. Julian departed for and returned
from the south with five-and-twenty of the most famous
wrestlers, and to stimulate public curiosity still further,
one was announced to be unconquerable — *L'homme
masqué.* Soon all Paris was tremulous with curiosity to
know who was the mysterious person in black hose and
black mask, who came at the end of every performance

and overthrew the victor in the preceding contests. The movement and press of bodies strain forward, even to the great danger of the precarious building! Now the unknown man, his mask securely chained about his head, has appeared. See, he throws down his white glove to any who may choose to accept his challenge. In the abandonment of the moment Sculpture awakes from her sleep of ages, and the circus seems like the frieze of an antique temple.

A member of the Jockey Club paid Cœur de Lion a thousand francs to tear off the mask, but the heralds were able to intervene in time; spies were stationed at all the exits, *l'homme masqué* was followed by the swiftest horses, pursued far into the country, and when his carriage was overtaken it was found to be empty. It was said at the time that Julian himself was *l'homme masqué*, and to prove that this was not true he showed himself among the spectators while *l'homme masqué* was in the arena.

At the end of the season Julian found that he had cleared over a hundred thousand francs. It would have been well if he had then sent the wrestlers home and sold the circus for firewood, for the novelty of the entertainment had worn off, and the heat in the following year was tropical. Julian lost all the money he had made, and once again he had to turn to painting as a means of livelihood. He bethought himself of pupils, and becoming a tenant of the whilom halls of the illustrious Markouski, waited in the company of a model as patiently as he might. Julian was then a stout man of about thirty. The legs short and slightly bowed, the trunk that of a Hercules, an enormous width of shoulders, short, heavy arms. A dark beard covered the lower part of the face; large brown eyes interested you, likewise a voice soft and flexible; add to this the charm of much visible strength, and the

gracious, winning manner of the sensual south.
Although without capital and friends who could assist
him, nature had, as the following anecdote will show,
intended him to succeed in this new enterprise. Day
after day passed ; Julian trembled at every noise on the
staircase . . . a pupil? One had come, that is to say,
one was hesitating on the threshold. The model
yawned over her knitting, the easels were set out in line-
like squadrons as if on a review day, the chairs were
empty. It was a solitude comparable to that of the
auditorium of the Odéon on a night when a tragedy
is being played. Julian saw that the pupil was hesitating, that he was frightened by the mournful silence,
and was seeking escape. Poor pupil ! full of faith in
the old legend he had expected the noise and gaiety of
youth. Julian called him back gently, and in a voice
tremulous with emotion said, "You are going, sir ;
what is there that you do not approve of? Tell me
what you wish to have changed and it shall be changed
immediately." "Oh, nothing, but . . . " "If you do
not like the model she shall be changed." "Oh no, on
the contrary, I like the model very much." "Then
I think I can guess your reason ; because you don't see
any one here ; but you will be able to work better
without neighbours ; besides I did not engage to provide
you with neighbours." "No, no, that is quite true."
"Well, then, remain."

Do we not see clearly that such qualities of tact
and *bonhomie* would stand Julian in good stead, and win
for him many subsequent victories? Three or four
pupils, then a dozen. After the war, when work was
resumed, the studio numbered about twenty. It was
then, about the year 1872, that Julian succeeded in
persuading Jules Lefebvre and Boulanger to pass round
the room amongst the easels, giving words of advice on
alternate weeks. But notwithstanding this advance in

artistic tuition, the studio had not yet lost its character
of a little family gathering; nearly all who worked
there were Julian's intimate acquaintances, if they were
not his friends, and he used to go with us to Meudon
and Bas Meudon, and after a long day spent in painting
some picturesque old staircase, full of sunlight, or a quiet
waterway lost in the shadows of an island, we would
dine together in some humble river-side *auberge*, and
then not unfrequently, as we sat smoking in the porch,
the hot evening would awake in Julian some memory of
his beloved South, and he would tell of his first years
in Paris, when, a lone boy, with only Balzac for a friend,
he would pass along the cemeteries, stopping to peer
through the railings, trembling lest he might meet the
ghost of Rastignac or La Palfarine; or he would tell the
story of *l'homme masqué*, and then his descriptions
taking fire in our hearts, we demanded instructions
in attack and counter-attack, and soon the moon-
light was filled with straining and prostrate forms.
But as the studio filled with new faces Julian found
it necessary to withdraw from companionship with
us, and his last confidence to us I remember was
when the Government had closed the schools in
the Beaux-Arts for some cruelty or barbarism more
than usual perpetrated by a jocular student. Then
Julian said to a friend with whom he was walking
in the Salon: "One day all this will belong to me."
On being questioned as to his meaning, he answered:
"Now that they have closed the Beaux-Arts, all the
great painters that the next ten years may produce
will come from my studio." It is hardly to be thought
that Julian entertained at the time even a remote
suspicion that he was speaking but the plain and
literal truth. The closing of the Beaux-Arts could
not but prove to his advantage, and he interpreted
the chance that had come to him as any other Gascon

would have done. Do not all who come from the
south, in Zola's books, speak of *La Conquête de Paris*?
A few weeks after Julian appeared at the studio with
a medal in his hand.

To succeed in England you must offer a new reading
of the Book of Genesis; to succeed in France you
must offer medals.   There are as many societies for
the distribution of medals in France as there are
associations in England for the propagation of dissent.
We laugh at our religious crazes, our friends across the
Channel laugh at their medals, but neither our national
characteristics nor theirs are affected thereby.   We
distribute tracts, the French distribute medals.   Hair-
dressers and tailors have academies which award medals.
The societies of mutual help, gymnastic and shooting
societies, choral and philharmonic societies have medals,
palms, and crowns.   The members of the various
societies for the preservation of human life are covered
with medals; these medals are purchased; the Belgian
diplomas cost from eight to ten francs, and on St
Nicholas-day every one walks about proudly, his breast
covered with medals and multicoloured ribbons; yet
not one out of every ten ever saved a fly fallen into
a milk-jug from drowning.   Pork butchers, bakers,
the makers and the sellers of insect powder, rag-
pickers, and itinerant musicians, all have medals.
Without this explanation of a Frenchman's love of
medals it would not be possible for the English reader
to realise the genuine emotion produced in the studio,
when Julian appeared at the door of his private room
leading into the studio, holding a medal in his hand.
He said, "Everywhere in France there are medals!
why should there not be medals in my studio?   I
have therefore decided to offer a medal each month
for the best drawing or painting.   Those who wish
to compete will send in their drawings and paintings

on the last Saturday of the month, and on the following Monday M. Lefebvre will award the medal. And knowing well the necessities and temptations of a student's life, and foreseeing that the winner of a gold medal might find himself forced to dispose of it, and as he would get nothing like the original value for it, I have decided to give a hundred francs and a bronze medal. The first competition for this medal begins to-day."

Julian's appeal to the instincts of his countrymen met with immediate response. Before three months had passed every square foot of parquet was occupied by an easel, and Julian had to seek for new premises; the fame of his medals soon reached England and America; every mail brought him new students. Events, too, were running in his favour. Wearied by the constant protestations of the artists against its administration of the Salon, the Government, in 1881, surrendered its right to nominate the jury, giving up the Palais de l'Industrie to the artists, with full power to manage their own affairs. Art was at last in the hands of the artists, art was free at last, no more oppression, no more injustice, no more lagging behind in the mire of old æstheticisms. This time there were to be no mistakes. The exhibiters should elect their own jury. It is difficult to imagine anything more frankly democratic. But in art the democratic is always reactionary. In 1830, the democrats were against Victor Hugo and Delacroix. When the *Pall Mall Gazette* started a plebiscite to determine which was the worst picture in the Academy, the intelligent "middles" selected a very fine portrait by Mr John Sargent; and when the three thousand exhibiters elected their own jury, their selection proved to be no more than a consecration of the art of M. Bouguereau. When we learn who are the three

thousand exhibiters, no one will wonder. All people
who have once in their lives exhibited a drawing
have a right to vote. Among the three thousand are
found waiters in cafés, hackney - coachmen, lawyers'
clerks. An elderly spinster copies a drawing, it is
accepted by accident, and she obtains a vote. Sketches
are done by an artist and sent in the name of one
of his models, so that he may have many votes for
those who, he thinks, will look after his interests. The
Salon had not enjoyed democracy more than three
years when it came to be noticed that the best places
were occupied by pictures painted by *les élèves de
Julian*, and that a large proportion of the medals were
distributed among them. Julian had turned his business
into a company, of which he was managing director,
at forty thousand francs a year ; M. Bouguereau received
ten thousand francs a year for his professorial services,
and it is said that more than one of the professors
has money invested in the studio. Branch-establish-
ments had sprung up in every quarter of the town,
eighteen in all, some of the larger ones numbering two
hundred pupils. A large proportion of these students
could do a piece of painting that would pass muster ;
those who could not, had drawings done for them, and
so it came to pass that *les élèves de Julian* elected a
jury devoted to their interests, and headed by their
own professors. In return for the honour paid them,
the professors gave the best places to their pupils and
covered them with medals. The more medals the more
pupils, and so the studio waxed prosperous.

Julian had conquered. He was omnipotent in the
Salon. But a turning-point comes in the affairs of all
men, and the Universal Exhibition was to Julian what
Leipzig was to Napoleon. The Universal Exhibition
being Government business, the election of the jury

became the duty of one of the Ministers. It was undertaken by M. Proust, whose knowledge of art and advanced æstheticism are well known, and he elected a jury more representative of France than of Julian's studios; and this jury, being unconcerned with any but national interests, awarded some four hundred and odd recompenses, including medals, *exempts, hors concours*, and *mentions honorables*, to foreign artists. These *exempts* and *hors concours*, unless they meant free admission into exhibitions at the Salon, would mean nothing whatever, unless they were considered as so many practical jokes played upon foreign exhibiters. But MM. Bouguereau, Lefebvre, Tony Robert Fleury, Benjamin Constant, and the many other professors of painting and sculpture in Julian's studio, thought that it was far more important that *les élèves de Julian* should have good places in the Salon than that the foreign exhibiters should not be publicly insulted, and it was voted, at a meeting of Le Comité de la Société Française, that neither medal, nor the *exempts*, nor the *hors concours* awarded by M. Meissonier's jury at the Universal Exhibition should have effect in the Salon. Very naturally M. Meissonier, and those who had sat with him on the jury of the Universal Exhibition, protested very bitterly, denying the right of the committee to pass any such resolution. It therefore became necessary to call a general meeting of La Société des Artists Français; in other words, of the three thousand exhibiters whose claim to artistic suffrage I have already alluded to. They assembled in their thousands — café waiters, hackney-coachmen, professional models, etc. Needless to say that a "whip" marked urgent had been sent round the studios, and at the head of many hundreds Julian arrived in person at the Salle Jean on one of the last days of December. This big man with bowed legs and colossal shoulders, this shepherd from the South, this ancient wrestler, a sort of modern Tamerlane, directed the applause and urged his men to the ballot-boxes without further parley. It was the fight of a studio for its life — one of those dramatic scenes of contemporary life with which Zola has irrevocably associated his genius.

The mutterings of an approaching storm were heard along the extremities of the vast hall, and the annual reports of work done were listened to with indifference. It was not until M. Tony Robert Fleury spoke of the Universal Exhibition that he succeeded in obtaining public attention. Then you might have heard the proverbial pin drop. He wound up his speech with a solemn appeal for the maintenance of peace and mutual agreement. "Do not forget the value and "power of the association; think of the way we have "trodden together now for several years; think of the "difficulties we have surmounted together. Think "calmly of the best means of arriving at some agree-"ment, and let us, my dear colleagues, unite in one body, "so that we may defend this society which, in a burst "of enthusiasm, we founded to guard our interests, "our dignity, and our liberties." This peroration was received with unanimous applause. Then M. Bouguereau, in the name of the Committee, submitted to the assembly Clause 7 in the orders of the day.

Here is the clause :—

"The Committee ask the General Assembly to decide "by a *yes* or a *no* whether the awards given at the "Universal Exhibition will prevail in our Annual "Exhibitions, that is to say, will they carry with them "the right of *hors concours* and *exempts*?"

In turn, and sometimes together, M. Bouguereau, M. Tony Robert Fleury, and the many other professors and shareholders in Julian's studio, urged the meeting

N

to vote that the awards given at the Universal Exhibition should carry with them no right in the annual exhibition at the Salon. Their argument was :—

"During the nine years—this year 1890 is the tenth "—that the artists have managed the Salon, there have "been distributed each year about 85 medals: paint-"ings, 40; sculpture, 21; architecture, 12; engraving, "12; and this brings the sum-total of *hors concours* and "*exempts* to 1,586; if there be added to this sum the "493 given to foreign artists in the Universal Exhibition, "we obtain a total of 2,079 *exempts* and *hors concours*.

"As each of these has a right to send two works "to the Salon, if they use their rights, we obtain a "total of 4,158 works that are passed without examina-"tion by the jury.

"In 1876, there were 2,095 paintings exhibited; in "1881, 2,248; and in 1888, 3,586; this gives an average "of 2,310 works exhibited yearly in the Salon; there "would therefore be 1,848 *exempts* and *hors concours* for "which places could not be found. We should aim at "the opposite result; for, in the opinion of the com-"mittee, 1,500 places are necessary for the young "artists."

To this Meissonier replied :—

"My dear Colleagues, I must tell you that the high "distinction which has been accorded to me is a decora-"tion which is shared by you all; it is a manifestation "which places the arts on a level with the most beautiful "things.

"I must explain to you that the new awards cannot "cause any prejudice to the members *non-exempts* of the "Société des Artistes Français; the *exempts*, who, it is "true, have the right, will not all send two works. To "prove this, it is only necessary to read the figures of "the last three years. In 1887 there were 875 *exempts*; "they only sent 621 canvases and 21 drawings; in 1889

"there were 929; they only sent 562 canvases and 89
"drawings. You see that the new *exempts* are less
"terrifying than you were led to believe; and in
"architecture and sculpture, without fear of falling
"wide of the mark, we may base our calculation on
"these figures.

"A great deal too much has been made of the 493
"foreigners, and it has been used as a means to frighten
"you. But an equal number cannot be found again
"for the next ten years. It would require a universal
"exhibition. Foreigners will not find every year govern-
"ments and syndicates to pay for the transport of their
"works."

M. Meissonier could not continue; his speech was
interrupted by the Julian cohorts massed in front,
and by cries of "Tais ta gueule" on his right. Turning
to them, he said: "Mes chers confrères, car je veux
bien vous encore appeler ainsi;" but with still more
horrible cries he was howled down, and in the unearthly
din Julian was seen urging his legionaries to the ballot-
boxes. A few of the committee declared that they
would resign. Fearing, however, that they might re-
consider their determination, Roll asked them to sign
their names; and there were but nine, including
Meissonier, Puvis de Chavannes, Carolus Duran, Duez,
Dagnan - Bouveret, Gervex, Roll, Walter. A few
minutes after, Meissonier reascended the platform:
and having read out the names of the dissident
members of the committee, and stated again the reason
of their resignations, he said:—

"But before I leave you, my dear colleagues, let
"me tell you it is deplorable that artists should band
"together as you are doing; that men of heart and
"honour, Frenchmen before all, cannot rise to a region
"sufficiently high to understand that above the interests
"of particular groups and societies there is a sentiment

"of patriotism which, after the triumph of the Universal
"Exhibition, ought to overrule all, and that France by
"no faction of her children should seek to diminish the
"value of the awards that foreigners received thankfully
"at our hands with public acknowledgment."

This protest, delivered, it appears, with all the fire
and energy of Gambetta in his best moments, was
received with some slight applause in the midst of an
extraordinary tumult which Tony Robert Fleury and
Garnier strove vainly to calm. Then again did Julian
excite his legionaries onwards to the ballot-boxes.
But without waiting for the poll to be taken Meissonier
left, declaring "that from no point of view could he
"admit a vote upon a question in which our national
"honour was compromised."

He retired with his followers to Ledoyen. There
happened at that moment to be a man distributing
the prospectuses of some obscure studio. "Never mind
your prospectuses," said Roll, "here are four francs,
and keep shouting for the next hour that M. Meissonier
has retired to Ledoyen to arrange the constitution of
a new society." Roll spoke at random, but the words
were happily chosen, and, half-an-hour after, some
fifty or sixty eminent painters had severed their connection with the old society and given their adhesion
to the new and yet unborn society. This number of
painters included some twenty-five members of the
committee of the Société des Artistes Français, and
it was resolved that these should go, with Meissonier
at their head, and explain how they had come to
resign their connection with the old society of fine
arts, and their plan for the founding a new and truly
national one, which would be able to offer that
hospitality to the foreign artists which the Salon had
refused. M. Meissonier spoke as brilliantly as before,
but his eloquence could not prevent the question:

How many are you? twenty-five out of how many?
eighty-five? M. Tirard, who had till then been listening with singular satisfaction to all that Meissonier
had to say in defence of the national honour, could
not but feel himself obliged to advise the twenty-five
dissidents to return and arrange their differences as
best they could. He was, it appears, on the point of
dismissing the delegation, when one of those comic
incidents occurred which so often turn the scale. Some
one, it never was discovered who, cried out, at the
last moment:—" Mais toute la province est avec nous."
" Then," cried M. Tirard, rising as if he were impelled
by the sudden loosing of a spring, " if the provinces
are with you, I am with you too. I will speak, and
you are at liberty to make my words public." He
told them that they had his entire sympathy; he
authorised them to make known the step they had
taken. The same delegation proceeded immediately
to M. Fallières to explain to him the reasons that
brought about the dissidence. M. Fallières answered
that the society in progress of formation had all his
sympathy: and he shortly after placed at its disposal
the galleries of the Exhibition in the Champ de Mars.

Every day fresh artists withdrew from the old and
went over to the new society; the secession increased,
and the Société des Artistes Français, seriously alarmed,
called another meeting, where a resolution, proposed by
M. Garnier, to do away with all exempts, was unani-
mously adopted. This being done, MM. Guillaume,
Garnier, and Bonnat called on Meissonier to name a
commission that might suggest a way out of the
difficulty. But Meissonier refused categorically to
enter into discussion with the old society. " The new
society," he said, " has been founded; its statutes have
been approved of; it is too late for compromise." This
phrase afforded Meissonier's followers much gratification;

it shows the amount of animus that existed, and it is probable that, if all their demands had been granted, they would not have returned to the Salon under the headship of M. Bouguereau. Until then the plea of patriotism had alone been put forward as the motive of the secession, but under the elegant phrases about the honour of France and justice to the foreigners who had contributed so largely to the success of the glorious exhibition, there lay a second motive, as important in determining the action of the dissidents as the first. The first was flown in the face of the world, a pennon; the second was sunk deep in the heart, an anchor. And a good stout anchor too, did hatred of Julian's studio prove in the swift-running tide of secession. Deep fixed it lay, unmoved, keeping the vessel's head well off shore, and never alluded to in public speech until all shoals and sandbanks were cleared. "The plan of Julian's studio," said Meissonier, "since it has become necessary to name it, was prepared long ago, and executed in every detail. Even those who proposed the adjournment of the meeting, ran to the ballot-boxes, Julian himself exciting the waverers."

And it is in fact Julian's studio that endows the secession of the French Artists in the Salon with a deep and grave significance, that raises it from the triviality of a petty dispute and makes of it a matter of national, perhaps I should say international, importance. Very little does it matter to us whether M. Bouguereau and M. Meissonier hold different exhibitions in the Champs Elysées and the Champ de Mars, or abjure their differences, and in perfect communion open one exhibition to the artists of the whole world; but what does concern us, and very deeply indeed, is that we should preserve unsullied our own beautiful English art traditions—I mean the eighteenth-century traditions bequeathed to us by Gainsborough and Reynolds, and

worthily continued even unto the present generation by
Millais and Orchardson.

Twenty years ago the mischief began. It began
then to be generally regarded as a truth that it was
necessary to go to Paris to learn painting. Twenty
years ago we began to tire of the *naïveté*, the quaint-
ness, the simplicity of our English drawing, because
it did not measure so correctly with the model as
that done in the Beaux-Arts; and we became infected,
about the time I speak of, with a desire of construction,
that is, the mapping out of the figure into so many
dioramic shapes, some to be filled with light, some with
shadow. We began then dimly to understand that the
figure should be " built up," that to draw by the character,
as we had hitherto been content to do, was but the
infancy of art, whereas to draw by the " masses " was
its manhood and apotheosis. So we went to France
to learn to draw by the " masses," and there we
heard of " solid painting," and we were told that all
other painting was primitive and barbarous. The
special temperament of the artist, we learnt, was nothing
to the point; there was *la bonne peinture, la peinture au
premier coup*, which was produced in such and such a
way, and if we could not learn the trick, it was clear
that nature had not intended us to be artists. And
we were introduced to the nude model, propped up
on boxes, or standing in a conventional pose, hand on
hip. We were told to count the number of heads, and
to mark them off on our paper; then with the plumb-
line we were shown how to determine the sway of the
figure. It drops through the ear, the right breast, the
hip-bone, passing, let us say, through the heel. The
leading measurements and general lines being thus
obtained, note was taken how much of the body fell
to the left and right of our plumb-line, and we were
instructed to sketch in, drawing by the masses of light

and shade. This was the way, and the only way, to
learn to draw, we were assured; we needed not to
think of anything but the studio model; the world in
the fields and the streets, that living world full of
passionate colour and joyous movement, was but an
illusive temptation; the studio model was the truth,
the truth in essence; if we could draw the nude, we
could draw anything. For the success of the studio
it was necessary that this should be accepted as an
article of faith. In the highest sense to draw the
nude is well-nigh impossible; in another sense, it is
almost as easy to draw from the nude as from the
flat. I have seen hundreds draw the posed studio
model fairly well, but to catch the movement of a
man's hands, say, as he lights a match, is quite another
thing. To do that at all satisfactorily demands great
skill and knowledge, and no one can learn of another
to do it well.

But it will be argued that those who are geniuses
of the first rank will separate themselves from Julian's.
This is not so certain as some of us think, but I will let
the point pass; I am concerned rather with the preservation of the character of our art as a whole than with the
genius of the favoured few, and I will ask those who think
this of no consequence to look at some ordinary English
work done fifty years ago and compare it with the best
work done at Julian's. The English work is simple and
racy of the soil, full of an engaging ignorance, "au moins
les figures ne sont pas bien construites." The French
work is cosmopolitan and pedantic. A drawing by
Westall, for instance, would not measure very correctly
with the model, but Westall's drawing is homely and
English, and we love it for its old-fashioned air, for the
sentiment of the time that it reflects so naïvely; and
in the decoration of a room it takes a hybrid place,
existing somewhere between an artistic *bibelot* and a

work of art, something more than one, something less than the other. But what charm will any of the mechanical drawings and paintings done in Julian's studio have in fifty years' time? not more I think than that of a machine-painted plate. Another example: Stubbs was not a great artist, but his pictures exhale an English air that will always be pleasant; and this particular air he acquired by remaining at home, by remaining ignorant of all but English influences. The artists of the last century and the artists of the beginning of this century were content to till one plot of ground, planting there always the same flower, they were content with the only true genius—*le génie de terroir*. Only by being parochial, in the first instance may any man's art become ultramontane in the end.

Our art came to us from Holland. Vandyck inspired Reynolds and Gainsborough, and from them proceeded all that is worthy and valuable in English art. Alone among English painters, Turner succeeded in the golden romantic Italian manner, and though we may not deny his *Carthage*, we may ask with excellent reason if the grey, sad, meditative note which came from Holland, and which he professed with so exquisite an art, is not preferable and more valid.

I had seen a beautiful Gainsborough at an Exhibition des Portraits du Siècle at the Beaux-Arts, and speaking to Sir John Millais one night I told him how much it had been admired by French artists. Sir John said: " Ah, yes, they would understand Gainsborough—they would understand him through Watteau." This remark seemed to me to be just one of those magical criticisms which no one but a great artist could make. The truth of Sir John's words was obvious, but why, I asked myself, should Watteau enable Frenchmen to understand Gainsborough; and if I had asked Sir John how the resemblance came about—Watteau a painter of court life in the reign of Louis XV., Gainsborough a painter who had never left England—he might have been puzzled to say. Sir John may have been content merely to note an analogy without troubling himself as to the cause of it. However this may be the idea haunted me, and I sought an explanation of a fact which seemed to defy explanation until one day while examining a picture of Watteau, my thoughts turned suddenly into some remembrances of Rubens' palette, and I recognised the analogy between Rubens and Watteau. I then recollected that Watteau was born in or on the confines of Flanders, and that the first pictures he saw were Rubens'. Rubens was Vandyck's master, and it was Vandyck who founded the English school.

The influence of Vandyck on Reynolds and Gainsborough was about the same, the genius of both was about equal, but Reynolds went to Italy, and Italian influence destroyed in part his native English simplicity, as it had destroyed that of many a Dutchman; and just as Italian influence destroyed the art of the Low Countries in the sixteenth century so French influence is destroying English art in the nineteenth. But how much more disastrous is the journey to Paris than the journey to Rome! Reynolds went to Rome when he was in full possession of his art, he went there to see great works, to muse, to think, to reflect. But to-day young men go to Paris knowing nothing; and they go there not to visit the Louvre but to shut themselves up in a studio from eight to ten hours daily, accepting blindly an elaborate system of education organised on principles as purely commercial as those at the Bon Marché. Is such expatriation and such instruction suitable to the preservation and the development of English talent?

Those who think that it is not must agree with me that the first step in the artistic education of this country, is to persuade students that it is not necessary to go to Paris. If this cannot be done, I would save them at least from Julian's studio, where, as we have seen, all is corruption and commercialism.

It is well that the dignity of art should be upheld, and our *confrères* should have our full sympathy in their efforts to wipe away all suspicion of intrigue and favouritism from their exhibitions; but our concern in the matter lies far deeper than theirs, far deeper than the false distribution of a few medals, for we are concerned to preserve what remains of our artistic tradition. The commercialism of Julian's studio is the most flagrant, its appeal to England and America the loudest, but its influence on our art is hardly more detestable than that of another Parisian studio. True, had I to choose I would accept Duran's instruction in preference to Bouguereau's, but, exercised on English talent, or even genius, both are disastrous, for both are un-English. So, if it behoves French artists to separate themselves from all alliance with Julian's studio, it is doubly desirable that English artists, English art critics, all interested in English art to whom the ways of public speech and writing are open, should, forgetting all internecine broils, unite in upholding our own Academy, which at least is not corrupt, and endeavour to teach love of England to the youths within and without its walls, who, discontented with the naïve simplicity of our tradition, are turning their eyes towards Paris.

UNE RENCONTRE AU SALON

IN the May of '85, as I stood before a bust by Rodin, lost in admiration, saying to myself, "What an admirable portraitist he is, though he be nothing more!" I heard some one behind me mutter:

"*Michel-Ange à la coule. . . .*"

The words caused me to turn suddenly, and I found myself face to face with a handsome young man, thoughtfully dressed, and yet there was something in his blue cloth jacket buttoned across his throat, in his manner of wearing it (or was it the large trousers cut somewhat after the pattern of the white ducks of a house painter?), that suggested the artisan.

"*Alors pour vous Rodin est un Michel-Ange à la coule? Vous êtes donc sculpteur?*"

He avoided answering my question, and I did not press him to do so, knowing well that the phrase *Michel-Ange à la coule* was a sculptor's; and we walked about discussing the groups, single figures and busts, myself interested in the young man's hatred of Salon sculpture, and curious to hear him tell why he hated it. For a long time he was indefinite, saying at last:

"I don't see any choice of material here. Wherever I look I see glaring white marble."

"You don't like marble?"

"It isn't so much that I don't like it, but it is isn't the only material. It suited the Greeks very well, enabling them to express their ideas, but not one of the sculptors here has ever thought that he might express himself better in terra-cotta, in bronze, or in wax ; he chooses marble from habit, and works it as if it were his slave instead of his collaborator."

"You like bronze better?"

"It is more suitable to a modern house. But if you would care to see sculpture of a different kind I will show you some. A young friend of mine, a provincial, is exhibiting his work in Passy. . . . A lady who is interested in his work has allowed him to show his things in her house."

We got into a cab and were driven to a real French villa, a Passy villa hidden away under chestnut trees, at that moment all in flower, the white blossom shedding itself over the sunlit steps leading to the portico. As we passed through the house we caught sight of tapestries through the open doors, and the corridors were lined with painted and gilded tables, laden with Italian porcelain ; and, going up a rich staircase, we came to the drawing-room, hung — or, shall I say, festooned?—with pink silk.

"I don't care for variegated ceilings, do you?"

My companion did not answer ; he was thinking of the sculpture which filled the drawing-rooms ; some twenty-five or thirty pieces, wax models, bronzes, and wood carvings were all around me, and picking up a block, seemingly a huge paper-weight, on which was carved the head and throat and breast of a Sphinx, I said, "You don't always disdain marble. This example of your work helps me to understand your art better than anything you have said. You looked at this piece of marble as a Chinaman looks at a piece of jade, thinking what form the grain of the stone was prone to take, and throwing back accordantly the arms like wings ; and you have worked the marble with such loving care that it has become as beautiful as a piece of jade."

This appreciation satisfied the young man, and he began to talk of the Aubusson carpet, whose roses were as real as coloured thread allowed them to be.

"We must always seek reality, but we must seek it within the limitations of our material. If these roses——"

A faint rustling sound was heard; a lady came into the room, and he went towards her and muttered a rapid explanation which I did not catch. She came across the room, smiling graciously, and he said:

"This English gentleman is much interested in sculpture, and feeling sure that you would not mind if I brought him here——"

"On the contrary, I am most pleased. I should be sorry if he returned to England without having seen anything but the marbles exhibited at the Salon."

"It was very kind of this gentleman to bring me to see his friend's sculpture."

A slight smile appeared in the lady's face, and my companion took his leave abruptly, asking me if I would meet him an hour hence at the Café de l'Etoile. I promised to do so, and turned to the lady for information regarding her *protégé*. But the lady avoided answering my questions, and when it seemed to me that I had praised the sculpture sufficiently I thanked her for her kindness in allowing me to see it, and bade her good-bye.

"There is something in him," I said to myself; "something that will transpire later on . . . perhaps. He is at present thinking too much of the material, and for that reason his sculpture is a little empty."

In the street there was a great glare of light, and Passy is a long way from l'Etoile; and in pursuit of ideas I wandered up a very long and hot street, Rue

de la Pompe, arriving tired and hot at l'Avenue du
Bois de Boulogne, my inflamed feet hardly able to
carry me across it. My young friend had told me that
I would find the Café de l'Etoile at the corner of
l'Avenue de la Grande Armée. For a long time it was
sought in vain, but at last a *garçon* said to me: "*C'est
ici, monsieur,*" and I wondered why my companion
had directed me to a café not much better than a
marchand de vins; in fact, a *marchand de vins* it was,
and nothing more, with three workmen lounging over
a zinc counter, and outside a few chairs under an
insufficient awning.

On one of these I sat, resting my inflamed feet on
another, thinking what folly it had been to come all this
way. And for why? L'Avenue de la Grande Armée
is one of the least interesting avenues in Paris; it
contains three or four little roadways, and between each
one is a line of trees, very small, uninteresting trees, and
the houses are small and insignificant, and the avenue
extends away and away in a straight line into an
uninteresting district called Neuilly. We never see
anybody interesting in l'Avenue de la Grande Armée,
nobody one knows, and as soon as I was rested and my
thirst assuaged I fell to thinking of art to pass the time.

All great art, all valuable art, is inspired by the
surroundings in which men live. For instance, there
would have been no frescoe painting if there had been
no Gothic cathedrals. The romanesque cathedrals were
gloomy, tomb-like places, and mosaics were sufficient
ornamentations; but the Gothic cathedral was graver;
men's minds were arising out of the gloom of the real
Middle Ages, and as soon as the cathedrals were built
the sculptors of the twelfth and thirteenth centuries
began to carve statues; and when the niches were
filled the artists of the fourteenth and fifteenth centuries
covered the walls with saints, angels, and ecclesiastics.

At the end of the fifteenth century interest in the Mass began to decline, and men began to build palaces for their pleasure in this world; and just as the cathedral had brought saints, angels, and ecclesiastics into art, the palace brought voluptuous women in embroidered gowns and young men in chain armour with velvet cloaks thrown about their shoulders. About the middle of the seventeenth century feudalism was a declining force; men began to build houses, and the house introduced family life into art; it inspired the Dutchmen continuously for nearly seventy years; they painted everything that could happen in the house and everything that could happen in the fields around the house. Their inventions include local colour, truth of effect and chiaroscuro; and upon Dutch art we have been living ever since; and we must wait for some architectural change before we can hope to find a new pictorial formula.

The villa! We have invented the villa. The word is the Italian for house, but in English it carries a suggestion of a somewhat archaic structure standing in the middle of a garden. When we go on Sunday to lunch with our friends who live in Surrey, long before we arrive at their suburban station we have in mind gable ends, tiled roofs, and false beams showing between the trees; and when we jump out of the train we find pa and ma and the girls and the boys all waiting to meet us, and we go up the smooth wide road together, a pleasant ten minutes' walk from the railway station, hearing all the while that the morning and evening trains are excellent. Kent, Sussex, and Surrey are crowded with villas, all run up within the last fifty years, and the question arises if our English villa will create an art peculiar to itself, as the cathedral, the palace, and the house have done.

Nothing seems more probable than that it will, for

the younger generation has begun to perceive that the
Royal Academy prices are incompatible with parties;
and a drove of Highland cattle driven across the moors
is relinquished at mother's instigation.   She reminds
father that the girls have been promised a month at
Boulogne at the end of the summer.   Father admires
the work of the Academician, but mother finds a
resolute supporter in Julia; Julia's opinions have to be
considered, for she goes to Camden Town three times
a week for lessons in painting, and her advice to her
father is that quality, not subject, should be sought for,
and Highland cattle in heavy gold frames are out of
place, she says, in white-painted rooms hung with
chintz and muslin; she suggests to her father etchings
in pretty Whistlerian frames for the drawing-room.
" And she would agree with the young man whom I
met in the Salon, and for whom I am waiting in this
very hot and detestable little café, that if father is to
buy sculpture at all it had better be in terra-cotta, or
wax, or in bronze. . . ."

It was pleasant to close one's eyes and to listen to
Julia and the young man discussing the beauty of the
material and its limitations till Julia begins to weary
of Theseus and the Venus de Milo, and to long for talk
about men and women. . . .

" We may be," I said, " on the eve of a new artistic
formula.   We must be, for we can't go on painting
Highland cattle and seagulls screaming round wintry
rocks for ever and ever; and our houses are becoming
more and more unsuited to marble.   That is the
discovery of the young man whom I am waiting for."
And I fell to wondering how it was that I had not
perceived at once that he was aiming at Oriental art.
His love of the material for its own sake came to him
from the East, and his dislike of marble as a medium of
sculpture is derived from his knowledge that no Oriental

O

sculptor has used marble, and perhaps from some religious sense going back to ancient Egypt, where granite and porphyry were used in preference to marble, these materials being more solemn, more disposed to inspire awe. Marble went westward; the Greeks were the first secularisers, and ever since the secularisation of the world has been going on continuously. On such an idea one can dream a long while, and five seconds or half an hour may have passed before I awoke and saw again the miserable aspects of the Avenue de la Grande Armée. After a little stare I muttered aloud:

"It is strange that I should not have thought of these things before. I'll speak to my young friend about the religious aspects of porphyry and granite as soon as he arrives. He will have to admit, I think, that both are too solemn for modern consumption. But I am with him; yes, I am with him altogether when he says that we do not consider the material sufficiently, and have but little interest in the handicraft on which the Oriental sculptors rely to make beautiful material seem more beautiful. He is quite right when he says that we have not a sculptor to-day who can wield a mallet; Rodin never raises one: he sends his plaster casts to Italian copyists, and the public prefers these copies to the bronze castings, though the bronze contains the sculptor's thought unadulterated."

Strange, is it not, that man should be so conventional? Any originality he ever attains to is the result of circumstance, and therefore it is quite possible that the villa will bring a new art along with it, an art dependent on the material employed and the use it is put to rather than upon ideas. The mark of a chalk pencil on a sheet of Whatman is not beautiful in itself, but a beautiful texture can be obtained with a chalk pencil, and it is certain that a drawing may give pleasure in which there is nothing but beauty of touch. No one is blinder to proportions, anatomies, and gestures than Walter Sickert; from the point of view of—shall we say Ingres?—his drawing does not exist at all; he has only "quality," and his cleverness consists in always keeping well within his limitations, putting down upon paper and canvas only that which he can express well. It will be noticed that he always chooses subjects which do not tax his powers of drawing—street corners, for instance. A street corner may present much perplexing drawing, but Walter Sickert avoids these, choosing for preference a simple gable end. It taxes his capacity, but he gets it down, and once he has it down the rest is easy, for his art does not include values. Whosoever says "values" suggests chiaroscuro, and chiaroscuro brings endless difficulties into art, and Walter Sickert has discovered that it is unnecessary to seek a true relation between his gable end and his sky. According to his æstheticism, any grey tint will do for the sky provided the paint is nicely laid on, and with brown and a little Indian red the roofs and the shadows can be achieved. His one pre-occupation is beauty of touch, and he gets it in the curve of the pavement. He has invented a formula which leaves out almost everything, and is therefore suitable to his own talent and to the talents of a large following, principally ladies. For the last seven summers his pupils have been painting in our streets, and they have left London seeking gable ends in all the old English towns; they have spread over the Continent; Dieppe has not a wall left unpainted; they have reached Venice, and St Mark's affords endless opportunities for their art; they have gone on to Constantinople and to Egypt, applying their method unembarrassed by the fact that in Egypt the relations of the sky and earth are the reverse of what they are here. Here the sky is pale and the earth dark; in Egypt the sky is dark and the earth light. But truth of effect does not trouble them. The strip of grey that sets off the tower in Smith's Square, Westminster, furnishes an equally truthful background for the domes and minarets of Egypt ; and hundreds of small pictures of unvarying merit are brought back—faint designs in gold frames, inoffensive always, and sometimes soothing to the eye. A considerable number of their pictures are to be seen in the exhibitions of the New English Art Club, but not all, and this is a grievance which has been to some extent removed by the organisation of vast picture-shows at the Albert Hall. It is reported that as many as a thousand street-corners have been exhibited there ; and among this somewhat bewildering array of gable ends we find portraits of chairs, jugs, basins, and brooms. The Dutchmen relied upon a ray of light or a shadow to give interest to some such simple object, but these ladies rely entirely on Mr Sickert's recipes.

The master is, however, a little more venturesome than his pupils ; he sometimes leaves his street-corners for music-halls, and his method is as applicable to interiors as it is to exteriors. The stage box at the Bedford is represented by a patch of slate-colour— white broken with blue-black, and a gold arabesque ; and his recipe for gold is a foundation of yellow ochre, with raw umber for the shadows, and Naples yellow for the high lights. Figures are sometimes introduced into the music-hall pieces, and he talks so well about the drawing he has omitted that we forget to examine what is there, and the stuttering and the stammering among the gallery boys are forgiven him for he never altogether lacks quality, and it is not easy to get quality in oil paint. No material is more rebellious, but he has tamed it.

" He must meet the young man whom I met this morning in the Salon," I cried to myself. " They have

many ideas in common." "Before a dressmaker designs
a dress," Sickert will say to him, "he asks himself what
material the dress is to be made of, and I think we
should do the same." And the two will agree heartily
about the necessity of cheap art for the villa.

In his articles he has always advocated cheap art,
deriding his friends in Chelsea for selling their pictures
at high prices, for painting chintz in winter and castles
in summer; and his friend Mortimer Menpes is also
working for the villa, neglecting proportions, movement,
and gesture, all that it was once the fashion to regard as
the essentials of drawing, and thinking much more of
the effect of a sheet of Whatman in a gold frame and
the relation of the gold frame to the wall. Like Walter
Sickert he was a pupil of Whistler, and Whistler was
the first to draw the attention of the Western world
to Oriental art. He has been in Japan and many other
countries, and has brought back a great deal of local
colour; he has given us not only Japanese, but Indian
and Turkish, and, for all I know, Circassian dresses;
spots of colour very often laid upon a gold background.
He is also addicted to etching and, like Walter Sickert,
leaves out all that he has not understood. The gold
frame that he took from Whistler, and into which he has
introduced many modifications of his own, enhances the
beauty of the old Dutch paper laid upon a sheet of
Whatman. And Helleu's etchings are nearly as suitable
to the villa as Menpes's. In an indulgent moment Degas
described Helleu as *un Watteau à vapeur*; and thinking
how his etchings are appreciated in villadom, I remembered a man whose merit is that he works in silver
point, a medium so difficult that he claims dispensation
from all drawing and design. "And there are others,"
I said. But it was too hot to seek out names, and my
thoughts drifted on, dismissing the drawings of Conder,
Brabazon, and Aubrey Beardsley as being too recondite

for the taste of the villa ; " and too expensive," I added.
" *Garçon, encore une limonade* ! "

Walter Sickert is an economist as well as an æsthete, and foresees that in about fifty years all and sundry will be living in villas, and that there is no end to the art that will be required for those who come after him. It is only here that we feel inclined to join issue with him. Is the villa the end of art? The last word? We think not. The bungalow will succeed the villa, and after a little while the bungalow will become a tie, and man will wander over the earth again, but not on a camel's back by day, sleeping in a tent by night ; he will wander in railway trains, in Pullman cars, and the traveller returning to Paris from Cape Horn, *viâ* Behring Straits, will need pictorial refreshment. Pictures will——. As the art of the Pullman car was about to rise up before me my reverie was interrupted by the sculptor whose acquaintance I had made that morning in the Salon before Rodin's bust.

" *A quoi rêvez-vous ?* "

" *Je veux bien vous raconter mes rêves ; seulement ce sera long ;* " and while walking round the Arc de Triomphe he listened to me telling him the gradations by which we should reach the end of the Art age. " You kept me waiting so long in that café that I have had time to think out the question of nationality in art from end to end."

My companion laughed sympathetically, and encouraged by his laughter I continued my theory of nationality in art, telling him that if the Greeks had had the compass their ships might have reached the Red Sea, for a canal existed in ancient times ; and through the Red Sea their ships might have wandered eastward, and if one laden with marbles had been wrecked off the coasts of Japan in the year 200 B.C.

we should not have had Japanese art; Hokusai and Outamaro would not have existed.

"Degas would agree with you that segregation is the source of the artistic river."

"Degas! You know Degas?"

"Yes, I have known him for some time, and I met him soon after leaving you, and told him about our meeting in the Salon. He asked me to tell you that he is dining at the Nouvelle Athènes. He hopes you will come."

"Who would miss an evening with Degas!"

We walked down the Avenue Friedland together, talking of the hordes of young English and Americans who come to Paris to learn to paint, thinking that there is but one painting and no other, and that if they can get the recipe they will be able to produce the article required.

"A sort of international art; that is what the world is making for," my companion said. "International cooking is with us," and he related how he had asked the manager of the Splendid Hotel if the cooking in his establishment was international, and, smiling, the manager assured him that he could count upon the cooking as being of the very same quality as the Splendid Hotel in Rome, in Aix les Bains, in Munich, in Geneva; in fact, in all the capital cities of Europe. "*Et vous n'avez pas de plats locaux !*" I said to him.

"He began to suspect that you were poking fun at him?"

"A moment later he did, and assured me that notwithstanding international cooking they were still prepared——"

We laughed together, and our thoughts reverting to the subject of our conversation of international art, I said:

"If you send a Japanese artist to Ville d'Avray he

will bring you back a piece of Japan, and if you send a French artist to Japan he will bring you back a piece of Ville d'Avray."

"I'm afraid that isn't so," my companion interposed.

"How is that?"

"You forget that Eastern artists have already begun to imitate the Western. Japanese art ended with the opening up of Japan to Western ideas; and now all that Japan can do in the way of art is to imitate us or its old masters."

"Yes; isn't it sad? Art ended once before in the fourth century; a new idea came into the world, and from the fourth to the thirteenth there was no art except the cathedrals, no sculpture, no painting, no literature. Another new idea has come into the world, locomotion; and railways and steamboats have made art impossible; every man knows his neighbour; man is an imitative animal, and if he can imitate he will. There will be plenty of international art, and man's lot will be worse than ever."

"*Pas de plats locaux.*"

"No," I answered, laughing sadly. "Great geniuses will be born in vain. Men of talent were born in the Middle Ages, but there was no artistic formula, and they remained mute and inglorious. Nature is always the same. What is art but intellectual formulæ, and it requires three or four generations living in an obscure corner of the world to create an artistic formula. One of these corners still exists; we are going to the Place Pigalle, and the artists we shall see there to-night— Degas, Pissaro, Renoir are the last; Monet is in the country, so is Sisley, and together they are developing the Impressionistic formula. To-day there are no buyers for their pictures, but in about fifty years' time almost any price will be paid for them; the worst will be a masterpiece then. I didn't think of it before, if we only had a few hundred pounds we could invest it at a thousand per cent., and our children would be millionaires.   But we have no money."

"We have better than money or children," my companion answered, "for if all that you say be right we have immortality; not on account of any merit we possess, but because of the mediocrity that will follow us.   We are the demi-gods, and the demi-gods are to-night going to dine with the gods, with the last of the old world's gods."

DEGAS

ONE evening, after a large dinner party, given in honour of the publication of *L'Œuvre*, when most of the guests had gone, and the company consisted of *les intimes de la maison*, a discussion arose as to whether Claude Lantier was or was not a man of talent. Madame Charpentier, by dint of much provocative asseveration that he was undistinguished by even any shred of the talent which made Manet a painter for painters, forced Emile Zola to take up the cudgels and defend his hero. Seeing that all were siding with Madame Charpentier, Zola plunged like a bull into the thick of the fray, and did not hesitate to affirm that he had gifted Claude Lantier with infinitely larger qualities than those which nature had bestowed upon Edouard Manet. This statement was received in mute anger by those present, all of whom had been personal friends and warm admirers of Manet's genius, and cared little to hear any word of disparagement spoken of their dead friend. It must be observed that M. Zola intended no disparagement of M. Manet, but he was concerned to defend the theory of his book—namely, that no painter working in the modern movement had achieved a result equivalent to that which had been achieved by at least three or four writers working in the same movement, inspired by the same ideas, animated by the same æstheticism. And, in reply to one who was anxiously urging Degas' claim to the highest consideration, he said, "I cannot accept a man who shuts himself up all his life to draw a ballet-girl as ranking co-equal in dignity and power with Flaubert, Daudet, and Goncourt."

Some four, or perhaps five, years after, one morning in May, a friend tried the door of Degas' studio. It is always strictly fastened, and when shaken vigorously a voice calls from some loophole; if the visitor be an intimate friend, a string is pulled and he is allowed to stumble his way up the cork-screw staircase into the studio. There are neither Turkey carpets nor Japanese screens, nor indeed any of those signs whereby we know the dwelling of the modern artist. Only at the further end, where the artist works, is there daylight. In perennial gloom and dust the vast canvases of his youth are piled up in formidable barricades. Great wheels belonging to lithographic presses— lithography was for a time one of Degas' avocations— suggest a printing-office. There is much decaying sculpture—dancing-girls modelled in red wax, some dressed in muslin skirts, strange dolls—dolls if you will, but dolls modelled by a man of genius.

On that day in May Degas was especially anxious for breakfast, and he only permitted his visitor to glance at the work in progress, and hurried him away to meal with him—but not in the café; Degas has lately relinquished his café, and breakfasts at home, in an apartment in the Rue Pigalle, overlooking a courtyard full of flowering chestnut-trees.

As they entered the apartment the eye of the visitor was caught by a faint drawing in red chalk, placed upon a sideboard; he went straight to it. Degas said, "Ah! look at it, I bought it only a few "days ago; it is a drawing of a female hand by Ingres; "look at those finger-nails, see how they are indicated. "That's my idea of genius, a man who finds a hand

"so lovely, so wonderful, so difficult to render, that
"he will shut himself up all his life, content to do
"nothing else but indicate finger-nails."

The collocation of these remarks by Zola and Degas
—two men of genius, working in the same age, floating
in the same stream of tendency, although in diverging
currents—cannot fail to move those who are interested
in the problem of artistic life. Perhaps never before
did chance allow a mutual friend to snatch out of the
oblivion of conversation two such complete expressions
of artistic sensibility; the document is sufficient, and
from it a novelist should be able to construct two
living souls. Two types of mind are there in essence;
two poles of art are brought into the clearest appre-
hension, and the insoluble problem, whether it be
better to strive for almost everything, or for almost
nothing, stares the reader in the face; we see Zola
attempting to grasp the universe, and Degas following
the vein of gold, following it unerringly, preserving it
scrupulously from running into slate. The whole of
Degas' life is in the phrase spoken while showing his
visitor the drawing in red chalk by Ingres. For no
man's practice ever accorded more nearly with his
theory than Degas'. He has shut himself up all his
life to draw again and again, in a hundred different
combinations, only slightly varied, those few aspects
of life which his nature led him to consider artistically, and for which his genius alone holds the artistic
formulæ.

Maupassant says in his preface to Flaubert's letters
to George Sand:—"Nearly always an artist hides a
"secret ambition, foreign to art. Often it is glory
"that we follow, the radiating glory that places us,
"living, in apotheosis, frenzies minds, forces hands to
"applaud, and captures women's hearts. . . . Others
"follow money, whether for itself, or the satisfaction

"that it gives—luxuries of life and the delicacies of
"the table.

"Gustave Flaubert loved letters in so absolute a
"fashion that, in his soul, filled with this love, no other
"ambition could find a place."

With the single substitution of the word "painting"
for "letters," this might be written with perfect truth
of Degas. To those who want to write about him
he says, "Leave me alone; you didn't come here
"to count how many shirts I have in my wardrobe?"
"No, but your art, I want to write about it." "My
"art, what do you want to say about it? Do you
"think you can explain the merits of a picture to those
"who do not see them? Dites?... I can find the best
"and clearest words to explain my meaning, and I
"have spoken to the most intelligent people about art,
"and they have not understood—to B——, for instance;
"but among people who understand words are not
"necessary, you say—humph, he, ha, and everything
"has been said. My opinion has always been the same.
"I think that literature has only done harm to art. You
"puff out the artist with vanity, you inculcate the taste
"for notoriety, and that is all; you do not advance
"public taste by one jot. . . . Notwithstanding all your
"scribbling it never was in a worse state than it is at
"present. . . . Dites? You do not even help us to
"sell our pictures. A man buys a picture not because
"he read an article in a newspaper, but because a friend,
"who he thinks knows something about pictures, told
"him it would be worth twice as much ten years hence
"as it is worth to-day. . . . Dites?"

In these days, when people live with the view to
reading their names in the paper, such austerity must
appear to many like affectation; let such people
undeceive themselves. Never was man more sincere;
when Degas speaks thus he speaks the very essence

of his being. But perhaps even more difficult than the acceptation of this fact will be found the association of such sentiments with a sweet genial nature, untouched with misanthropy or personal cynicism. Degas is really cynical only in his art, and although irony is an essential part of him, it finds expression in a kindly consciousness of the little weaknesses of human nature when directed against those he loves. For instance, when he is in company with any one who knew Manet, his *confrère* and compeer in realistic pictorial art, and the friend of his life, he loves to allude to those little childishnesses of disposition which make Manet's memory a well-beloved, even a sacred thing.

"Do you remember," Degas said, as he hurried his friend along the Rue Pigalle, "how he used to "turn on me when I wouldn't send my pictures to the "Salon?   He would say, 'You, Degas, you are above "the level of the sea, but for my part, if I get into an "omnibus and some one doesn't say "M. Manet, how "are you, where are you going?" I am disappointed, "for I know then that I am not famous.'" Manet's vanity, which a strange boyishness of disposition rendered attractive and engaging, is clearly one of Degas' happiest memories, but all the meanness of *la vie de parade*, so persistently sought by Mr Whistler, is bitterly displeasing to him. Speaking to Mr Whistler, he said, "My dear friend, you conduct your-"self in life just as if you had no talent at all." Again speaking of the same person, and at the time when he was having numerous photographs taken, Degas said, "You cannot talk to him; he throws his cloak "around him—and goes off to the photographer."

A dozen, a hundred other instances, all more or less illustrative of the trait so dominant and decisive in Degas, which leads him to despise all that vain clamour which many artists are apt to consider essential, and without which they are inclined to deem themselves unjustly treated or misunderstood, might be cited. One more will, however, suffice. Speaking to a young man hungering for drawing-room successes, he says, and with that jog of the elbow so familiar in him, " Jeune M——, dans mon temps on n'arrivait pas, dites?" And what softens this austerity, and not only makes it bearable but most winsome and engaging, is the conviction which his manner instils of the very real truth, of the unimpeachableness of the wisdom which he expresses by the general conduct of his life and by phrases pregnant with meaning. Nor is it ever the black wisdom of the pessimist which says there is no worth in anything but death, but the deeper wisdom, born it is true of pessimism, but tempered in the needs of life, which says : " Expend not your " strength in vain struggling in the illusive world, which " tempts you out of yourself; success and failure lie " within and not without you ; know yourself, and seek " to bring yourself into harmony with the Will from " which you cannot escape, but to which you may bring " yourself into obedience, and so obtain peace."

In accordance with this philosophy, Degas thinks as little of Turkey carpets and Japanese screens as of newspaper applause, and is unconcerned to paint his walls lemon yellow ; he puts his æstheticism upon his canvases, and leaves time to tint the fading whitewash with golden tints. They are naked of ornament, except a few *chefs-d'œuvre* which he will not part with, a few portraits, a few pictures painted in his youth. Looking at *Semiramis Building the Walls of Babylon*, Manet used to say, " Why don't you exhibit it, *cela fera de la variété dans votre œuvre ?*" There is a picture of some Spartan youths wrestling which Gérôme once ventured to criticise ; Degas answered, " Je suppose que ce n'est pas assez turc pour vous, Gérôme ?" Not in his dress

nor in his manner will you note anything glaringly
distinctive, but for those who know him the suit of
pepper-and-salt and the blue necktie tied round a loose
collar are full of *him*. For those who know him the
round shoulders, the rolling gait, and the bright, hearty,
essentially manly voice are brimmed with individuality;
but the casual visitor of the Café de la Rochefoucauld
would have to be more than usually endowed with the
critical sense to discern that Degas was not an ordinary
man. To pass through the world unobserved by those
who cannot understand him—that is, by the crowd—
and to create all the while an art so astonishingly new
and so personal that it will defy imitator, competitor,
or rival, seems to be his ambition, if so gross a term
can be used without falsifying the conception of his
character. For Degas seems without desire of present
or future notoriety. If he could create his future as he
has created his present, his future would be found to
be no more than a continuation of his present. As he
has in life resolutely separated himself from all possibility of praise, except from those who understand him,
he would probably, if he could, defend himself against
all those noisy and posthumous honours which came
to the share of J. F. Millet; and there can be but little
doubt that he desires not at all to be sold by picture-
dealers for fabulous prices, but rather to have a quiet
nook in a public gallery where the few would come to
study. However this may be, it is certain that to-day
his one wish is to escape the attention of the crowd.
He often says his only desire is to have eyesight to
work ten hours a day. But he neither condemns nor
condones the tastes and the occupations of others; he
is merely satisfied that, so far as he is concerned, all
the world has for giving is untroubled leisure to pursue
the art he has so laboriously invented. To this end he
has for many years consistently refused to exhibit in

the Salon ; now he declines altogether to show his pictures publicly.

In old times, after a long day spent in his studio, he would come to the Nouvelle Athènes late in the evening, about ten o'clock. There he was sure of meeting Manet, Pissaro, and Duranty, and with books and cigarettes the time passed in agreeable æstheticisms : Pissaro dreamy and vague ; Manet loud, declamatory, and eager for medals and decorations ; Degas sharp, deep, more profound, scornfully sarcastic ; Duranty clear - headed, dry, full of repressed disappointment. But about the time of Manet's death the centre of art shifted from the Nouvelle Athènes to the Café de la Rochefoucauld. Degas followed it. He was seen there every evening, and every morning he breakfasted there — every year looming up greater and more brilliant in the admiration of the young men. Latterly Degas has abandoned café life. He dines with Ludovic Halévy and a few friends whom he has known all his life ; he goes to the opera or the circus to draw and find new motives for pictures. Speaking to a landscape-painter at the Cirque Fernando, he said, " A vous il faut la vie naturelle, à moi la vie factice."

From the quotations scattered in the foregoing paragraphs the reader has probably gathered that Degas is not deficient in verbal wit. Mr Whistler has in this line some reputation, but in sarcasm he is to Degas what Theodore Hook was to Swift, and when Degas is present Mr Whistler's conversation is distinguished by " brilliant flashes of silence." Speaking of him one day, Degas said, " Oui, il est venu me voir." " Well, what did he say to you ? " " Rien, il a fait quelques coups de mèche, voilà tout." One day, in the Nouvelle Athènes, a young man spoke to him of how well Manet knew how to take criticism. " Oui, oui,

Manet est très Parisien, il comprend la plaisanterie."
(" Yes, Manet is a true Parisian, he knows how to take
a joke.") Speaking of Besnard's plagiarisms, " Oui,
oui, il *vole* avec nos propres ailes." Speaking of Bastien-
Lepage's picture, *La recolte des pommes de terres*, " C'est
le Bouguereau du mouvement moderne ; " and of Roll's
picture of *Work*, " Il y a cinquante figures, mais je ne
vois pas la foule ; on fait une foule avec cinq et non
pas avec cinquante." (" There are fifty figures, but I
see no crowd ; you can make a crowd with five figures,
not with fifty.") At a dinner at Bougival he said,
looking at some large trees massed in shadow, " How
beautiful they would be if Corot had painted them ! "
And speaking of Besnard's effort to attain lightness of
treatment, he said, " C'est un homme qui veut danser
avec des semelles de plomb." (" He is a man who
tries to dance with leaden soles.")

Of Degas' family history it is difficult to obtain any
information. Degas is the last person of whom inquiry
could be made. He would at once smell an article,
and he nips such projects as a terrier nips rats. The
unfortunate interlocutor would meet with this answer,
" I didn't know that you were a reporter in disguise ;
if I had, I shouldn't have received you." It is rumoured,
however, that he is a man of some private fortune, and
a story is in circulation that he sacrificed the greater
part of his income to save his brother, who had lost
everything by imprudent speculation in American
securities. But what concerns us is his artistic not
his family history.

Degas was a pupil of Ingres, and any mention of
this always pleases him, for he looks upon Ingres as
the first star in the firmament of French art. And,
indeed, Degas is the only one who ever reflected, even
dimly, anything of the genius of the great master. The
likeness to Ingres which some affect to see in Flandrin's

work is entirely superficial, but in the *Semiramis Building the Walls of Babylon* and in the *Spartan Youths* there is a strange fair likeness to the master, mixed with another beauty, still latent, but ready for efflorescence, even as the beauty of the mother floats evanescent upon the face of the daughter hardly pubescent yet. But if Degas took from Ingres that method of drawing which may be defined as drawing by the character in contradistinction to that of drawing by the masses, he applied the method differently and developed it in a different direction. Degas bears the same relation to Ingres as Bret Harte does to Dickens. In Bret Harte and in Dickens the method is obviously the same when you go to its root, but the subject-matter is so different that the method is in all outward characteristics transformed, and no complaint of want of originality of treatment is for a moment tenable. So it is with Degas; at the root his drawing is as classical as Ingres', but by changing the subject-matter from antiquity to the boards of the opera-house, and taking curiosity for leading characteristic, he has created an art cognate and co-equal with Goncourt's, rising sometimes to the height of a page by Balzac. With marvellous perception he follows every curve and characteristic irregularity, writing the very soul of his model upon his canvas. He will paint portraits only of those whom he knows intimately, for it is part of his method only to paint his sitter in that environment which is habitual to her or him. With stagey curtains, balustrades, and conventional poses, he will have nothing to do. He will watch the sitter until he learns all her or his tricks of expression and movement, and then will reproduce all of them and with such exactitude and sympathetic insight that the very inner life of the man is laid bare. Mr Whistler, whose short - sightedness allows him to see none of these beauties in nature, has declared that all such excellencies are literary and not pictorial, and the fact that he was born in Baltimore has led him to contradict all that the natural sciences have said on racial tendencies and hereditary faculties. But there are some who still believe that the *Ten O'clock* has not altogether overthrown science and history, and covered with ridicule all art that does not limit itself to a harmony in a couple of tints. And that Degas may render more fervidly all the characteristics that race, heredity, and mode of life have endowed his sitter with, he makes numerous drawings and paints from them; but he never paints direct from life. And as he sought new subject-matter, he sought for new means by which he might reproduce his subject in an original and novel manner. At one time he renounced oil-painting entirely, and would only work in pastel or distemper. Then, again, it was water-colour painting, and sometimes in the same picture he would abandon one medium for another. There are examples extant of pictures begun in water-colour, continued in gouache, and afterwards completed in oils; and if the picture be examined carefully, it will be found that the finishing hand has been given with pen and ink. Degas has worked upon his lithographs, introducing a number of new figures into the picture by means of pastel. He has done beautiful sculpture, but not content with taking a ballet-girl for subject, has declined to model the skirt, and had one made by the nearest milliner. In all dangerous ways and perilous straits he has sought to shipwreck his genius; but genius knows no shipwreck, and triumphs in spite of obstacles. Not even Wagner has tested more thoroughly than Degas the invincibility of genius.

If led to speak on the marvellous personality of his art, Degas will say, "It is strange, for I assure you no

" art was ever less spontaneous than mine. What I do is
" the result of reflection and study of the great masters ;
" of inspiration, spontaneity, temperament — tempera-
" ment is the word—I know nothing. When people talk
" about temperament it always seems to me like the
" strong man in the fair, who straddles his legs and asks
" some one to step up on the palm of his hand." Again,
in reply to an assurance that he of all men now working,
whether with pen or pencil, is surest of the future, he
will say, " It is very difficult to be great as the old
" masters were great. In the great ages you were great
" or you did not exist at all, but in these days every-
" thing conspires to support the feeble."

Artists will understand the almost superhuman genius
it requires to take subject-matter that has never received
artistic treatment before, and bring it at once within
the sacred pale. Baudelaire was the only poet who
ever did this ; Degas is the only painter. Of all
impossible things in this world to treat artistically, the
ballet-girl seemed the most impossible, but Degas
accomplished that feat. He has done so many dancers
and so often repeated himself that it is difficult to
specify any particular one. But one picture rises up in
my mind—perhaps it is the finest of all. It represents
two girls practising at the rail ; one is straining forward
lifting her leg into torturous position — her back is
turned, and the miraculous drawing of that bent back !
The other is seen in profile—the pose is probably less
arduous, and she stands, not ungracefully, her left leg
thrown behind her, resting upon the rail. The arrangement of the picture is most unacademical ; the figures
are half-way up the canvas, and the great space of bare
floor is balanced by the watering-pot. This picture is
probably an early one. It was natural to begin with
dancers at rest ; those wild flights of dancers — the
première danseuse springing amid the coryphées down

to the footlights, her thin arms raised, the vivid glare of the limelight revealing every characteristic contour of face and neck—must have been a later development, The philosophy of this art is in Degas' own words. "La danseuse n'est qu'un prétexte pour le dessin." Dancers fly out of the picture, a single leg crosses the foreground. The première danseuse stands on tiptoe, supported by the coryphées, or she rests on one knee, the light upon her bosom, her arms leaned back, the curtain all the while falling. As he has done with the ballet, so he has done with the race-course. A race-horse walks past a white post which cuts his head in twain.

The violation of all the principles of composition is the work of the first fool that chooses to make the caricature of art his career, but, like Wagner, Degas is possessed of such intuitive knowledge of the qualities inherent in the various elements nature presents that he is enabled, after having disintegrated, to re-integrate them, and with surety of always finding a new and more elegant synthesis. After the dancers came the washerwoman. It is one thing to paint washerwomen amid decorative shadows, as Teniers would have done, and another thing to draw washerwomen yawning over the ironing table in sharp outline upon a dark background. But perhaps the most astonishing revolution of all was the introduction of the shop-window into art. Think of a large plate - glass window, full of bonnets, a girl leaning forward to gather one! Think of the monstrous and wholly unbearable thing any other painter would have contrived from such a subject ; and then imagine a dim, strange picture, the subject of which is hardly at first clear ; a strangely contrived composition, full of the dim, sweet, sad poetry of female work. For are not those bonnets the signs and symbols of long hours of weariness and dejection ?

and the woman that gathers them, iron-handed fashion
has moulded and set her seal upon. See the fat
woman trying on the bonnet before the pier-glass, the
shopwomen around her. How the lives of those poor
women are epitomised and depicted in a gesture!
Years of servility and obeisance to customers, all the
life of the fashionable woman's shop is there. Degas
says, "Les artistes sont tellement pressés! et que nous
faisons bien notre affaire avec les choses qu'ils ont
oubliées." ("Artists are always in such a hurry, and
how well we manage with what they have forgotten!")

But perhaps the most astonishing of all Degas'
innovations are his studies of the nude. The nude has
become well-nigh incapable of artistic treatment. Even
the more naïve are beginning to see that the well-
known nymph exhibiting her beauty by the borders
of a stream can be endured no longer. Let the artist
strive as he will, he will not escape the conventional;
he is running an impossible race. Broad harmonies of
colour are hardly to be thought of; the gracious mystery
of human emotion is out of all question—he must rely
on whatever measure of elegant drawing he can include
in his delineation of arms, neck, and thigh; and who
in sheer beauty has a new word to say? Since
Gainsborough and Ingres, all have failed to infuse new
life into the worn-out theme. But cynicism was the
great means of eloquence of the Middle Ages; and
with cynicism Degas has again rendered the nude an
artistic possibility. Three coarse women, middle-aged
and deformed by toil, are perhaps the most wonderful.
One sponges herself in a tin bath; another passes a
rough night-dress over her lumpy shoulders, and the
touching ugliness of this poor human creature goes
straight to the heart. Then follows a long series
conceived in the same spirit. A woman who has
stepped out of a bath examines her arm. Degas says,

"La bête humaine qui s'occupe d'elle-même; une chatte qui se lèche." Yes, it is the portrayal of the animal-life of the human being, the animal conscious of nothing but itself. "Hitherto," Degas says, as he shows his visitor three large peasant women plunging into a river, not to bathe, but to wash or cool themselves (one drags a dog in after her), "the nude has always been "represented in poses which presuppose an audience, "but these women of mine are honest, simple folk, "unconcerned by any other interests than those involved "in their physical condition. Here is another; she is "washing her feet. It is as if you looked through a "key-hole."

But the reader will probably be glad to hear of the pictures which most completely represent the talent of the man. Degas might allow the word "represent" to pass, he certainly would object to the word "epitomise," for, as we have seen, one of his æstheticisms is that the artist should not attempt any concentrated expression of his talent, but should persistently reiterate his thought in twenty, fifty, yes, a hundred different views of the same phase of life. Speaking of Zola, who holds an exactly opposite theory, Degas says: "il me fait l'effet d'un géant qui travaille le Bottin." But no man's work is in exact accord with his theory, and the height and depth of Degas' talent is seen very well in the *Leçon de Danse,* in M. Faure's collection, and perhaps still better in the *Leçon de Danse* in M. Blanche's collection. In the latter picture a spiral staircase ascends through the room, cutting the picture at about two-thirds of its length. In the small space on the left, dancers are seen descending from the dressing-rooms, their legs and only their legs seen between the slender banisters. On the right, dancers advance in line, balancing themselves, their thin arms outstretched, the dancing-master standing high up in the picture by the furthest window. Through the cheap tawdry lace curtains a mean dusty daylight flows, neutralising the whiteness of the skirts and the brightness of the hose. It is the very atmosphere of the opera. The artificial life of the dancing-class on a dull afternoon. On the right, in the foreground, a group of dancers balances the composition. A dancer sits on a straw chair, her feet turned out, her shoulders covered by a green shawl ; and by her, a little behind her, stands an old woman settling her daughter's sash.

In this picture there is a certain analogy between Degas and Watteau, the grace and lightness and air of fête remind us of Watteau, the exquisite care displayed in the execution reminds us of the Dutchmen. But if Degas resembles Watteau in his earlier pictures of the dancing-classes at the opera, he recalls the manner and the genius of Holbein in his portraits, and nowhere more strikingly than in his portrait of his father listening to Pagano the celebrated Italian singer and guitarist. The musician sits in the foreground singing out of the picture. Upon the black clothes the yellow instrument is drawn sharply. The square jaws, the prominent nostrils, the large eyes, in a word, all the racial characteristics of the southern singer, are set down with that incisive, that merciless force which is Holbein. The execution is neither light nor free ; it is, however, in exact harmony with the intention, and intention and execution are hard, dry, complete. At the back the old melomaniac sits on the piano stool, his elbow on his knee, his chin on his hand, the eyelid sinks on the eye, the mouth is slightly open. Is he not drinking the old Italian air even as a flower drinks the dew ?

Another great portrait is Degas' portrait of Manet, but so entirely unlike is it to any other man's art that it would be vain to attempt any description of it. It shows Manet thrown on a white sofa in an attitude strangely habitual to him. Those who knew Manet well cannot look without pain upon this picture; it is something more than a likeness, it is as if you saw the man's ghost. Other portraits remind you of certain Spanish painters, the portrait of Mlle. Malot for instance; and in his studies of the nude there is a frankness which seems borrowed from the earlier Italians. Degas' art is, as he says himself, based upon a profound knowledge of the great masters. He has understood them as none but a great painter could understand them, and according to the requirements of the subject in hand he has taken from them all something of their technique.

The following anecdote will give an idea of Degas' love of the great masters. In 1840, Degas set up his easel in the Louvre and spent a year copying Poussin's *Rape of the Sabines*. The copy is as fine as the original.

Degas now occupies the most enviable position an artist can attain. He is always the theme of conversation when artists meet, and if the highest honour is to obtain the admiration of your fellow-workers, that honour has been bestowed on Degas as it has been bestowed upon none other. His pictures are bought principally by artists, and when not by them by their immediate *entourage*. So it was before with Courbet, Millet, and Corot; and so all artists and connoisseurs believe it will be with Degas. Within the last few years his prices have gone up fifty per cent.; ten years hence they will have gone up a hundred per cent., and that is as certain as that the sun will rise to-morrow. That any work of his will be sold for twenty thousand pounds is not probable; the downcast eye full of bashful sentiment so popular with the uneducated does not exist in Degas; but it is certain that young artists of to-day value his work as far higher than Millet's. He is, in truth, their god, and his influence is visible in a great deal of the work here and in France that strives to be most modern. But it must be admitted that the influence is a pernicious one. Some have calumniated Degas' art flagrantly and abominably, dragging his genius through every gutter, over every dunghill of low commonplace; others have tried to assimilate it honourably and reverentially, but without much success. True genius has no inheritors. Tennyson's parable of the gardener who once owned a unique flower, the like of which did not exist upon earth, until the wind carried the seeds far and wide, does not hold good in the instance of Degas. The winds, it is true, have carried the seeds into other gardens, but none have flourished except in native soil, and the best result the thieves have obtained is a scanty hybrid blossom, devoid alike of scent and hue.

THE NEW PICTURES IN THE
NATIONAL GALLERY

WE are proud of our National Gallery. We know that it would be hard to name another so uniformly instructive and so pleasant to walk through. In the National Gallery bad pictures are surprisingly scarce, and good ones are visible almost everywhere. All the schools are well represented, and before we enter on the many wonders of our own adorable eighteenth century we are greeted by one of the most beautiful pictures ever painted—a picture that is a unique delight of imaginative design and colour—a picture as truly exquisite as any in the world. I mean the family group by Gainsborough which stands on the staircase. But though a magnificent prefatory page, there are many pages within the swing-doors that its beauty cannot discount—the Turners, the Constables, and the Cromes.

From the first days almost to the present hour the finest judgment has been almost always exercised by those who were and who are responsible for the collection in Trafalgar Square. So heavy is our debt of gratitude, not only to those who have gone, but likewise to him who now guides and induces the decisions of the Trustees, that it is with much reluctance and much diffidence that I take on myself the task of questioning the wisdom of many late purchases and the acceptation of many modern works as worthy of place in our National Gallery. And if I undertake the task of

236

criticism, it is because inevitably there springs out of my admiration of what has been done to improve and perfect the collection a deep and sincere regret for the several grave errors which, in my opinion, have disfigured these last few years of management. Had only one error, or even two, been perpetrated, I should not have spoken, but error begets error, and the list of mistakes now threatens to become a long one.

The mistakes which I am about to criticise in detail began with the purchase of the Raphael for £70,000. The mistake was a popular one, and this is of itself a sufficiently grave impeachment, for it were surely a monstrous thing that the taste of the general public should be allowed to find expression in the National Gallery; and that is precisely what is happening, and flagrantly, as we shall see. The truth about Raphael is that he is far more popular with the general public than with artists. Art reached its height with Michael Angelo, and began to slip into decadence with Raphael—a great artist, no doubt, but so far as his genius is represented in England and France, he is nowhere sublime except in the Cartoons; there, the beauty of his genius may tempt us into the folly of thinking him worthy of comparison even with Angelo. No doubt there are among his too numerous Madonnas some passages of exquisite colour and drawing; if it were not so, Raphael could not continue to hold the high place to which popular admiration has exalted him. Even in his most commonplace Madonnas there is always a distinction of line that commands the admiration of artists. But in this £70,000 picture the artist seeks in vain for some justification of the money and the applause that have been lavished upon it. Indifferent in design, indifferent in colour, indifferent in drawing, it bears, in truth, the same relation to the Cartoons as Tennyson's prize poem does to *The Lotos-Eaters*. It is not possible to point to a distinctive passage in it, or, indeed, to any passage that foreshadows, however dimly, the genius to which he attained so soon afterwards. Whether it was painted before or after *The Marriage of the Virgin*, it is certainly in every way inferior to this picture. *The Marriage of the Virgin*, though feeble compared with some of the Madonnas, and puerile compared with the *Parnassus*, is, nevertheless, exquisitely original in design, and exquisitely graceful in treatment; but in this £70,000 picture I fail, and I have examined it again and again with the greatest care, to discover anything but an antiquarian interest; it is a document showing how Raphael painted at a certain period of his life, and no more. The student will not learn from it a single technical secret of his trade : any one of Raphael's drawings would prove infinitely more inspiring. Think of those drawings, so exquisite in their spontaneous grace—those that render the assent of the staircases of South Kensington a matter of such a long time. Ask any artist which has stirred him the most deeply, those drawings or that picture. And if a picture is not instructive and not a thing of beauty, its interest, if any, must be antiquarian. It will be said : admitted that it is not a good picture, calculated neither to inspire the student nor to delight the amateur, still it was necessary to possess a picture painted in Raphael's first manner. Frankly, I cannot admit the necessity. I repeat that the National Gallery is only in a very limited sense a museum, and if a picture is not a good one it should find no prominent place there. Above all, such sums should be paid for nothing but artistic work of the first class. £70,000!! What a sum, and when we think what we might have had for a half, a quarter, a seventh part of it. In the beginning of this year possibly the finest cattle-piece in the world was offered to the National Gallery for £10,000. I mean *La*

Vallée de la Tonque, by Troyon.   The acquisition of this picture would have been a brilliant page in a chapter wholly missing in our collection—that phase of modern French art which is the direct result of the English influence which agitated France in the beginning of this century—namely, *le plein air*.

What is known as *plein air* was invented by the Dutchmen about 1630, notably by Paul Potter, who was the first to attempt to paint cattle as part of the landscape, quite a different thing from the method practised till then, which consisted in introducing cattle into a landscape.   The moment it was perceived that animal life is but a part of nature, and not a centre round which nature revolves, a decisive and memorable step had been taken.   If we look back, we find that he who gave the East its philosophy enounced the truth two thousand five hundred years ago.   Paul Potter was, however, the first to introduce it into painting.   But with Paul Potter and the Dutch school, the secret of atmospheric effect died, or rather it was allowed to slumber until Constable revived it.   A great number of Constables went to France, there being but little sale for them in England, and they instantly inspired Troyon, who either consciously or unconsciously took up the art of Paul Potter exactly at the place where he had left off.   For it must not be forgotten that Potter was only three-and-twenty when he painted his bull, and that he died four years afterwards in the midst of his glory, but before he had acquired his trade. And this is the only cattle-piece of great size that could for one moment be compared with the superb *Vallée de la Tonque*.

The prodigious Dutchman was entirely self-educated, and was educating himself when he died; and it was only in his very last works that we lose sight of the engraver.   In all that preceded the last few pictures the steel point is felt, even where the paint is thickest. Nor will it be denied that the composition of the picture of the bull is of the poorest kind. The picture has neither beginning nor end; the sheep are lumps of plaster; and as for the shepherd—no one attempts to defend him. Only two parts of the picture hold together—the immense sky and the bull. The *Vallée de la Tonque* is, on the contrary, one of the most perfect and the most complete works it is possible to imagine. How the sensation of the thunder-storm is represented in the unquiet grouping of the cattle round the brook that flows down the middle of the picture! In the foreground two cows descend into the water; from the left the great bull advances bellowing; in the middle of the picture a black cow stands looking at the thunder-cloud that hangs in the silvery sky; further away, horses gallop to and fro in the lurid gleams that stream across the landscape. The picture is but the song of the earth, the murmur of unending existence. In the atmosphere is hidden the secret of life, and it makes of the lowing cattle, the neighing horses, the growing grass, and the flowing brook, not several things, but one vague, dim mystery, manifesting itself in many forms of life. And yet this admirable picture was passed over— a picture of such historical importance in the history of English art, of such intense artistic beauty and so full of instruction for those who are still seeking for some way out of that mystery of mysteries—*le plein air*.

To-day everything is painted out of doors, Teniers-like scenes—scenes that should be placed amid the darkness —are now painted in clear tints. Artists have forgotten that, irrespective of *le plein air*, there is such a thing as *une atmosphère de tableau*, and that by suppressing all shadow they have suppressed all balance, all weight. Objects float through their pictures like feathers. But the great bull in the Troyon picture could push down a barn-door. He is a ton weight if he is an ounce. Troyon painted *le plein air*, but he was an artist great enough to see that in every picture there must be weight. A tree in a picture by Corot carries the whole landscape away, a hand in a portrait by Manet brings the whole body down with it. But on this subject it would be easy to write a volume. I have said enough for my purpose, which is to show that it would have been better to have bought the *Vallée de la Tonque* for £10,000, than to have paid £70,000 for a Raphael, which teaches nothing and which does not call forth the faintest emotion in any one.

We have now to consider the latest purchases, their artistic value, and the price paid for them. £55,000 have been paid for three pictures—a portrait of a man by Velasquez, a portrait by Moroni, and a portrait-group by Holbein. Was the Director of the National Gallery well advised in asking the Trustees to spend so much money on these pictures?

The portrait by Valasquez represents a man about forty years of age. He is dressed in trunk hose (the effect is of black velvet knicker-bockers). The sleeves of the doublet are in a soft white material slightly stuffed ; over the shoulders falls the wide lace collar, and a narrow white sash crosses from the collar to the sword-handle ; tied round his waist is a crimson sash ; in his left hand he holds a broad-brimmed hat, in his right hand what looks like a large ruler in some pale-brown wood. The black hair hangs in thick, heavy masses about his neck, and has been lavishly painted with the brush full of paint : the background is pale-yellow, fading sometimes to green, and the green tints have been swept into the black hair, and at the same time just above the crown, the drawing of the hair is marked with the most direct and incisive strokes. The picture is

extremely interesting as a revelation of Velasquez'
method of work. It is in perfect preservation, and I
understand how it was done just as if I had seen him
paint it. The palette is abundantly spread with a few
colours—ivory, black, flake white, light red, vermilion,
lake, yellow ochre, raw sienna, terre verte, ultramarine;
perhaps a little blue was used, but it happened to be on
the palette. It was not put there for the picture. I
think that is all. The face was painted twice or else
it was painted over another picture; but the greater
part of the picture was painted *au premier coup*. I am
only uncertain whether Indian red or light red was used
in the painting of the face; on the one hand it seems
impossible to obtain such richness with light red, and
on the other it would be difficult to get such a softness with Indian red. The small eyes, entirely over-
shadowed by heavy eye-brows, are masses of frowning
shadow painted entirely with raw umber. The moustache
curls triumphantly; the jaw bone and quarter side of
the face appear, if you look into the picture, not to be
too strongly drawn; but when you get to a proper
distance every line holds its place with an exactness
that can only be described by the word defiant. The
scheme of colour is perfectly well preserved throughout.
The background is reflected in the hair, the fawn-
coloured clothes repeat it, and the light brown coloured
ruler remotely echoes it. The face repeats the crimson of
the sash. A single dominant chord is the great green
hat, faintly muttered through the background, in the hair,
and in the heavy shadow lying on the floor.

But is the portrait equal to that of Philip IV.? I
could not decompose that silvery enchantment and
show you the palette. But in this new picture I can
not only show you the palette but the exact frame
of mind in which it was painted. Agreed that it was
painted in one of Velasquez' great pictorial moods,

still I feel sure that the mood trended towards a coarseness that verged on insolence. Painting is the most indiscreet of all the arts ; the *ennui* of painting, the pleasure of painting, the model that bores you, the model that inspires you—all these things are told on the canvas, and I read in this picture a desire to parade the power and knowledge that the painter then held within him. I find nowhere an inspiration transmitted directly from the model to the painter. As I understand the picture, the model merely stimulated a mood already existent in the painter, and, swelling with arrogance in the consciousness of his power, he went ahead, his hand reproducing his mental state with astonishing fidelity, and the result is a piece of pictorial rhetoric of the finest possible kind, but for all that no more than a piece of pictorial rhetoric. We do not look, it is true, to Velasquez for *naïveté*, for simplicity ; but in the presence of the king he lost himself in a dream of silver and aristocracy, and in this mood the hand forgot to display its strength so ostentatiously. I have only seen the new picture once, but I shall not like it better when I see it again, possibly less. Its beauty is apparent at first sight, too apparent, but the *Philip* is looked on with an ever-deepening interest and an ever-increasing emotion. As a work of art, the new portrait cannot compare with the *Philip*. It is nevertheless a pure *chef-d'œuvre*, and as it represents Velasquez in an aspect different from any in our possession, it was of high importance that the picture should be bought for the National Gallery.

By the side of the Velasquez hangs the portrait by Moroni, and there is very little to be said about it. It represents a gentleman in black hose, only not nearly so well painted as the other gentleman by him, also in black hose, that hangs in the next room. In the new picture, the gentleman is entirely in black, without those delightful white notes which enchant us in the other portrait.   This time the Italian gentleman stands against a marble wall, rising above his head, but relieved on the left by a small space of sky.   On a broken column he has laid his helmet, and on it rests his left hand.   The head is very small, and the cheeks and chin are covered with a red beard.   The drawing is generally indolent, the painting is woolly, and the work betrays the indifference of the painter. Only in the expressive look in the dreamy eyes and in the drawing and painting of the left arm, which is clothed in chain - armour, do we find interest.   We have seen it all before; no new thing has been said; and if we look through certain repaintings, it is impossible to think that it was, even in its best days, anything but an inferior work.   No one will pretend that it can for a moment be compared with the three other pictures by Moroni which hang within a few yards of it.   Then why was it purchased?   Because it could be had cheap?   There could be no other reason for buying it, and that reason is no reason.

We have now arrived at the most important question —the vast sum that was paid for the Holbein.   As I examined the Velasquez and the Moroni I caught sight of *The Ambassadors* once or twice, and even these involuntary and casual glances told me that I should not be able to acknowledge the merits that are imputed to this picture.   I am aware that it is celebrated, and that, if it were put up again for auction, it would again fetch as much as was given for it.   But, looking at it carefully, without hurry, and without consideration for anything except what I see and what I know of Holbein's greatest works—the portrait of the man writing in the Louvre, the portrait of the woman in black hanging in the next room, above all that wholly

miraculous series of drawings exhibited last winter in
the New Gallery—I find myself at a loss to account
for the reputation that this picture possesses.

The work is ugly and ill-conceived. The painting
is monotonous, heavy, glaring, and dry. The
Ambassadors are dwarfs if they are standing up, and
they are—for a moment I was not certain that the
man in ermine was not sitting; neither is more than
six heads high. True, the Ambassadors may have
been dwarfs, but if they were, the spectator is not
made to feel that they were; he is left rather under
the impression that in composing the picture from
drawings done by the master, some one slipped into
an error of measurement. The Ambassadors stand
on either side of a high table. The one on the left
is in crimson and white fur; the crimson is at once
thin and glaring in colour, the white fur is dirty and
uninteresting in execution; and the green curtain
which forms the entire background is false in value,
and thin and repellent in colour. The light comes
from every side, and yet there is no light in the picture.
The table is covered with a red-and-white tablecloth,
in which there is not a single decisive bit of drawing or
a single touch of living colour; the green globe is
dull and lifeless; cubes are strewn all over the table,
and not one fascinates the eye; under the table there
is a musical instrument, equally uninteresting in drawing and in colour, and something lies on the floor
the nature of which I am unable to verify. Many are
the accessories, and yet the picture is not composed.

The man on the right is wrapped in a brown robe.
He likewise looks straight out of the picture; you
may notice the emphatic drawing of the thick lips,
but the modelling of the face is round, shapeless, and
even more uninteresting than the rest of the picture.
And from him the eye wanders back over the vast

surface of the painting without finding a single point of interest. That it was painted by Holbein, I believe there is no doubt; if it were not, Sir Richard Burton, who is an expert, would not have acquiesced in the purchase; at the same time it is a fact that the *Ronde de Nuit* in the National Gallery, although it is known to be a copy, is still labelled Rembrandt. Looking again at *The Ambassadors*, I see that it is not wanting in what the French call *allure*. The Ambassador on the left is admirably placed in the picture, the silhouette is rhythmical and ample. Concentration there is, but it is attained by a false lighting of the face which starts out of the picture. The drawing is in Holbein's most brutal and most angular manner. There is power, but none of that incisive sweetness which endears his work to us. Go into Room XI. and look into the face of the woman in black—look into the thin pale oval of the face. Obviously the hand that drew that woman's face drew every one of that series of miraculous drawings exhibited in the Stuart Exhibition. But is it obvious that the hand that drew the face of the woman in black also drew the picture of *The Ambassadors*, so clumsy, so monotonous, so wanting in that alertness of observation without which no picture, even though drawn by Holbein, can be called a Holbein?

In the beginning of this article I have alluded to certain flagrant concessions that have lately been made, and that disgrace the harmony of the galleries, which, until a few years ago, were but a gracious expansion of genius from end to end. The authorities in Trafalgar Square have thought fit to fill one of the first rooms with pictures by Frith, E. M. Ward, Landseer, and Armitage. I write these lines with reluctance, but unless the noble tradition of critical judgment that has so long obtained in Trafalgar Square is to be overthrown, we must sternly resist all pandering to contemporary vanities—Trafalgar Square, at least, must not be allowed to drift into an advertisement for painters. It is unseemly that the works of any living artist should be exhibited there, and to save our galleries from the influence of the dealer, it would be well if fifty years were allowed to elapse between the death of the painter and the time when his works might be admitted. Fifty years may be too long; twenty-five generally winnows most of the chaff from the wheat. Twenty-five years may gain for Mr Frith an esteem which we do not extend to him to-day. Be this as it may, the verdict of our time is that his pictures are shockingly out of place in the National Gallery. It is, no doubt, well that nursemaids should be amused, but this desirable end can be attained by more legitimate means than hanging *The Derby Day* in the National Gallery. The pictures by E. M. Ward cannot be said even to amuse the nursemaids, and as art they are quite as bad as *The Derby Day*. Landseer was an artist, though he was not a great artist, and we could well bear with one or two pictures by him. But surely the celebrated Newfoundland dog lying on the quay is an anomaly in the National Gallery—indeed, the presence of so many Landseers, none of which rise above mediocrity, does much to discredit a very real though somewhat superficial talent. And last, and worse than all, worse even than *The Derby Day*, is a picture by Armitage—*Judas offering to give back the Shekels of Gold*. Macaulay's schoolboy, even had he been educated in the most obscure Board School, would be able to advise the authorities rightly with regard to this picture.

Printed at
The Edinburgh Press,
9 and 11 Young Street.